From the Reviews of the First Edition

'[Lewis's] approach to life, his anecdotes, his observations have more content than t̶ ̶ ̶ ̶ ̶ reminiscences of several contemporary sailors, ̶ ̶ ̶ ̶ ̶ ̶ ̶ ̶ ̶ ̶ ̶ ̶ ̶ ̶ ut not nearly as honest or plai̶ ̶ ̶ ̶ ̶ ̶ ̶ ̶ ̶ ̶ ̶ ̶ ̶ Severin

'What an extraordina̶ ̶ ̶ ̶ ̶ ̶ ̶ ̶ ̶ ̶ ̶ ̶ ̶ none. A storyteller who can give goosebumps when relating real-life experiences.'

Sir Peter Blake

'David Lewis has lived and loved with a capacity for adventure and experience sadly lacking in conventional modern society. His ability to be different, often disapproved of but true to himself, should be appreciated and applauded.'

Dame Naomi James

'It's humbling that David Lewis has done more since he turned seventy than I have done in my entire life ... Autobiography is an intrinsically egotistical enterprise, but Lewis somehow manages to avoid any trace of self-aggrandisement. He is an engaging storyteller, with a lovely turn of phrase. Lewis is the epitome of the can-do independence upon which the Kiwis pride themselves. His is an inspiring story.'

John McCrystal, *Evening Post* (NZ)

'It is [Lewis's] wry, self-deprecating humour and his frank accounts of human love affairs that are the charm of this book but, as with Jesse Martin's *Lionheart*, it is the courage of the human spirit that is its inspiration.'

Boating New Zealand

'[Lewis's] excellent book will shame every couch potato who gets it for Christmas.'

Gordon Parry, *Dunedin Star*

'*Shapes on the Wind* could well be the inspirational handbook for people planning to grow old disgracefully and vibrantly.'

Lindsay Wright, *Daily News*, New Plymouth (NZ)

'In these couch-bound times, it's wonderful to read stories like that of David Lewis ... and what a life it has been (and still is) ... Lewis writes with charming frankness about the deliberate challenges he set himself, each adventure being as much against himself as against the physical challenges of nature. In overcoming his own fear and limitations he exhibits his true heroism.'

Margie Thomson, *New Zealand Herald*

'Unlike most Kiwi heroes, Lewis is articulate and self-observant, an eloquent writer with a dry wit ... Highly recommended, then, to everyone who yearns to lead a less mundane existence (but doesn't know where to start).'

Anne French, *New Zealand Books*

'There is something almost incandescent about David Lewis's energy and enthusiasm ... "I seem," he reflects in this book, "to have lived an unconscionable number of lives in disparate places." You can say that again. But it is not the least quality of this engaging autobiography that gives us a good idea of these different lives and how they reflect on the whole man — not just the prototype valiant seaman or intrepid explorer or dedicated scholar ... This is scarcely the place to judge, but the nobility of his character in every respect emerges so clearly that one is bound to conclude that he must be deeply loved, in a wide variety of cultures. What man could ask for more?'

Michael Richey, *Navigation News* (UK)

shapes ON THE wind

UPDATED EDITION

DAVID LEWIS

HarperCollins*Publishers*

To the star-path navigators of Oceania

HarperCollins*Publishers*

First published in Australia in 2000
Reprinted in 2001
This updated edition published in 2002
by HarperCollins*Publishers* Pty Limited
ABN 36 009 913 517
A member of the HarperCollins*Publishers* (Australia) Pty Limited Group
www.harpercollins.com.au

HarperCollins*Publishers*
25 Ryde Road, Pymble, Sydney, NSW 2073, Australia
31 View Road, Glenfield, Auckland 10, New Zealand
77-85 Fulham Palace Road, London W6 8JB, United Kingdom
Hazelton Lanes, 55 Avenue Road, Suite 2900, Toronto, Ontario M5R 3L2
and 1995 Markham Road, Scarborough, Ontario M1B 5M8, Canada
10 East 53rd Street, New York, NY 10022, USA

National Library of Australia Cataloguing-in-Publication data:

Lewis, David, 1917-2002.
  Shapes on the wind
  Updated ed.
  Includes index.
  ISBN 0 7322 7662 4.
  1. Lewis, David, 1917-2002. 2. Sailors – Biography.
  3. Voyages and travels. I. Title.
910.45

Author's note: Nautical miles have been used when describing sea distances.

Permission to quote from *Seven Pillars of Wisdom* kindly granted by Trustees of the
Seven Pillars of Wisdom Trust.

Permission to quote from *The Seal Oil Lamp* kindly granted by Dale De Armond.

Permission to quote from 'Do Not Go Gentle Into That Good Night' from *Collected Poems* by
Dylan Thomas, published by J. M. Dent, kindly granted by David Higham Associates Limited.

Design and internal maps by Luke Causby/HarperCollins Design Studio
Typeset by HarperCollins in 9.5/13 Ehrhardt MT
Front cover and spine photograph courtesy of Barbara and Garry Satherley
Back cover photograph courtesy of David Lewis

Printed and bound in Australia by Griffin Press on 79gsm Bulky Paperback

8 7 6 5 4 3 2 1   02 03 04 05

About the Author

The late Dr David Lewis (DCNZM) was born in Plymouth, England, in 1917. At the age of two, he moved to New Zealand with his family and went to school in Tapu on the west coast of the Coromandel Peninsula and Titikaveka in the Cook Islands. Later, he attended Wanganui Collegiate School and Otago University Medical School, but completed his medical degree in Leeds, England, graduating with a MB, ChB in 1942.

During the Second World War, he was a Parachute Battalion Medical Officer in the British Army and served in Normandy and Palestine. After the war, he moved to Jamaica to be near his plantation-owning parents, and became a port doctor and a physician in a leper colony. After his father died, he returned to England and set up a general practice in the East End of London, where his first two children were born. In 1964, however, he quit his practice to sail with his second wife and two children around the world in a catamaran, *Rehu Moana*, the first multihull circumnavigation of the globe.

Sailing was not a new pursuit for Lewis. As a teenager, he had canoed 430 miles from his school at Wanganui to his home in Auckland. In 1960, he had placed third in the first single-handed transatlantic race, won by Francis Chichester, and had raced again in 1964. In 1963, he had led the Greenland Sea Expedition. But it was after the three-year-long *Rehu Moana* adventure that Lewis began a new chapter in his life, cut off from a nine-to-five job and conventional limitations. It was a period of both great adventure and scientific and personal discovery for Lewis, and his activities centred on two mysterious parts of the globe: the Pacific and the Antarctic.

In the late 1960s, Lewis spent nine months with his son Barry sailing with the traditional star-path navigators of the Pacific Islands on the gaff ketch *Isbjorn*. Then, in the mid 1970s, he joined the crew of the double-hulled canoe *Hokule'a* for a 2500-mile voyage without conventional navigational aids from Hawaii to Tahiti. He also made several expeditions into the deserts of Central Australia, documenting the wayfinding secrets of the Australian Aborigines.

In the early 1970s, Lewis made the first-ever single-handed voyage to Antarctica in the yacht *Ice Bird*, and followed that up with three other Antarctic expeditions in the late 1970s and early to mid 1980s. The subsequent two decades were largely spent on scientific expeditions in the Soviet Far East, Alaska, Melanesia and Polynesia.

In 1993, aged seventy-six, he once again sailed single-handed, this time from the Solomon Islands to Australia. In 2000, aged eighty-three, he attempted to sail his yacht *Taniwha* to the Caroline Islands in Micronesia in order to return an ancient *rokeyok*, or sacred navigator's vessel, to its traditional custodians but the yacht foundered and sank off Tryphena Bay, Great Barrier Island, near Auckland. Sadly, Lewis was forced to make the trip by more conventional means — by air. In late 2000, he began fitting out a new yacht, *Leander*, with the help of friends and benefactors and, with no firm plans in mind, began sailing up the east coast of Australia.

On 22 October 2002, Lewis passed away in Gympie Hospital, Queensland. He was eighty-five. His last piece of writing, *Apocalypse Tin Can Bay*, is published for the first time in this updated edition of his autobiography.

David Lewis was the author of twelve books and contributed fiction to *Argosy* magazine, and articles to *National Geographic*, *Playboy*, *Oceania*, *The Lancet*, *The British Medical Journal*, *Medical World*, *Exploration Medicine*, the *Journal of Pacific History*, the *Journal of the Polynesian Society*, the *Journal of the Royal Institute of Navigation* and *Hemisphere*. He was the recipient of the following honours: Honorary Citizen of Newport, Rhode Island (1964); Francis Chichester Trophy from the Royal Yacht Squadron (1965); Bernard Fergusson Trophy for New Zealand 'Yachtsman of the Year' (1965); Daily Telegraph Award as 'Traveller of the Year' (1967); Royal Cruising Club Seamanship Medal (1967 and 1975); Honorary MSc from Leeds University (1967); Fellowship and Gold Medal of the Australian Institute of Navigation and the Royal Institute of Navigation (1975); Superior Achievement Award of the American Institute of Navigation (1975); Honorary Life Member of the Royal Burnham Yacht Club, the Royal Western Yacht Club of England, the Royal Cruising Club, and the Little Ship Club; Blue Water Medal of the Cruising Club of America (1982); attachments to the University of Alaska (1988–91) and the University of Auckland and National Maritime Museum of New Zealand (1990–96); Australian Geographic Society's 'Adventurer of the Year' (1998); Member of the Society to Study Human Performance in Extreme Environments (1999); Distinguished Companion of the New Zealand Order of Merit (2001); and Honorary Fellowship of the Royal Institute of Navigation (2002).

He is survived by four adult children, three grandchildren and one great-grandson.

Books by David Lewis

The Ship That Would Not Travel Due West (1961)
Dreamers of the Day: An Arctic Adventure (1964)
Daughters of the Wind (1967)
Children of Three Oceans (1969)
We, the Navigators: The Ancient Art of Landfinding in the Pacific (1972)
Ice Bird: The First Single-handed Voyage to Antarctica (1974)
From Maui to Cook: The Discovery and Settlement of the Pacific (1977)
The Voyaging Stars: Secrets of the Pacific Island Navigators (1978)
Voyage to the Ice: The Antarctic Expedition of Solo (1979)
The Maori: Heirs of Tane (1982)
Icebound in Antarctica (1987)
Shapes on the Wind (2000)
Shapes on the Wind: Updated Edition (2002)

Acknowledgments

To my longtime friend and agent, Tim Curnow, whose refusal to be put off by 'he's old hat' or 'never heard of him' I owe the best of publishers, and the staff of Curtis Brown.

John Ferguson and Ian Watt, both formerly of HarperCollins, were instrumental in bringing the original edition to fruition, and for this new edition I extend my sincere thanks to Jesse Fink, who pressed for HarperCollins to consider updating the book and who once again has been my long-suffering editor and guide, and designer Luke Causby, who created a new map for the chapter *Apocalypse Tin Can Bay*.

Howard Whelan of *Australian Geographic* gave the book his most generous support, and his organisation honoured me with their 'Adventurer of the Year' award.

Closer to home, my son Barry and my daughter-in-law Ros unearthed long-forgotten items from old photo albums. My youngest daughter Vicky spent endless hours correcting my deplorable spelling, and Robyn Stewart and Ros Demas were indefatigable proofreaders and critics. For their research into the O'Neill family history I thank my cousin Lloyd Speedy, and Waitakere historian and former Miss New Zealand Mary Woodward.

Further afield are major players in my story: Dick Smith, for one; the late and much-missed Sir Peter Blake; the editors of *National Geographic*; and my former wife Dr Fiona Lewis, who never allowed our differences to stand in the way of cooperation over the children and support for my own ventures.

I am enormously grateful to Gordon Lewins and Steve Ramsey who helped rebuild *Leander*, along with James Couston and Gary Henschel, and I would like to acknowledge the help and support of Larry and Heidi Bardsley, Mike and Denise Harrison, Brian Sweeney, Jill and Janet Blake, David Edmondson and Jo Solomon.

And last but not least, thanks must go to Anne Cross, to whose endless patience in deciphering four audio tapes and, even worse, writing, I owe *Apocalypse Tin Can Bay*.

Contents

Introduction

Clouds in long columns driving before the trades; towering
thunderheads of unimaginable power and portent that herald
hurricanes; the ever-changing seascape that makes over the marine
world anew each day, so completely, as calm succeeds storm, that
you can hardly credit it as the same sea. I have long been moved at
the wonder of it all. Yet fresh perspectives keep being revealed to
me by such unlikely candidates as Arctic reindeer herders and
Siberian Eskimos, television censor Mary Moos on our 1995
Tasman Sea winter crossing and, after six months sailing the South
Pacific, sculptor/potter Robyn Stewart. I owe to her artist's eye a
deeper perception. The title of this book acknowledges, in small
measure, my debt to her.

In Maori, *koro* means 'grandfather'. Bay of Plenty Maori expand
the term to mean 'respected elder'. Indeed, I was so-called on board
the double-hulled *waka* (travelling canoe) *Te Aurere*, during our
voyage without instruments from Rarotonga in the Cook Islands to
Aotearoa (New Zealand) in November 1995. *Koro* introduces what
is perhaps the central theme of this book, the challenge of ageing.
It seemed particularly appropriate to explore this in my eightieth
year, the age I was when I began writing this book in 1997. In the
late 1990s events such as John Glenn's return to space and a
growing appreciation of the buying power of the 'grey market' had
revealed oldies to be potential social assets rather than garbage to be
discreetly disposed of, and so preempted part of my thesis.

The challenge of ageing! While the shapes sculpted by the South
Seas winds may well remain exotic to people half a world away and
the ocean less appealing than land, the age challenge comes to all of
us in time. By *challenge*, what do I mean?

As our functions come to be eroded by the accumulated wear and
tear of life, it is all too easy to grossly overestimate the *degree* of
resulting deterioration and give up. 'You mustn't expect to still be

able to do it now' is a false imperative dictated by outdated and regrettably negative social expectations and voiced often by people, especially social and medical workers, whose experience of ageing is largely confined to the *sick* aged. Such negative attitudes are particularly inappropriate today, when life expectancy is steadily increasing and all manner of props are increasingly available, like glasses (a boon not always available in the Third World), artificial corneal lenses, hearing aids, and a host of prostheses. I admit to having a number of such props myself. My 'tin and tupperware' hip replacement, for instance, the legacy of a skiing accident, has stood the test of close on two decades of hard usage in the Arctic and Antarctic and over many miles of ocean.

In fact, if we don't pamper ourselves too much and continue to exercise our bodies and minds, we deteriorate very little, sometimes hardly at all, in the absence of disease. We can still do all or most of what we used to do, albeit perhaps more slowly, balancing with conscious care where once spontaneous reflex guided our footsteps. There is an insidious tendency to assume that just because some activity is harder than it was, and probably deemed socially inappropriate for our age group (orgasms, for instance), we should, therefore, simply 'give it away'. The only way to be certain if we're up to it, it seems to me, is to periodically test our limits. Invariably, we will then find we can still do much more than we had thought possible. (My father understood this, too, when in late middle age he told me that this was the time of life to take risks, and proceeded to prove the point by leaving New Zealand for Jamaica and the heavy challenges of a totally new and demanding career — running a plantation.)

Mountains had loomed very large in my youth, but have since become higher and steeper, a process aggravated by a detached retina and sundry other visual disabilities, including loss of central vision in my right eye, that materially impair my distance perception and balance, making me, according to a young cousin, 'doddery'. I owe a huge debt to climbing friends who chivied me, in my late seventies, into vertical challenges that ultimately revealed what a wimp I had become. (The spinoff is that I am still tramping the Waitakere West Coast bush tracks with, among others, the acerbic young cousin.)

The first occasion, I remember, was a climb with crampons and twin ice axes up a frozen waterfall in Alaska. I felt considerable relief when my mentor pronounced the ice unstable and we retreated, to the benefit of my trembling calves and overstretched nerves. Then came a climb on the 3285-metre Mount Baker in Washington State, where I was pleased to discover that steep snow slopes and crevasses were of little concern and only a wrong route, taken earlier, had robbed us of the summit. More recently, a young sailing friend, Tim Brokenshire, who is a Sydney rock-climbing instructor, led me up one of the Three Sisters pinnacles at Katoomba in the Blue Mountains west of Sydney. The experience left me quaking at the realisation that simple cowardice was my problem. Physically, I could do it easily.

But since what I know best is the ocean, it was at sea in 1993 that I undertook the first deliberate challenge to test my limits. This was to sail the 1400 miles from the Solomon Islands to Australia alone in the 32-foot gaff cutter *Gryphon*. I had last sailed single-handed on the *Ice Bird* twenty years earlier. In the intervening years, the donkey work had been done by fit, young male and female companions. Could I still climb the mast in an emergency and manage all the rest on my own? I duly set out to find the answer.

I seem to have lived an unconscionable number of lives in disparate places, so that circles of even the most significant friends rarely intersect. Seeing that I must roam rather widely in space and time in this book, a chronological format is essential to avoid hopeless confusion. At the same time *Shapes on the Wind* is not intended as a comprehensive autobiography. I have no wish to revisit dreary blind alleys nor to agonise fruitlessly over past instances of my own selfishness, obtuseness or unkindness, so reserve the right to be selective. Thus, significant incidents and individuals may receive no mention at all. To them I tender my apologies.

xiv shapes ON THE wind

I have often been asked about my marriages, for instance. This is not so simple as it sounds. In the first place, my adult life began long before the word 'partners' was invented, in the days when Woolworths mock 'wedding rings' and doctored names in hotel registers were the norm. Then, there were marriages of pure convenience to allow residence in another country; so, all in all, my 'real' total is three.

One problem I have faced is how much to include from earlier works. After all, some of them have dealt with my life's high spots. But since my other books are all out-of-print, with the exception of *We, the Navigators* and a number of new international editions of *Ice Bird*, I have felt free, when appropriate, to recapitulate.

I also offer any apologies for possible errors in dates and the spellings, and sometimes omissions, of people's names. It is not only my short-term memory loss that is responsible for this, but the unfortunate circumstances that saw poor *Taniwha* take with her to the ocean floor my background material for this book, magazine articles, my two 1970s short stories, every last copy of my résumé, and, less hard to bear, all my income tax receipts.

This book is less about particular personal incidents than about the themes that have informed my major endeavours. The extraordinary precision with which nameless men and women managed to find their way across oceans and deserts has fascinated me ever since my imagination was fired as a child by my cousin Tumu Korero in Rarotonga. It has led me to travel over the years through many Pacific islands, Indonesia, Australian deserts, and the Arctic tundra of Chukotka. Then there have been my explorations of wild places, especially Antarctica. Both obsessions have necessarily involved rejection of 'proper' life stages. For many years now I have been 'too old' for what I have been doing, and still do — rising to the ongoing challenges that life continues to offer so abundantly.

o n e

New Zealand and Rarotonga

My father, Trevor Alyn Lewis, came from a prominent family in Bangor, North Wales. His father, Sir Henry Lewis (I long thought his name was 'Tyde', which is Welsh for grandfather) was Mayor of Bangor and principal of the local university, as well as being involved in religious and temperance activities. Newspaper clippings of the time make him sound so model a citizen as to be phenomenally dull. But I believe this to be quite unfair: he was the epitome of genuine goodness, not conformity. His imaginative scope is revealed in his role as a founder of Colleg Harlech, an adult education institution for miners and quarrymen that was revolutionary and groundbreaking for its time. Henry was a flour miller until forced out of business by large-scale monopolies in the 'rationalisation' that accompanied the First World War. 'Henry' is perhaps a misnomer: 'Arise Sir *Harry* Lewis,' Edward VII proclaimed. 'I will not knight you as *Henry*, that is a foreign French name!'

The foundations of the Lewis family's modest fortune had been laid by Henry's father, my great-grandfather, Thomas, known as 'Lewis Palestine' — a Welsh joke, since Palestine was about the only country he had not (then) visited. According to my father's account — Trevor was prone to exaggeration — Thomas, a poor boy from an Anglesy village (true), came to work at the Bangor flour mill, ultimately marrying the mill owner's daughter (true). She was so ill-favoured and bad-tempered that no one else would have her, so Thomas set out to travel the world (very doubtful). Thomas, in fact, was a deeply religious man and a Welsh nationalist, as we would say today. He was a pioneer of the Welsh settlement of Patagonia, where the aim was to preserve the language and the nonconformist faith. He later became MP for Bangor.

My father, on leaving school, worked as a cowboy, or young jackaroo, to use the Australian term, on a ranch in Oregon, which was owned by Jim Rice, an émigré from Bangor who had made good. A huge photograph of Windsor Castle adorned one wall of his ranch's dining room. With a sob in his voice and tears in his eyes, Rice would point to the photograph and theatrically exclaim, 'My old home!'

So convincing was Rice's performance that Trevor, who knew full well the tiny Bangor cottage that his employer had really come from, still felt a lump in his throat. But despite such foolery, these were rough times on the high plains. Teenaged Trevor, who did not drink, had to drive a wagon to town on Saturday nights to bring home the brawling drunken ranch-hands from the saloon. First, however, he had to prudently collect their guns and stow them in the box under his seat. It was not unknown for a solitary cowhand or lonely shepherd to be found shot to death out on the range.

Trevor loved riding the open prairie that rolled unbroken to the distant snow-capped pyramid of Mount Hood. He often recalled the meals around the chuck wagon, where outdoors-honed appetites made short work of heaped flapjacks drenched in maple syrup and mugs of strong American coffee. He had a less pleasant experience on his way home, however, when he was robbed of his wages in a Chinese theatre in San Francisco. Luckily, he found work in a road gang to help raise his fare home.

Back in the UK, my father studied at the Camborne School of Mines to become a mining engineer. Unlike me, he excelled at sports and even played in a rugby trial for England. His first engineering job was at a mine in Kalgoorlie, Western Australia. The mining town was several days inland by stage coach. During a stopover Trevor was naïve enough to inquire about bathing in a nearby lake that he had seen on a map. Everyone was eager to help and Trevor, with his bathing suit over his arm, was followed by a crowd of interested spectators. The lake, of course, was a vast, dry salt pan: it hadn't seen rain for seven years.

Trevor's next job was in Burma, on the oil fields. He loved the country and its people but unfortunately contracted dysentery and typhoid and became so debilitated that he was advised to find a more salubrious climate. He chose Fiji and the sugar plantations of Vanua Levu. This was in 1914.

Trevor had four brothers and sisters: Nelly, Arthur, Roger and Nora. Arthur was a ship's captain under sail, who had trained on HMS *Conway*. While Trevor was working at a refinery in Mandalay, Arthur had temporarily abandoned the open ocean to skipper an 'Irrawaddy Flotilla' steamer on the run from Rangoon to Mandalay. The captains on these steamers were ruthlessly competitive, and thought nothing of ramming each other. My father was very fond of his big brother, so I am at a loss to account for this remark by Nelly: 'Your dear grandmother was so worried when she heard your father and uncle were in the same country. She was sure they would kill each other!' Whatever did she mean? Even allowing for the fact that Nelly was then more than a shade ga-ga, there must have been something mysterious behind this statement, extreme even for the hot-tempered Lewis family.

Ultimately, Arthur was to lose his life in the First World War while leading an Indian cavalry charge outside Baghdad. Not one to

be overawed by authority, he was due to be court-martialled for
sending his Indian wife to England on a troopship without
permission. Arthur's son, Allan, migrated to a farm in New
Zealand. He was later to lose half his hand as a rear gunner in the
Second World War. I will always remember a visit he paid at the
hospital where I was an intern while awaiting my call-up.

'Who *is* he?'

The tall, dark, handsome, wounded RNZAF officer quite
devastated the nurses, who thronged to meet him. I have never
been so popular in a hospital before or since. Allan, no longer able
to farm, became a medical auxiliary back in New Zealand. His son,
my namesake, an ex-helicopter pilot, lived until recently in Rotorua.

The youngest brother, Roger, after being severely wounded in
the First World War, became a lawyer in Cheshire. Trevor's younger
sister, Nora, of whom I became exceptionally fond, never married,
and devoted her considerable energies to women's institutes in New
Zealand (with an ancient Morris car and a tent). She was also a
teacher in the mountains of Kentucky in the United States. One of
my earliest memories, I must have been all of five, is of my father,
who was, I think, rather afraid of his radical sister. He explained to
me that 'ladies who don't get married get knotted up inside like
your aunt Nora'. I watched her intently thereafter but, to my
intense disappointment, there was no sign of the knots.

Much later, Nora was sharing a home in Wales with Nelly, by
then a widow and very deaf indeed. Nelly was in bed, nursing a
broken leg. 'You mustn't get out of bed, Nelly.' Nora's penetrating
shriek could be heard clearly through two feet of Welsh stone wall.
'You mustn't be like that silly Mrs Williams Ellis of Abersoch.
She broke one leg, then she fell down and broke the other. Wasn't it
lucky she only had two!'

My mother, Carinna Augusta Barry O'Neill, became a doctor in
the days when female doctors were few and far between. Only two
English medical schools would accept women at the time, the Royal
Free and Durham. Carinna studied at the latter. Even there she
encountered prejudice. During her final oral examination one

professor went so far in expressing his disapproval of female doctors as to turn his back on her and stare out of the window, leaving it to his colleague to conduct the 'distasteful' examination on his own. Less than encouraging, one would think, for a nervous student facing her greatest ordeal! To balance things a little, she was a favourite pupil of the famous physician Rutherford Morrison, who inscribed one of his books to her.

Carinna was dark, very pretty and wavy-haired, and it has always been a disappointment to me that I inherited my father's sandy colouring. Carinna was shy to a degree all her life, but was exceptionally strong-willed nonetheless.

The O'Neills' New Zealand history began with Carinna's grandfather, James O'Neill of Manor Hamilton in County Leitrim ('full of old iron works, peaty hills,' says my daughter Anna, who has stayed in the town) who, like his own father Dr John Henry O'Neill of Tyrone, was an apothecary/chemist/doctor. He landed by steamer from Sydney at Kororareka in the Bay of Islands (now Russell) in 1839, a year before the Treaty of Waitangi, two years before Heke's and Kawiti's remarkably successful Northern War. He returned to Ireland for a time, then went back to New Zealand in 1842 on the sailing ship *Pilgrim* together with his brother Allan and their families. James and Allan landed at New Plymouth. At the time, Kororareka was being sacked by the formidable Heke (oddly with the participation of many of its Pakeha inhabitants), so was not available as an entrepôt. The brothers and their families walked to Auckland. James's wife was Catherine Barry, hence my mother's middle name and our relationship with Kevin Barry, the IRA lad tragically hanged at eighteen, and hero of the ballad:

> ... *Another martyr for old Ireland,*
> *Another murder for the crown* ...

The New Zealand O'Neills only recently found out that a third brother, Louis, went to Philadelphia, where he changed his name to Neil in deference to the anti-Irish sentiment of the time.

More recently, David Hopkins, one of his descendants, migrated to New Zealand and founded a vineyard at Matakana in Northland. A family reunion was held there in January 1999. While some eighty O'Neill descendants attended, ironically none of us bore the O'Neill surname.

Over the last few generations the O'Neills have drifted far and wide — to Australia, South Africa, and the tropical Pacific. One such was a part-Maori, Mary O'Neill, from Mauke in the Cook Islands. She married a Cowan and later we will encounter my cousins George Cowan in Rarotonga and Francis Cowan in Tahiti. Regrettably, I have been unable to find out exactly where she fits into the family network. She may or may not have been the same striking, dark-complexioned old lady that I fondly remember from my childhood, Mary Henrietta O'Neill Cowan of O'Neills Bay and Te Henga on the wild west coast of the Waitakere Ranges near Auckland. Her farm was the scene of wonderful Maori *hungi* (earth oven feasts).

Carinna was born in Italy, where her father, Dr Jack O'Neill, painted monumental oils of rocky defiles and opulent ladies in classical settings. His medical education had consisted of an apprenticeship in Ireland, where fledgling physicians used to fight over whose turn it was to pull teeth or lance abscesses, so academically his training left something to be desired. In any case, he was much more interested in being a painter. Eventually, he moved to New Zealand. The years 1913 and 1914 found Carinna, who had graduated from medical school more conventionally, taking ship to New Zealand to urge Jack to rejoin his first wife, Carinna's mother, in England. He presented Carinna with greenstone carvings, but was deaf to her entreaties, for he was firmly attached to his second wife Hoanna Te Waka, a Maori lady noted for her beauty, her stature and the number of her husbands (five, I believe, of whom grandfather Jack was the last). They had a son, Jack, who was the apple of his father's eye and who chose to be identified as a Maori. The family must have had some money in those days, for young Jack studied at Duntroon Military College, Australia's Sandhurst. Subsequently, the handsome young infantry lieutenant could be observed spending his leaves at London's Ritz Hotel. Jack was killed in 1916, a lieutenant in the Te Hokowhitu a Tu, the fighting detachment of Tu, the god of war, the real name of the Maori Pioneer Battalion. (I dedicated my book, *The Maori: Heirs of Tane*, to his memory.) His son's death devastated my grandfather and he did not long survive him.

Taking ship back to England to work in a wartime hospital, Carinna encountered Trevor who, his health now restored, was en route from Fiji to join the army. They fell in love and were married in some style (the British prime minister, Lloyd George, a 'hometown boy', was a friend of the Lewis family) in St Margarets, Westminster, under the crossed swords of the Royal Welch Fusiliers. (A splendid Welsh dragon, a replica of the one passed round the mess to light after-dinner cigars with its meths-flamed breath, was a wedding present from the regiment, and in later years came into my possession.) Trevor served in Mesopotamia, and Carinna in a London hospital where later Trevor, watching her perform an appendicectomy, disgraced himself by fainting.

I, myself, was born in Plymouth, England, on 16 September 1917. What my mother was doing there I have no idea. All I know of my first two years is anecdotal. Thus, I was apparently addicted to raw rhubarb and would howl with frustration if my pram was wheeled past a greengrocer without stopping. My mother's embarrassment was compounded by soldiers chanting, 'Who stuck a pin in the baby?' We were in Yarmouth when the town was shelled by German warships. My mother told me she had wondered anxiously whether my pram would float, as she had contemplated escaping across the harbour.

When I was two years old we sailed to New Zealand aboard the liner *Bremen*. My first memories are of Orua Bay in Manukau Harbour, and, naturally, of the beach. Spearing flounder in the shallow water, our two cats would follow us, crying piteously but unable to resist the smell of the fish. I once found a beautiful iridescent creature at the tideline. Naturally I poked it curiously, then ran howling up the beach — it was a Portuguese man o' war, or bluebottle, whose sting, as I found to my great regret, is most painful.

The dirt roads near Manukau Heads would become virtually impassable in winter, so much so that Carinna often had to visit patients on horseback. I remember sitting proudly on the saddle in front of her. Regrettably, bowing to then-fashionable ideas of a mother's role, she rarely practised medicine thereafter. A dreadful waste of talent that would have delighted her surly examiner! It has taken me many years to realise it, but my wonderful parents were trapped between two worlds: the Edwardian mores of *noblesse oblige* — you simply do not take work when others need it more (an attitude they were to hold more strongly during the Depression) — and the ethos of greed that is so lauded today.

The memory of my first sail remains vivid. I can still recall sitting on the bottom boards of a dinghy in the hot sunshine, watching with awe while my almost grown-up cousin, Val Edgecombe, set sail and steered us confidently out to sea. Deeply etched in my memory, too, is the look on my father's face after he had rescued us. Years later I mentioned the incident to my mother.

'I suppose Val was about eighteen?' I asked.

She looked at me quizzically. 'Well, not quite, you were five and he was eleven.'

When I was about six and a half, I broke my left elbow falling off a pony — I have never been much of a rider. The seemingly endless trip to Onehunga and the hospital was by launch. Here, I disgraced myself by howling in terror at the x-ray machine, which for some unknown reason I was convinced was going to cut off my arm. About this time, I paid my first visit to a dentist. I well remember my outrage at the unexpected agony and the equally shocked dentist shaking a blood-stained finger and angrily addressing my mother: 'Madam, a child's bite goes septic!'

Subsequently, we moved to Whalebone Creek, near Tapu on the Coromandel Peninsula north of Thames. Here I first went to school, a one-teacher establishment with twenty-five pupils. I clearly remember the long daily walk to school — about three and a half kilometres, as I recall, skirting awesome cliffs on the way. I revisited Tapu last year in company with blond, athletic Fran Gosnell, daughter of a former fellow pupil at both Tapu and Otago Medical School. We were mightily amused to find that the 'large' bungalow where I had lived had unaccountably shrunk to a mere bach (small holiday home); the walk to school measured not three and a half kilometres, but half a kilometre on the odometer; the tall cliffs were only two metres high. With the best will in the world, memories can sometimes play us very false indeed.

I vaguely remember a lady in the village giving me lunch, invariably a boiled egg and bread and butter, on school days. I still cannot bear the nauseating smell of boiled eggs. Apparently my aversion was even greater then, for an elderly O'Neill relative reminisced at a family gathering some thirty years ago: 'You were such a polite little boy. You would eat your egg, then turn around and vomit it up, before quietly going on with your bread and butter.'

I was an introverted child given to daydreaming. I still recall the time I arrived at the village post office only to find my hands, which had been clutching a bunch of letters, were empty — a line of them stretched back accusingly across Tapu green. From that day, I have remained a daydreamer, though more than once my dreams have been gripping enough for me to devote myself to some all-consuming enterprise or take a change of direction in my life. Thus, the sagas of the Maori voyagers, that shortly were to be related to me, would bear fruit many years later in nearly half a century's exploration into maritime prehistory, while dreams of adventure inspired my first all-absorbing project, a kayak traverse of New Zealand, and later, mountain, sea and polar ventures.

It was not until around 1962 in the aftermath of the first single-handed transatlantic race that I came across these words of T. E. Lawrence in *Seven Pillars of Wisdom*, and found them relevant:

All men dream: but not equally. Those who dream by night in the dusty recesses of their minds wake in the day to find that it was vanity: but the dreamers of the day are dangerous men, for they may act their dream with open eyes, to make it possible.

For a generally mild and often timid person such as myself, it sounds rather pretentious, but I suppose I really am one of those 'dangerous men' after all.

My parents treated me as a *person* from a very early age, just one more reason I have to be eternally grateful to them. At one time I was an ardent collector of cigarette cards.

'Have you any cigarette cards, sir?' I asked a Chinese market gardener, who was smoking in his cart. When he drove away, my parents laughed and said something like: 'Fancy calling a Chinese market gardener "sir"!' I was deeply shocked. 'You taught me to call all grown ups "sir" — what difference does it make if someone is Chinese?' My parents apologised. Racism was an insidious disease, they explained, compounded of unconscious false assumptions. They were very ashamed at having fallen into the trap themselves. Not many adults, I feel, would have shown such integrity — and humility.

The tropics beckoned my father. He had been doing rather desultory work for oil companies and increasingly hankered after something more challenging, as well as tropical. I must have been around seven and a half when, some time around 1925, we sold our Tapu home and went to live in Rarotonga in the Cook Islands, where Trevor leased a small coconut plantation, I think, from one of Carinna's Cook Islands cousins. At the time there were separate Maori and European schools on Rarotonga and, fortuitously, my parents sent me to one of the former, the Titikaveka village school. The sallow white children had to wear shoes and socks and sometimes even pith helmets, while we trailed our toes luxuriously through the dust on the warm roads, clad only in shorts or *pareus*.

Our favourite haunt was the reef, where we hunted the yellow-banded sea snakes and dived for *arere* shells. Admittedly, we were forever limping from coral cuts and sea urchin spines. There were moonlit nights when, from the shelter of the scrub, we surreptitiously watched parties of silent men illegally poisoning lagoon fish with crushed *utu* fruit; or equally secretly from under the palms, watched the hula dancing, the provocative nature of which was mysteriously disturbing to even a naïve child such as myself.

I remember, too, the great rat controversy. The colonial government was paying a shilling each for rats' tails, and the ever-optimistic islanders were cutting them off and letting the rats go, in the hope they would grow fresh ones. Could they or couldn't they? Experience answered the vexed question in the negative, and the government underlined the point by transferring the bounty to rats' heads.

My education, in academic terms, left something to be desired. Even then, I rather suspected something was awry in our Niuean teacher's assertion that 42 and 24 were the same thing. But many things I learned were beyond price. Not least were the ancient voyaging sagas told to my father by our cousin Tumu Korero (also known as Charlie Cowan), Keeper of Traditional Knowledge. Tumu spoke of legendary heroes like Kupe, the reputed discoverer of New Zealand, and other fabled voyagers.

Ko Kurahaupo
He waka ururu kapua

'A canoe to dare the clouds of heaven' was the *karakia* or prayer of the captain of the great double-hulled canoe *Kurahaupo* before he guided her across 2000 miles of ocean in Kupe's wake. Such oral traditions are poetic reflections rather than literal history, though modern scholarship has done much to validate them. But men like Kupe really did exist. They truly 'dared the clouds of heaven', and theirs is an exalted place in the story of seamanship. It was not until the early 1960s that glib academic pronouncements, appealing to the land-bound mind but making no sense to the small-boat sailor, were to revive with a vengeance my fascination with Kupe's legacy.

Our stay in Rarotonga ended abruptly. Trevor was never one to tolerate abuses and his somewhat intemperate remarks on the grave shortcomings of the island's medical service ('no better than drunken murderers') led to our expulsion by the colonial government. Back in New Zealand, my father was charged with slander, but despite his witnesses being prevented from leaving Rarotonga, the jury disagreed, going far towards validating his allegations.

We then lived in the Auckland suburb of Takapuna, where, in the Takapuna Sea Cubs, I received my only formal training in seamanship. I missed Rarotonga very much. My two 'sisters', Naomi and Christina Hosking, daughters of friends of my parents who came to live with us in New Zealand, while only a few years older than me, were already young women. I was fond of them, but hardly as companions until we met again as adults, for the gulf between child boy and teenage girl is immense.

Sometimes I found the mores of New Zealand hard to understand. I recall meeting a young woman who was about to get married visiting my mother. I was a generally well-mannered little boy, so I enquired politely, 'What will you do with your baby when you get married?' In rather shocked tones I was informed that it was customary to have babies *after*, rather than before, marriage. 'But in the Islands girls always have a baby when they're about seventeen, and when they get married they give it to an older sister or someone else to look after. Everybody in the Islands loves to have babies,' I said. My mother patiently explained that this civilised custom was frowned upon in New Zealand. Many years later I had a Tongan girlfriend, who had 'adopted' two separate women as her mother. I was often not a little confused as to which 'mother' she was talking about. It is perhaps no coincidence that, given the strength of the extended family network, I have never come across an unwanted child anywhere in the Pacific.

A rather shy and solitary boy, I was a great collector of all manner of objects. I housed them in the crate in which my Aunt Nora's Morris car had been shipped out from England. Particular treasures were a small Solomon Islands canoe and some poison arrows (confiscated by my mother, to my extreme distress) that had been given to me by my cousin Charlie Cowan (not the same Charlie as Tumu Korero, but a trading skipper involved in the labour trade and other activities in the Santa Cruz archipelago). I must have been a favourite of Charlie for, apart from the aforementioned gifts, he took me on sea trials on his schooner *Navanora* after her periodical refits in Auckland. During these trials I could be observed clinging ecstatically to the foremast hounds as the schooner pitched over the swells of Hauraki Gulf.

My schooldays culminated in two years of boarding school at Wanganui Collegiate School. I was an undistinguished pupil. In the first place, I found the idea of 'training an elite', which would of necessity be based on income, to be distasteful and inappropriate to a new and democratic country. This was when I began to think independently about social matters for the first time. Then, I was a dreamer and a poor mixer. I had indifferent hand-eye coordination, so was bad at organised games, which in any case I found pointless in a land full of forests, mountains and wild rivers. In 1928, when I was eleven, my father revealed a new world for me by taking me to the volcanic Mount Ruapehu. It was the first time I had ever seen snow. Subsequent holidays were spent skiing, climbing and tramping over the North Island volcanoes. In 1934, when I was seventeen, I celebrated my last days at boarding school by building a canoe/kayak and informing the headmaster that I was going home in it at the end of term — 430 miles across New Zealand by river, portage, lake and sea. His prompt veto was undermined by my parents' written permission. But at what cost to their peace of mind? After all, I was their only child. Since no one else would come with me I set out alone.

It was on this fifty-day trip that I first experienced the fulfilment that comes with enforced self-reliance in struggling towards a goal. Looking back, it is now obvious that this undertaking was to set the tone for much of my future life. How did I ever come to dream it up in the first place? Even now, I really have very little idea. I only know that it popped up in my mind somehow, and that I immediately recognised it as a great idea, something crying out to be done. I would do it. Only afterwards did secondary matters intrude on my plans: I knew nothing of kayaks (answer: build a very light one out of boxwood, laths and aircraft fabric; fit a spray dodger) and nothing about rivers either (answer: study maps, read accounts, ask around).

So it was that my first adventure came to fruition, and others that came to follow took shape in much the same way with sometimes mixed results. This sequence of dream, obsession, commitment to doing it, and only then trying to work out *how*, seems to have set up a lifelong pattern. I am sure that in this manner came about my abortive, ineffectual and illegal attempts at Arab/Israeli *rapprochement* in 1945–46, the single-handed transatlantic races of 1960 and 1964 (Blondie Hasler's idea, not mine, but which gripped my imagination nevertheless); the *Rehu Moana* circumnavigation of 1964–67; my ongoing exploration into the heroic past of pre-instrumental maritime navigation and wayfinding; the 1972–74 *Ice Bird* voyage and subsequent Antarctic adventures up to 1984; and my time in the Russian Arctic in 1988–90.

Back to that very first adventure. There were times, like a capsize in the icy Tongariro River — that I was to learn later had only been shot once before — when I came close to losing heart. To haul the light craft on long portages I constructed a trailer with bicycle wheels. Anticipating frequent wettings, I carried no blankets and slept wrapped in a ground sheet. More by luck than good management, for reliable information about the river was then hard to come by, I managed to haul out and avoid the major Waikato rapids. The final legs were coastal: across the tidal Manukau Harbour to near where the international airport now stands, across New Zealand by the reputed Tainui canoe portage (the country is exactly one and a half kilometres wide at this point) to the Tamaki River, the Waitemata Harbour and home. But when I did eventually reach Takapuna I had an empty feeling, as if an essential ingredient of endeavour was somehow missing, left behind somewhere in the rapids of the Tongariro.

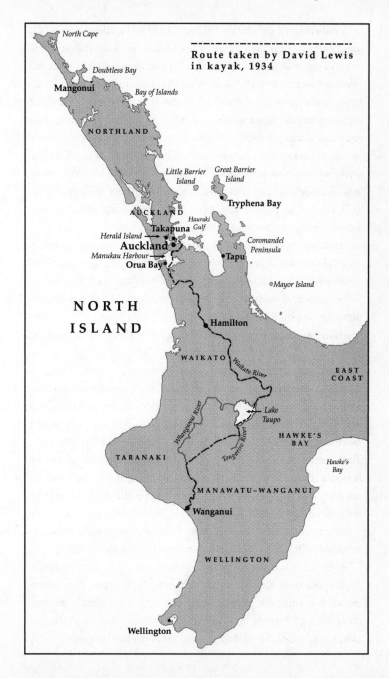

North Cape

Doubtless Bay

Mangonui

Bay of Islands

NORTHLAND

Little Barrier Island

Great Barrier Island

Tryphena Bay

AUCKLAND

Hauraki Gulf

Takapuna

Herald Island

Auckland

Coromandel Peninsula

Manukau Harbour

Tapu

Orua Bay

©*Mayor Island*

NORTH ISLAND

Hamilton

WAIKATO

Waikato River

EAST COAST

Whanganui River

Lake Taupo

HAWKE'S BAY

Tongariro River

TARANAKI

Hawke's Bay

MANAWATU–WANGANUI

Wanganui

WELLINGTON

Wellington

Route taken by David Lewis in kayak, 1934

I rediscovered it between 1935 and 1938 while taking part in the ascent of nineteen unclimbed peaks on the South Island, where I went to medical school in Dunedin (one of these mountains in the Olivine Range I called Mount Carinna after my mother). These Otago mountains are difficult of access through heavy bush and across mountain streams that all too readily become dangerous torrents, rather than being necessarily technically difficult. As a very junior member of the Otago Section of the New Zealand Alpine Club, my role was as a follower rather than leader. My first season was spent guiding and portering on the Fox Glacier in Westland, an experience that seemed not quite real, for I could not get over actually being *paid* for enjoying myself so much.

Looking through some old photographs recently, my son Barry came upon some images of two naked youths riding across the Fox Glacier floodplain on horseback; one was carrying a very large eel.

'What was that about?' he asked. I told him. 'Then you have to put it in the book,' he insisted.

'But you don't want to make your father out to be a law breaker, do you?'

'Why not?' he said, unsympathetically.

The Sunday fishing excursion recalled by the picture had begun with a raid on the Public Works store to obtain gelignite and detonators. Fortunately, I had the gelignite but not the detonators when my horse bolted, strewing sticks of explosive along the track. There remained enough to go on with, though we found to our disappointment that you must almost hit a fish with a half stick of gelignite in a fast-flowing stream to get any results. In fact, the large eel was the sum total of our catch.

'What about these photos, then? Looks like your little Ford was swept away in a flood,' said Barry, leafing through an old album.

Indeed it was. Doug Dick and I were coming back from climbing La Perouse from the west with Arch J. Scott. We came to a stream too deep for the car. Scott crossed on foot — he needed medical attention for a cracked bone in his elbow — and went on to the Fox Hotel. He wasn't at all happy with us; we hadn't shown him as much respect as he believed he deserved. In fact, when he described the climb to the Alpine Club of Great Britain he said he couldn't recall the names of his companions! So Doug and I turned back to find a good camping place till the water went down a bit. An almost empty creek we had crossed half an hour before looked the same to me, but it wasn't. It had washed out. As soon as we entered it the car started floating and bumping downstream. We couldn't get the doors open till it snagged in a fence and we got out. Immediately the fence broke and the car rolled over on its side and disappeared under water and logs. We could hardly credit how lucky we were. Next morning the creek was dry and the car was buried in trees, mud and branches. A truck hauled the car out for us and it took us a week to strip it down and clean it before we got it going again.

'Do you remember these cuttings? How long since you read them?'

Barry passed over a scrapbook. The yellowed newspaper clippings pasted inside were from the *Otago Times* and sixty years old. They were signed 'David Lewis. N.Z.A.C.'. One was headed 'The Ascent of Mount Underwood'.

'I guess I haven't looked at them since they were written. I remember the climbs though. Let's see how I was writing then.' I scanned the old article. 'Yes, that was the first ascent of Mount Underwood, the high peak that overlooks Milford Sound. Lindsay Stuart was leader, then there was Jack Warren and me. We approached from the Hollyford Valley.' I read on:

Suddenly the world fell away below, all round. Far below, the glassy mirror of Milford Sound basked in the sunlight. We were on the summit.

But there could be no loitering. Down the long snow slopes we ploughed again, up the flanks of Karetai, climbing automatically now like machines, very weary and sure-footed as cats in our weariness, for this is nature's gift to the mountaineer, that, as the brain loses control over every movement, forgets to fear, and sinks into a dull apathy of weariness, the body climbs on, never missing a

step or dislodging a stone. We found a ledge which led under the
summit. The peaks were flaming scarlet in the sunset as we saw our
camp like a tiny speck below. But our difficulties were over now; we
were nearly home.

'Not bad!' I muttered. It was uncanny. It was like I was reading
someone else's words; some young climber who had existed far back
in another time. But it was me, sixty years earlier.

The winter following our ascent of Mount Underwood, Ernie
Smith, Cedric Benzoni and I made the first winter crossing on skis
from the headwaters of the Dart River to the Rees. We broke the
journey up country at a hospitable back country farm, where the
toilet was the usual dunny out in the yard. What was not so usual
was the chain that hung down from the roof, an invitation to
unthinking townies. Of course, I fell right into the trap. I tugged the
chain, a great bell clanged, and the assembled occupants of the
homestead roared with laughter. After all, they had to make their
own entertainment in the back country!

Conditions were impossible at the head of the Dart, so we took
shelter in a prospector's wood-framed tent until the blizzards eased.
We made free with the comfortable mattresses and pillows that had
been left behind, even holding pillow fights to while away the
boredom. Eventually the storm subsided and we got over the saddle.
In Queenstown we encountered the prospector.

'You were welcome to the tent, but was my dynamite all right?
I stuffed it in the mattresses and pillows to stop it freezing; you
know how cold makes it unstable — liable to go up at a touch!'

We turned pale.

Another experience in the same region taught me a timely lesson
on impatience. Two of us had spent a week weatherbound in a tent
at the head of Lake Wakatipu, hoping to climb Mount Cosmos.
On our last day we foolishly decided to 'give it a go', though the
mountain was plastered with loose wet snow, which was
avalanching. Eventually, the sight of numerous wet snow avalanches
forced us to return to relative sanity and we agreed it was high time

to retreat. I was belaying on top of a snow-covered bluff, while my companion, at the end of twenty metres of rope, was crossing a snowslide-tracked gully down below. He futilely thrust the shaft of his ice axe into the ice as avalanching wet snow buried him, snapped the axe, and swept him unharmed into the lee of the rock bluff. I, meanwhile, was plucked from my perch like a fly on a string and tumbled down to land on my bottom on hard snow some fifteen to twenty metres down the slope.

We were a sore and sorry pair that picked our painful way down a stony creek bed to the lake. (I only found out much later, when parachute training had become an agony, that my fourth lumbar vertebra had fractured and impacted, effectively splinting itself but depriving me of half an inch of my already modest stature.)

The season after the Mount Cosmos debacle I had my revenge when, under Jack Holloway and John Jackson's leadership, we climbed every one of those virgin Wakatipu headwaters peaks, including my former nemesis. In a different category of difficulty were the first-ever traverses of Mount Aspiring and Mount Sefton, the former under the leadership of Harry Stevenson and Doug Dick, and the latter under Jackson. Conditions were perfect for Mount Aspiring. The unclimbed knife-edge south-east ridge soared above the rocky platform where we spread out our sleeping bags. The weather would never be better, so we doused our spare rations — cabin bread biscuits — in kerosene and warmed ourselves at the unconventional campfire. Dawn found us already well up the ever-steepening hard-frozen snow of the arête. By 8 a.m. I was alarmed and thrilled by the steepness and exposure — our crampons were barely holding; by nine we were on the summit. Just recently, a youth who had read of our climb, fresh from an Outward Bound camp in Mount Aspiring National Park, regarded me with awe as some sort of mystic hero. This was quite misplaced and undeserved.

The seven hours Jackson and I spent without a single adequate belay on the eastern arête of Mount Sefton, near vertical rotten rock blocks cemented together with ice, made me reluctantly realise, even more forcibly than Mount Aspiring had, that I had reached the limit of my ability and was attempting to climb well beyond it. This was a bitter pill to swallow for a youth so dedicated to mountaineering. But the writing was on the wall. I had not yet attained the skill and stamina to be a first-class climber, nor was it at all certain that I had the makings of one. I decided I had better backtrack, at least for the moment, and settle for easier climbs. Otherwise, chances were I would soon be dead.

Nonetheless, rewarding mountaineering escapades continued on lesser, wilder peaks and, indeed, still does after a fashion, for my spirit expands mightily in the vast spaciousness between peak and sky. Then there was skiing. No matter that New Zealand didn't have teachers or ski lifts then, and that I floundered about developing uncorrectable faults in technique (a beginner could learn in less than a week what we picked up over many years), we had lots of fun on Mount Ruapehu in the North Island while I was still at school and on the Rock and Pillar Range in Otago. This 2000-metre treeless escarpment lies some eighty kilometres inland from Dunedin. Arriving by car or chartered bus, our party would spend the night in an abandoned farmhouse at the foot of the range, then slog up 600 metres to the windswept ski fields next morning. It was all very rugged and most enjoyable. I am almost ashamed to admit having won the NZ Universities downhill in 1938, so abysmal was the standard in those days.

Given my engagement with the high hills, it is hardly surprising that my medical studies suffered. First-year chemistry and physics did not gel well with my interests. Zoology, however, I found enthralling and it became a lifelong interest. Physiology seemed a logical and reasoned subject, but anatomy involved too much pure memory work. This was never my strong point, for I have always needed to build chains of logic to make sense of anything and to remember it. No doubt this is why, though I am intrigued by the verbal interplay from one language to the next, I am very poor at retaining vocabulary.

An amusing postscript to those long past university days was when a fellow classmate of mine from Otago was interviewed for a documentary about my life.

'David and I met in the dissecting room,' he recalled. 'That was the first time I ever saw a naked woman — *what an experience!*'

It was not the first time for me but very nearly so. A combination of shyness and my preoccupation with climbing had effectively limited my relationship with girls, much as they intrigued me. It was an older woman, Rima, with her opulent, slim-waisted figure, who opened up a whole new dimension in my life. At first, I think, she was a little put off by my inexperience, but when she *did* decide to go on with our relationship, she mercifully made no allowances for my ignorance and 'pulled no punches', thus effectively imprinting on my senses forever the wonder of sensuous intimacy with an aroused mature woman.

After this I went overboard a little, bedding as many women as I could get hold of — women, rather than girls. Although gaining much experience sexually, I was still hopelessly naïve when it came to another fact of life. Brought up in the warm North Island, as I was, I had never realised that deciduous trees lost their leaves in winter. I had been gaily throwing used condoms into the tree outside my window all summer and was away in the mountains when the leaves began to fall. The innocent student upstairs was unfairly charged with the offence — 'It can't have been that nice, quiet Mr Lewis!' To his great credit he refused to dob me in.

Eventually, I was lucky enough to meet someone very special and, importantly, my own age. Dark, wild and beautiful, Jean Russell was a quarter Maori, and a treasure that I was far too callow to appreciate. Our relationship perforce withered when she moved to Central Otago for health reasons. We never did meet again.* I found consolation with Louise Phillips, a tall Texan university lecturer who taught me a great deal about art and literature. With her high heels and upswept hair, she was at least a head taller than me. We must

---

* Some twenty years after those Otago days, Jean Bell (nee Russell) wrote me a letter on hearing I was sailing back to New Zealand on *Rehu Moana*, sending pictures of herself and her children. She looked as lovely as ever, but this was deceptive. Shortly after we reached Auckland, before we could get in touch, an old skiing and climbing partner, Dot Smith, phoned me in tears. Jean had just died of breast cancer.

have looked a mighty odd pair, but as my youngest daughter assured me recently, 'Let's face it, Daddy, most women are taller than you.'

As I wrote earlier, my restless father, homesick for his beloved tropics, took up the challenge of immigrating to Jamaica to farm eighty hectares of mixed crops. I was eager to see the world beyond New Zealand, that great big unknown where everything seemed to be happening, so, seizing the opportunity, I arranged a transfer to a medical school in Leeds, England, where I could complete the last three years of my training and hopefully visit my parents in the long vacations. So it was that, in 1938 at the age of twenty-one, I accompanied my mother on a Shaw Saville liner via Panama and Trinidad to Jamaica.

The plantation, New Monklands, 600 metres up in the hills overlooking Morant Bay, was a place of enchantment. The house was strongly built of stone and massive bulletwood beams supported the ceilings. Great spreading shade trees sheltered our coffee crop and rows of sugarcane climbed the hillsides, interspersed with citrus, pimento and coconut. Bananas, however, were the main crop. It was all very new and exciting. In the three months I spent there I became a reasonably competent judge of banana suckers and the quality of coffee beans. I never ceased to be amazed at the aptness of the local dialect's turns of phrase, when I could understand it. Thus one off-road village was named 'Casion Call' because the track was so rough you did not call there unless you had ''casion to'. For a people who had emerged out of the nightmare of slavery in the 1830s only to be plagued with continuing poverty, theirs was a wry sense of humour.

The transformation in Trevor's physical wellbeing was striking. He had been short of breath and overweight in New Zealand. Now he was fit and hard, slogging daily up steep ridges in stifling windless heat and humidity, his Walther automatic thrust into his belt or in a shoulder holster, for the times were unsettled.

All too soon it was time for me to leave if I were not to miss the opening term at Leeds Medical School. I travelled to England aboard the liner *Reina del Pacifico* (subsequently sunk during the

Second World War), with stops at Havana, Nassau and Bermuda. The steerage fare was £18 and the language Spanish, which I had been assiduously learning. I could get along well enough then, but having an exceedingly poor verbal memory, despite many months in South and Central America since, I am no more fluent now.

Our three days in Cuba were, for me, the highlight of the journey. The ancient city of Havana, overshadowed by the looming Moro Castle, was my first sight of Europe, albeit Europe transplanted to the New World. Wishing to get away from the vast American gangster-controlled brothel that was the central city in those pre-Castro days, I took a train to the little cow and sugar town of Guines. My hotel room overlooked the plaza, where swarthy, unshaven men, brandishing huge sheathed machetes, rode stocky ponies with cowboy saddles and silver-ornamented bridles, and small boys circulated suicidally on rollerskates.

'*Americano?*' the hotel proprietor had asked me in a none too friendly tone.

'*No. Inglés.*'

He was all smiles at once: '*Usted debe tener calor* [you must be hot].' He then ushered me into a bathroom and produced a wrapped cake of soap. Of course, there was only a trickle of rusty water, but this in no way lessened the spirit of his gesture.

It was a cold and rainy day in March 1939 when we landed at Liverpool and I took the train to Leeds, marvelling at the endless rows of sooty houses and the skeletal leafless trees, an unreal, almost 'underwater' vista, it seemed, soaked by unremitting rain pouring down from grey overcast skies. I was later to learn to love the Yorkshire Moors and the Lakeland Hills, but I still remember that first encounter as an unremitting nightmare. Overwhelmed by loneliness, I pined for the sunshine of New Zealand, Jamaica and Cuba.

I was soon installed in digs and busy adapting to the new lifestyle and lecture routines. Everything was peculiarly unfamiliar — strange considering that this was the mother of all English-speaking countries. Accents were sometimes almost incomprehensible. Anti-Semitism — a social pathology I had never encountered before and found inexplicable — was rife. On the bright side, I began to enjoy the increasingly clinical nature of my studies. Particularly enjoyable breaks were outings to the gritstone tors of Ilkley Moor and spectacular Malham Cove with the university climbing club. Not that rock gymnastics was ever my strong point, but the rolling rock-strewn moors, knee-high in heather and bracken in summer and snow-streaked in winter, let one breathe after the grimy city. For a time the grim Victorian towers of Leeds Infirmary and the drab lecture theatres could be forgotten.

The long vacation offered an opportunity to see something of Europe, so I enrolled in a French history course at a summer school in Strasbourg. The medieval city and its cathedral were enthralling, quite outside my previous experiences. The course, too, was interesting and made me realise how narrow had been the scope of the history taught to me in school back in New Zealand. After classes, groups of us would cycle into the Voges, with its endless pines and ruined keeps.

'Let's bike across the Rhine and have a look at Germany,' I suggested to a fellow student.

'All right. But let's not get into trouble; they say they have a lot of secret fortifications over there.'

'We'll pretend we can't read their notices,' I replied airily.

This was what we did, crossing the international bridge and wending our way lightheartedly among the awesome defences of the Siegfried Line. Of course, the inevitable happened. We were arrested, interrogated — kindly enough, I might add — and escorted back across the frontier. Our young Nazi guards, with their guns and daggers and badges, seemed to us like children in fancy dress. We were not completely naïve. The sorry record of Chamberlain's appeasement, the betrayals of Spain and Czechoslovakia, had seen to that. But neither the stormtroopers nor the scruffy French infantrymen huddled in their machine gun emplacements across the river seemed quite real to us. This sense of unreality blinded us to the true horror of what was in store. The time was August 1939, just one month before the outbreak of the Second World War.

two

War and Peace —
An East End Doctor

Intense excitement gripped us at the school at the announcement that war had been declared. Six of us took time off from sandbagging the infirmary to go and join up, only to be firmly told to return to our classrooms and qualify as doctors first. It was not until wounded soldiers from Dunkirk started coming to our hospital and bombing began that a sense of reality began to intrude. Even then, bombing was no more than an exciting spectacle for us, with the probing searchlights and exploding anti-aircraft 'fireworks'; for me at least, the rising shriek of falling bombs provoked more a tingle of apprehension than real fear.

Visits to London were another matter. Here the devastation was obvious, as was the stubborn resolve and wry humour encountered everywhere — in crowded tube shelters, pubs and socialist student meetings and conferences.

The loud, vital East End, a microcosm of Jewish New York come to life and so different from anything that I had known in New Zealand or Jamaica, fascinated me. Here, despite the obvious poverty, the cultural heritage of Continental Europe — music, theatre, art, literature, and philosophy — could be found. The 'Battle of Cable Street', when Oswald Mosley's police-protected thugs had been stopped and defeated by the massed East End citizenry, was still on everyone's lips. I had yet to meet my first wife, but this was the community whence she came. Sadly, it is mostly gone now, obliterated by the bombing and, much later, through the renovation of docks and warehouses into fashionable apartments for refugees from the West End.

Our studies proceeded, in my case larded with a good deal of left-wing student activism, which made me a target for the conservative anti-Semitic Yorkshire majority. A horrible memory, that I would much rather forget, is of a drunken rabble of medical students howling for my blood at a students' meeting, and of the beating I sustained, not as I would like to think from the whole mob, but from a single pugilist among them. I was left bleeding, utterly humiliated and alone. Not quite alone. One student, a German refugee, stood by me and took care of me. He was later lost at sea.

But we put even the blackest experiences behind us in the course of time. More and more interesting and responsible clinical work came my way as our studies proceeded. I well remember an absurd incident in Casualty one New Year's Eve that almost made up for being on duty at so inauspicious a time. This was in those far off days when doctors, not always deservedly, were supposed to be 'clever', and avenging lawyers were unknown. A man came in with a crushed hand, and the house surgeon, quite unaffected, he was sure, by his modest libations, expertly put him to rights. Next morning the patient returned. He would not dream of questioning the clever doctor, he apologised, but one thing rather puzzled him, and perhaps the clever doctor would explain: why had he sewn all the fingers together? Many years later I was tactless enough to remind the by now distinguished, and knighted, surgeon of this event in his youth. He was not amused.

I qualified as a doctor in 1942. One subject in the finals, therapeutics, had been complicated by my inability to memorise drug doses, so I had awaited the oral with some trepidation. I need not have worried. 'What was it about your paper? Oh, yes. The spelling!' exclaimed the examiners. The two men rocked with laughter, and had such fun asking me to spell simple words that they quite omitted to examine me on the subject itself.

A friend of mine, John Spink, was so sure he had failed that he took himself off to a Lakeland farmhouse without even waiting for the results. In the event, we both passed. When my telegram addressed to 'Dr Spink' reached John he was in the middle of drying dishes in the farmhouse kitchen. In his shock, he dropped the lady of the house's two most prized plates. After the graduation ceremony, for which John had had to return, I joined him in the Lake District to stride over the fells, never tiring of calling each other 'doctor'. (I did not then realise that I had become the fifth doctor in a direct unbroken line from my great-great-grandfather Dr John Henry O'Neill of Tyrone.) The weather was perfect for climbing and the warm rock of Great Gable felt very good to our hands. We returned refreshed to Leeds, after which I enjoyed a stint as a general practice locum in rural Yorkshire. There followed an obligatory year's internship before I could join the forces.

I have often been asked why I chose the paratroops. The short answer is, of course, to travel comfortably by plane and avoid tedious marching. If so, I was doomed to disappointment. In reality the adventure was an attractive inducement but, more responsibly, I detested fascism and all its works and wanted to play as active a part as possible in its overthrow. Paratrooping seemed the best bet. Like my uncle Jack O'Neill, I was adopting a Maori mindset, dedicating myself once and for all to the god of war, Tu, so that nothing further could happen to me.

Regrettably, seeing that New Zealand had no paratroops, the obvious course, since I was in England, was to join the British forces. It seemed to me that about two-thirds of my fellow volunteers had chosen Airborne for the thrill, and about a third for ideological reasons — socialists like me, liberal anti-fascists and, terrible in their hatred, refugee German Jews, all renamed 'Smith' for their own protection if captured and all ruthless avengers of the Holocaust; and, in the Royal Army Medical Corps, volunteer conscientious objectors who were courageous, highly respected and generally humourless.

This was around the time I met my first wife, Perle Michaelson. She was a nurse, a gracefully curved, handsome young widow with a two-year-old son, Michael. In retrospect, I suspect I fell in love with her East End family background as much as I did with her. Also, in hindsight, because of my commitment to Tu, I had not much expectation of surviving the conflict and wished to leave something behind me. The idea of family and children appealed.

Perle's father, descended from a long line of rabbis in Lithuania, had walked across much of Tsarist Russia to escape the Black Hundred and Cossack pogroms. Penniless and weakened by typhus, he had ended up in Stepney, where he gained a reputation as an inventor. More interested in the workers' struggle than in cashing in on his inventions, he was still poor when he died, worn out by the hardships he had suffered. Perle's mother, Bella Michaelson, whose family came from Minsk, was a dedicated communist and the most warmhearted person I have ever met. She died of a massive cerebral haemorrhage among her beloved comrades during an anniversary celebration. Perle's younger brother Sidney was to become a scientist of some renown for his computer analyses of the Dead Sea Scrolls. He later became Professor of Computer Science at the University of Edinburgh, and died in 1991.

My timing in applying for the parachute branch of the Royal Army Medical Corps was poor. D-Day 1944 found me not heroically engaged in battle, but undergoing the rigours of parachute training at Ringway near Manchester. As the training intensified after the invasion, my bung lumbar vertebra became increasingly painful. Yet I could not report sick for fear of being grounded. Our last three jumps were performed in a single day.

As if the nervous strain and lumbar ache were not enough, on my final landing I slipped on a cow pat and dislocated my back. The sheer agony nearly made me pass out. As it was, I crawled to my parachute, bundled it up, and promptly burst into tears. Clearly, I was not of the stuff of which soldiers are made!

I duly reached Normandy in typically unheroic fashion by sea, to be placed in a holding camp near Caen together with nine other parachute-trained doctors. Nothing else happened. Then the word spread that we were to go into ordinary infantry units. Was all the suffering we had endured in our intensive training going to be wasted? This would not do at all. I was elected delegate to present our case to the brigadier and hitchhiked to the front, arriving at his dugout.

'Did you get permission to come here?' he asked me.

'No, sir.'

'Good, we need men with initiative. I will see what I can do about getting as many of you as possible assigned to us. Have you had lunch?'

'No, sir.'

'Well, sit down, you can have the major's dinner ... do you know any nurses at the hospital in Caen?'

I replied that I did.

'Capital. I will drive you back in my jeep.'

The brigadier was as good as his word. I was duly assigned to 224 Parachute Field Ambulance and seconded as MO to the 9th Parachute Battalion, my severely wounded predecessor having been evacuated.

My first taste of action was unedifying in the extreme. We were being deployed into a field, with me in the process of climbing a barbed-wire fence, when rounds from a Schmeisser machine gun rent the air. I gave a convulsive leap and came down firmly impaled on the wire.

'I would get down, sir, if I were you. They are shooting at you, sir,' came the voice of the sergeant-major who was grinning at me from a position of relative safety in the ditch, where the rest of the battalion had promptly taken shelter.

'What the bloody hell do you think I'm trying to do?' I gave a wild heave and tore loose from the barbed wire at the expense of my dignity and trousers.

One thing I learned very soon was the utter confusion of combat. There was the time I was directed to take my ambulances down a road that I found was covered by fixed German machine guns. Only the fact that I had made my own independent reconnaissance averted a disaster. A little later I was establishing a first-aid post when a white flag began waving from a tiny farmhouse nearby.

'*Que êtes-vous?*' Our American-type paratroop helmets were not unlike the enemy's.

'British,' we called back.

A few minutes later a little old couple clutching a coffee pot and bottles of Calvados came running towards us, heedless of the bullets that were flying around their heads and our own cries to go back. Mercifully, they arrived safely.

Leaving my sergeant in charge of the first-aid post, I went forward with the attacking company to see what was happening and what 'medivac' (to use a modern term) was needed. Soon I came upon a German soldier with a huge hole in his chest from a mortar bomb. Air entering the gaping wound had pushed his heart to one side. His heartbeat was faint and fluttering and he could barely breathe. I had inadequate dressings for the size of his wound and there was no time to waste so, seizing a handful of mud and leaves, I slapped it over the wound and strapped it in place with adhesive tape. At once the soldier's colour came back and he began breathing more easily.

'Come on, you lot,' called the sergeant to the enthralled attacking company. 'Get on with it. This is supposed to be a sodding battle not a fucking first-aid lecture!'

I was severely reprimanded by the base hospital. Not only had our casualties arrived blind drunk (and singing raucously, I was informed) at the Advanced Base Hospital, thanks to the hospitality of the old couple, but my treatment of the German soldier had been deemed deplorable.

'Will he live?' I asked.

'Yes,' said the base hospital officer grudgingly. 'But that is not the point.'

A frightening occasion that sticks in my memory was when I was called to the aid of a mortally wounded French Canadian sergeant. As I reached him, clearly identified by the Red Cross armband I was wearing, rifle grenades started bursting around me. I dived frantically for cover and ineffectually returned fire with my .38 revolver. The French Canadian company rescued me and soon brought in the two SS snipers who had killed the sergeant and deliberately set the ambush for the Red Cross. Fresh from the Eastern Front, their wallets contained such sinister souvenirs as photographs of men and women being hung, apparently on telephone wire, of executions before great pits, and other such degradations. The French Canadian soldiers gazed at the POWs in silence.

'We will take them to the prison camp, M'sieur,' offered the senior corporal. The prisoners and their escort moved off down the road and disappeared behind a wood. Soon we heard shots. This, however, did not necessarily mean anything — there was a lot of shooting going on at the time.

Once the iron ring around the Anglo–American bridgehead was ruptured we moved forward apace. We marched through village after village to the cheers of the excited inhabitants, their jubilation often premature as shells from German 88s came whistling over. How were the children coping with the occupation, I wondered? They were coping, I found, by playing. Despite the dangers posed by snipers and shelling, boys and girls armed with makeshift toy rifles would scramble over the rubble, shrilly debating who would play the partisans and who the unpopular Nazis.

Shortly after the breakout from Normandy our badly mauled division was returned to England and, to my dismay, I was posted to the Middle East, where fighting had almost ceased. I appealed to the friendly brigadier.

'Can't help, Lewis,' he said. 'Had the rocket of my life for messing up the high-up's plans. As for you, this is a disciplinary

posting to teach you not to query your betters' plans. No, I'm sorry
to lose you but there's nothing I can do.'

A bright spot before I sailed to Egypt was a message from the
colonel: 'The officers of 224 Parachute Field Ambulance will drink
a toast at your expense this evening.' My daughter Anna had been
born. It was 1945.

In Cairo, all manner of revolutionary groups were conflicting and
interacting. There were the Yugoslav Royalist and Tito camps, a
plethora of illegal Egyptian nationalist movements aimed at
overthrowing King Farouk, Pashas who would bribe army officers
over stores and who sponsored armed raiding gangs, and opposing
Greek factions EDES and ELAS, with whom I became peripherally
involved through my acquaintance on the troopship with a Greek
woman married to a British intelligence officer.

The pro-Communist, anti-monarchist Greek ELAS guerillas,
who had fought the Nazis, were anathema to British policymakers
but were supported by the thousands of Greek troops in Egypt,
among whom it was widely believed that the Gestapo, before
withdrawing, had passed on their files to British intelligence.
Whatever the truth of this rumour, the husband of the troopship
lady, well aware of his wife's lack of discretion, had given her a list
of known ELAS sympathisers in Cairo that she must avoid.

'You know her. You are the only one who can get us the list,' an
ELAS operative begged me. All very well, but a car smash had laid
me low with broken ribs, which I had not reported so as to avoid
compromising my last chance of active service. I promised to do
my best.

'Please come out with me; cheer me up, just for an hour or two.
I feel so bad,' I pleaded to the woman. In truth I could hardly stand
the pain, and must have looked as pathetic as I felt. Whether it was
out of genuine kindness of heart or her innate inability to say
no to a man, something that her husband was all too aware of,

she came. It was with relief that I handed her over to the exceptionally handsome young Greek freedom fighter who just happened to be waiting in the cafe. I was told later that his charm worked and he did get the list.

My batman at this time was a diminutive Italian POW named Luigi. He would inject himself intravenously with a concoction that, according to him, sustained his virility. Goodness knows what it contained, but I was unable to persuade him of its doubtful efficacy and undoubted danger to his health. Months later, long after we had lost track of each other, I encountered Luigi again as the mystery patient in a dermatology ward, where I had come to deputise for the specialist. The cause of his allergic reaction was not difficult to figure out. This time his concoction was confiscated and he promptly recovered.

While the little active service I had seen had spawned its fair share of nervous tension and fear, there were periods of extreme boredom and frustration. Useless tasks were invented by senior officers concerned with maintaining their establishments and rank. Troops being ordered to whitewash desert stones was a not-unheard-of contribution to the war effort.

I was lonely and missing Perle. With my New Zealand background and radical outlook, I had little in common with the British officers. I took myself to task. Whose fault was it if I could not get on with such essentially decent people? Mine, of course! I was determined to bridge our differences by establishing some common interests and soon discovered my colleagues were not really so bad, after all.

As a relief from boredom, I sometimes took to the hills that bordered the Suez Canal and towered out of the Sinai sand dunes. They were a far cry from the New Zealand peaks or even the Yorkshire fells — utterly stark, arid and treeless. My scrambles were solitary — no one else could be tempted to come — so, equipped with water bottles and revolver, I would sally forth, ever on my guard, for even my boots and watch were incitements to murder in that desperately poor land. Those outings were a lifesaver — my

spirit soared and everyday irritations ebbed into insignificance.
Once, miles from anywhere, where not a blade of grass grew, a great
plump fox slid out from behind a boulder and, unafraid, eyeballed
me. What on earth did he live on? Where did he drink? Unanswered
questions, but the sight of this self-confident animal affirmed for
me the tenacity of life.

In due course my old division was assigned to Palestine,
apparently to keep out the desperate and wretched survivors of the
Holocaust. My former colonel came to see me. Would I like to come
back to the parachute field ambulance with the rank of major, he
asked. I was flattered and tempted, for the boredom I was enduring
was deadly.

'Sorry, I can't. This Palestine fighting isn't what I joined up for.
You see, I have every sympathy with the Jews and with the Arabs, too.'

'Thought you might feel that way, Lewis. I am sorry, too.'

The details of what I was then involved in belong to a past era,
an episode of 'what might have been', of no historical import since
the course actually taken by history proved far different. It must be
clear to the reader by now that I have never respected authority for
its own sake, preferring to reason things out for myself and having
the moral courage to act on my convictions. No matter how flawed
my conclusions have sometimes turned out to be, I am convinced
this is by far the best way for us humans to apply our faculties.
In my case I have no regrets.

To sum up a very complex chain of events, through army
sympathisers with Egyptian anti-monarchist revolutionaries, I
came to be a delegate for the outlawed Arab League of National
Liberation in Cairo to left-wing Zionists in Jerusalem. The
moderate members of the two communities were more than ready
to share the country of Palestine and live together. Many young
Arab men, especially students, were marrying or living with well-
educated Jewish girls. One memorable character, the late Mufid
Nashashibi, was a highborn sheik, who was greeted respectfully by
bearded elders with 'Salaam ya Nashashibi', while the street
sweepers called him 'Mufid', for he was a popular communist.

He was equally notable for his girth and for his fondness for piled-up rice dishes. Before he died, he wrote a very moving book about his life in exile.

I had the unusual experience of visiting Christian holy places accompanied by Muslims and Jews, who found each other's and the Christians' beliefs rather amusing, while seeing nothing odd in their own. But, despite a good deal of shoddy commercialisation, I felt a genuine sense of awe and wonder in Jerusalem at actually being among those ancient hills which had shaped so much of our Western culture.

Of course, all our negotiations, all those interminable meetings over endless cups of thick Arab coffee in airless shuttered rooms, went for naught. So much for our youthful high hopes for rational solutions to the impasse. We grossly underestimated the blind fanaticism of the two sides. It has taken over fifty years for both the Israelis and the Palestinians to broker solutions that were clearly apparent way back then.

The war at length wound down and the time came for my release from the army. It was only then that my mother wrote that my father was gravely ill. They had had to give up New Monklands and were living in Kingston. After being reunited in England with Perle, Michael and little Anna, we sailed for Jamaica, where I was demobilised in 1946.

Trevor was indeed very ill with cancer; he was so confused that when I saw him he told me his son had been killed in the war. But I was unprepared for the sight of my mother. At a glance I could tell she was suffering from Paget's disease, a chronic bone disorder of unknown etiology that causes overgrowth and distortion of the skull and limbs leading, over the years, to crippling and deafness. Mercifully, she was, and remained, quite unaware of her disorder.

We moved to Port Royal, where I was appointed Port Medical Officer. My father had been a magistrate at Morant Bay, highly respected for his fairmindedness, while as doctor and nurse, Perle and I were popular too in the local community. Perle nursed Dad at home, for there was nothing more the hospital could do for him. When he died the neighbours rallied around for a wake, filling our house to overflowing. The night was passed with food, drink, hymns and compassion, all of which I found surprisingly comforting. The support of these near strangers helped mitigate the awful realisation that all those opportunities to reveal our feelings, missed through impatience or perhaps typical Anglo–Saxon emotional inhibition, and to demonstrate our mutual love for one another had been lost irrevocably. None of us, not even Carinna, who was closer to Jamaican custom, was prepared for the second wake on the 'Ninth Night', for that is when the soul returns to Africa. It is an old slave ceremony, rarely, if ever, performed for a white man. Trevor would have been proud.

My life in Jamaica was varied and busy. Medical work in the small, derelict Port Royal community was frustrating for its lack of facilities, not least in the lepers' penal colony across the bay that was under my charge. 'Delinquents' were sent there from the lepers' home, generally for three months, for such grave offences as visiting the women's compound, going off home, and the like. The conditions in the barbed-wire-enclosed compound were primitive in the extreme: no electricity, hence no lights at all, since oil lamps were considered dangerous for lepers; a diet of bread and water. It was hard to believe that this was the mid twentieth century.

Of course, there was no way the wonderful old black matron or I would tolerate such privations. The inmates were thus fed properly out of our own pockets, the gates were permanently unlocked, sea bathing was encouraged, and the only leprosy treatment then available, injections of chalmoogra oil, was instituted. To relieve the monotony, I would on occasion dispense with the customs launch and cross the harbour perilously in a dugout sailing canoe borrowed from a local fisherman.

In a lighter vein, it was in Port Royal that I encountered one of my most memorable patients. He was a charcoal-burner, about eighty-two years old, he thought. He had come for a tonic. He had two young wives, he explained, and was recently having difficulty satisfying them both. Moreover, he was getting out of breath climbing coconut palms. So please, would I give him a tonic to put things right? It would have been heartless of me to suggest to this gallant ancient that relentless ageing might be at work, so I mixed him the strongest tasting tonic I could devise. He went away happy. Some years later I heard he had been killed in a fall from a coconut palm.

Two-year-old Anna was everyone's pet, and would disappear into the local village for hours at a time. One time, we were rather startled to see her marching solemnly at the head of a religious parade bearing a lighted candle. Her blond hair had been dressed into tiny plaits. I often took her or Michael with me when I boarded incoming ships. On one particularly elegant white schooner yacht named *Zaka*, Anna was entranced with the captain's parrot, though uninterested in its owner. I am always rather slow on the uptake. Even when he signed the papers the penny did not drop. 'Any relation to the actor?' I asked stupidly. Errol Flynn just laughed.

Anna soon developed a heavy Jamaican accent. One of the most worrying occasions during our stay was when she was brought down with pneumonia and a high fever. On the night the fever broke, the heat had become almost unbearable. Anna was lethargic and unresponsive.

'It's baking in here,' remarked Perle.

Unexpectedly, a little voice piped up from the bed: 'Baking. I want baking — baking and hegg!'

The worst was over.

To Perle and me it was a truism that just as one person cannot — should not — own another, so nations should be likewise unconstrained. In my own lifetime many proud empires have collapsed — the Austro-Hungarian, German and Ottoman in my infancy, the quarter of the world that was the British Empire in my middle manhood, and recently, the Soviet, to which I was an eyewitness. Disastrous as so many post-colonial regimes have been (victims of Cold War politics, more often than not), I remain convinced that only the people themselves can hope to solve their own problems. Left alone, they usually manage well enough.

Given such a philosophy, it was inevitable that Perle and I became involved in the People's National Party, the Jamaican independence movement led by Norman Washington Manley. Outsiders can play but peripheral parts in national movements, and then only in helping them to get going. It was an enormous compliment, therefore, when we were accorded a reception at Accompong in Maroon country. The Maroons were escaped slaves who maintained their freedom in the wild Cockpit Country or 'Look Behind Country' in the face of repeated assaults by the British Army. Eventually, on the promise to return future runaways, their independence was recognised. After a dinner of salt fish, ake (a Jamaican nut), gungu peas (Congo beans) and rice cooked on open fires, an elder stood up in the flickering firelight and recited the epic of their history. The old gods of West Africa came alive as he chanted of Dombala, the Serpent, and broke into snatches of Asante war songs, in which the fierce rhythm had survived the centuries but most of the words had been lost. An unforgettable experience.

Being a New Zealander, I had always taken the sea for granted as part of one's life, so I was quick to take advantage of my contacts as port doctor to arrange a passage for Perle, Michael and me on *Haligonian*, a one-time Nova Scotian 'Captains Courageous' fishing schooner with gaff foresail and staysail and cut down main. She was from Cayman Brac, where we called en route to Honduras for a load of lumber, and infested with bed bugs and the largest cockroaches I have ever seen. A storm, which frightened me out of my wits, sent us scurrying for shelter into Coxen Hole in the Bay Islands of Honduras. Here, to my surprise, the native language of the fishermen and subsistence farmers was English, albeit rather archaic at times ('wessel' for vessel, for instance). I had not realised that the buccaneers who cut logwood and manufactured salted beef jerky along the coast from present-day Belize south through the Mosquito Coast and Bluefields, Nicaragua, to the Bay Islands, had been mainly English. Incessant fighting against the Spaniards meant arming their own slaves, and a slave with a musket and a machete is no longer a slave.

We loaded our cargo at Puerto Cortez, where the American head of the lumber company entertained us. 'People work for the government or they work for the company,' he said. 'If they don't like it, they go into the harbour with a weight round their legs.'

An alarming experience of a different kind in Honduras was a flight through cloud-enshrouded mountains to San Pedro Sulla in an incredibly decrepit DC3. By the time Perle and I returned from this excursion, the schooner's cargo was loaded and it was time to leave. On the outward voyage, breakfast had been corned beef and fried bananas, lunch corned beef and raw bananas, and dinner corned beef and boiled bananas, but in port the cook quarrelled with the skipper and went on strike, so that on the return leg we subsisted on a diet of corned beef and uncooked bananas three times daily.

Ultimately, our political activities did not endear us to the authorities in Jamaica, not least the Colonial Health Service. The crunch came when a leper, an old sailor, threatened with a return to my penal settlement, replied that he would be delighted, since Dr Lewis treated him far better than did the lepers' home. I was ordered forthwith to abide strictly by the regulations. I refused and was summarily fired without a reference. Only a lawyer's intervention brought forth the following glowing testimonial: 'Dr Lewis has worked for us for eighteen months.' Our political farewell was another matter; the People's National Party even went so far as to compose a hymn in our honour.

We sailed back to England in 1948 accompanied by my mother. England, rather than New Zealand, was our destination, as my mother's sister, Sybil Jerram, lived in Cornwall and Perle's family in London. The war and these Third World experiences had convinced me of the need to put aside my penchant for adventuring and become a socially useful citizen. I settled down, therefore, as a general practitioner in East Ham in London.

Our son, Barry, was born in 1948 soon after our arrival. Anna was protective of her baby brother and very proud of him. She had a purely feminine instinct for social nuances from a very early age. Only on rare occasions did she stumble. The following incident was one. We were visiting another family with a young baby, when Anna remarked with unwonted lack of tact: 'Our baby is prettier than your baby.' Sensing at once her faux pas, she looked meltingly at the baby's father: 'But you are prettier than my daddy!'

One thing seemed obvious to me when I settled in my practice: health reform was called for. So it was that I plunged headlong into a whirlpool of controversy.

The next few years were marked for me by the battles attending the birth of the National Health Service, in which I often found myself in a minority of one among my conservative colleagues. The incipient NHS had many bureaucratic faults — the artificial separation of GPs from hospitals and public health, for instance, was one of the worst — but reforms were brought about in the ensuing years. Direct access to pathology services and clinical assistantships in hospitals for GPs, for instance, was one such reform. As a representative of the Medical Practitioners' Union I was a member of the London Trades Council, and for a time sat on its Executive, where I was much impressed by the calibre of the union delegates, especially the secretary, the legendary communist Julius Jacobs. These were, in the main, dedicated and selfless people.

Once in the early 1950s, I cannot recall exactly which year, I was even deputed to lead the Trade Council's May Day march from Stepney to Trafalgar Square. Something like a century of working-class history was reflected in the banners waving behind me that commemorated struggles for a living wage, shorter hours, workshop safety and health all the way back to Marx and Engels's *Communist Manifesto*. I was deeply moved by the occasion.

Equally as praiseworthy as the trade unionists were the members of the local Hospital Management Committee, who would negotiate with endless patience and, if necessary, fight like tigers for an improved dishwasher or an extra maternity bed. Particularly aggressive in lobbying for improvements was a certain councillor; a pacifist once jailed for his beliefs, he was still more than willing to back his convictions with his fists.

An important development was the formation of the College of General Practitioners, the inspiration of Dr John Fry. I was repeatedly shocked by the suddenness with which a healthy middle-aged docker, after an attack of pneumonia one winter, would rapidly deteriorate, develop intractable emphysema, be forced to retire and die soon after — all in the space of two or three years. Statistics indicated that the death rate from chronic bronchitis/emphysema in social group five (unskilled workers) was *six* times greater than in social group one (professionals). Clearly this was a disease largely caused by social conditions and, therefore, preventable. I approached Fry and the newly formed college and served for some years on the research committee that was formed to evaluate treatments. In retrospect, our antibiotics and the like had much less positive influence than the general clean-up of London's air after the killer smog of the 1950s.

All too conscious of the isolation of GPs from the growing points of medicine in England, I took advantage of every opportunity for further education. There were clinical assistantships in general medicine and skin diseases, weekend refresher courses and the like. A mentor I particularly liked was a Cambridge pathologist. True to form, he wore battered tweed jackets with leather patched elbows, stained flannels, and mumbled through an unlit pipe. He was immensely learned. One Christmas he invited me to drinks in his laboratory. It was not an experience to be forgotten, or repeated. Selecting two beakers, he tipped out their contents, slices of liver and kidney, rinsed the beakers roughly, and filled them with cooking sherry. I may be maligning the wine, but somehow my taste discrimination was in abeyance.

Again, on an odd note, I had a rather startling chance encounter on a London street with a former fellow student from Leeds Medical School. He halted abruptly, gazed at me accusingly, and exclaimed, 'You are supposed to be dead. We stood for two minutes silence for *you*.' This was not the sort of enthusiastic welcome back from the grave that I might have anticipated; I felt I should apologise. I never did figure out how it got to be there, but sure enough, my name *was* on the University's memorial scroll. A few years later, my little girls, who had heard the story from me, could not find it — but then they were looking under 'D' for 'Daddy'.

Outdoor pursuits were hardly at a premium in the East End of London forty years ago. One welcome 'breathing space', however, was nearby Epping Forest, which Michael, Anna, Barry and I came to know intimately: the birds, the pond life, the squirrels, and the shy fallow deer that we always knew where to find. There were good days, too, in a hired sailing dinghy on the Blackwater Estuary, where we sometimes camped on the damp saltings. On the first few outings, we were accompanied by my wife, but Perle and I were finding ourselves more and more at loggerheads. Increasingly, she seemed to need to dominate, to manage, to confront; my style has always been low-key. I had remained strictly faithful throughout my long years of military service (even if I had hoped for female company, there was little scope for dalliance in the Middle East), as well as in Jamaica, where our differences were becoming more apparent. Back in England, the dam burst.

A dreary and acrimonious divorce was the final outcome. I am in no way proud of my insensitivity to the trauma of the children, and cannot bear even now to dwell on it. Michael naturally clove to his mother. Anna was very much her mother's daughter too, and antagonistic to me. Not wishing to tear her apart emotionally, I did not press for access, a terrible mistake, since she could only interpret it as me not wanting to see her. In truth, for years I could not bear to look at girls her age for missing her so desperately. It was not until Anna was sixteen and about to be married herself that we began to get to know each other again.

The years in East Ham were not all disappointing. Barry was with me often. With my marriage essentially over, women intrigued me more than ever, though I was no nearer showing even rudimentary commonsense when my heart took over from my head. There was a particularly ill-judged two-year relationship with a London model, whose beauty was only matched by the incompatibility of our interests and lifestyles. When she eventually found a far 'smoother' partner, I was affronted to the depths of my male ego that she could prefer someone else. But it was the deviousness with which she took advantage of my trustfulness that really hurt, and was for a long time to colour my relations with women. Nevertheless, at the back of my mind I was relieved at being free of an impossible relationship.

Other more pleasant, but equally much needed, lessons in love continued to come my way.

There were 'The Twins', identical twenty-one-year-old Jamaican twins, indistinguishable as far as I was concerned (with regrettable consequences). Their mixed East Indian, African and European ancestry had endowed them with extraordinary beauty, their figures redolent of the more exotic Indian temple carvings. Their upbringing, however, had been so narrowly restricted that their only reading matter had been the Bible and comics. In a moment of madness their proud father had sent in their photos to a beauty contest, which they duly won. Not surprisingly, the family home was then besieged by suitors. In desperation, their father sent them to England to become nurses.

One of these lovely girls was visiting me and, while firmly rejecting my blandishments, managed to stay until the nurses' home had closed, thus narrowing her options. When she visited me again, she seemed surprised at my taking our new relationship for granted, but was willing enough. Matters had progressed beyond the point of no return before I realised that this was the *other* twin. Tears and ultimate forgiveness, the wronged one having prayed for me, finally put things back together again. The two innocent girls remained more than a little dependent on me for advice and counsel, a circumstance that was later to raise the ire of my future wife Fiona.

It was around the mid 1950s when I found myself becoming more and more out of tune with my patients' outlook. Their aspirations, particularly those of young couples starting out on their own, were so extraordinarily limited and unadventurous. Fears of illness, insecurity and, apparently, the sky falling down obsessed them. Their parents' memories of the Depression played a large part, no doubt. But why did they cower in abject fear now, when they *had* security and the whole exciting world at their feet? Should this lack of empathy with my patients persist, I realised, then I would be morally obliged, sooner or later, to try to find another profession. Here was I, a middle-aged man who had no earthly idea of what he really should be doing, nor how to set out on a new road even if he could work out what it was.

For some time the sea and the mountains had been beckoning ever more imperiously. I did my best to put aside thoughts of free winds and open spaces, yet restlessness intruded from time to time. Lying in bed on foggy nights, I could not sleep for the hooting of ships' sirens that came clear across two miles of sooty rooftops through the frigid air. I tried to ignore the message that the sea was there waiting, still untamed and as free as it had always been, still beautiful and terrible in its impersonal anger. The mountains were out there too. Since the opening of the M1 motorway, the mountains of North Wales had become more accessible, if only on long weekends (even in my elderly but speedy MG TD), while the Essex estuaries were less than three hours drive away.

I had long made tentative approaches to the sea, like a sailing dinghy that I built myself, and a twenty-seven-foot, sixty-year-old barge yacht in which I had become acquainted with most of the sandbanks of the Thames Estuary, and later with the shoals off Holland. At first Perle had accompanied me, but she soon lost interest. I found other female sailing companions, thereby driving further nails into the coffin of our marriage.

But in general I pushed into the background any impractical longings for far horizons. Quite apart from the children, my mother's Paget's Disease was steadily getting worse. She was becoming increasingly handicapped and was totally dependent on me. I could never leave her for more than a few weeks at a time.

Nevertheless, critical self-examination during this period led to a conclusion that I could not but accept. This was that the link connecting that first schoolboy kayak, through mountain and forest to the old barge yacht, was in fact the essence of my character. I thereupon bought a pair of climbing boots and a ship's lifeboat (the barge yacht had had to be sacrificed at the time of my divorce). I was in danger of becoming embroiled in a love affair — with the sea.

Increasingly frail as she was becoming, my mother had lost none of her interest in world events and was steadily developing a more radical outlook while my own radicalism was becoming less focused. By the mid 1950s, however, I had become rather disillusioned with political parties. I have never been attracted to politics as such, only to issues, and have not had the slightest interest in holding a political office. I was then, and have remained, 'left wing', but am concerned more by particular issues, many of them 'green', than by necessarily short-term party programs. Around 1956, my mother joined the Communist Party and became an avid reader of the *Daily Worker*. Carinna's indomitable will and indifference to discomfort kept her active, rain or shine, in our little garden. Only in the last winter of her life did she consent to remain indoors.

The end came unexpectedly in 1958. A mild coronary was diagnosed by a visiting consultant, who advised nursing at home — this was long before intensive care. In a confused state, Carinna got out of bed, wandered to the stairs and slipped, fatally fracturing her already fragile skull. I have hated stairs ever since. That she had been ailing for some time did not make her loss any the less tragic, nor lessen my guilt at lost opportunities to communicate that were now closed forever.

three

Sea Fever

With some modest cruising aims in view I had been going about decking-in my lifeboat when a new challenge arose that fascinated but also appalled me with its difficulty. This was the first single-handed transatlantic race of 1960, the brainchild of Blondie Hasler (it was entirely his own idea; the myth of a bet between him and Francis Chichester is sheer nonsense). I sold the lifeboat and bought the 25-foot *Cardinal Vertue* with the help of a bank loan. I was then, in 1958, forty-two years old, when one should, according to conventional wisdom, be settling down and accepting that one's peak is past. What nonsense it is to suggest that 'life stages' are carved in stone, rather than being largely up to the individual. Nor was this any sudden 'mid-life crisis'. I had had increasingly itchy feet since my mid-thirties; only my responsibilities, especially to my mother, had held me back. I was certainly nautically naïve for a project of this magnitude. But no such silly objections! I would just have to learn.

I will always treasure a letter my Aunt Nora sent me when publicity about the race surfaced. 'I thoroughly disapprove,' she wrote, 'of such a foolhardy project. But if it *does* have to happen I am very proud that my nephew, and a Welshman, is taking part!'

A 500-mile solo qualifying trip was required by the race organisers. I chose Norway, so reminiscent of the mountain landscape back home in New Zealand and familiar to me from a skiing holiday in Tellemark. My navigational equipment was limited to a compass and radio direction finder, the accuracy of which, in the northern North Sea, was approximate at best. As yet I had no self-steering gear. The plan was to sail north to Stavanger with two companions and return alone. Things did not work out that way. One man's girlfriend vetoed his participation and, on the very last day, the remaining crewman issued an ultimatum: he would only feel safe enough to come if we harbour-hopped instead of heading up the middle of the North Sea. There was no way I could accept this unseamanlike alternative.

'Of course you won't go now. I *am* sorry,' he said.

'Of course not,' I agreed, and we parted amicably with mutual regrets. In fact, I was blazing with anger, scared stiff, but more determined than ever. Feeling anything but confident, I set sail alone from Burnham-on-Crouch at midnight.

Dawn and low tide found me nosing a sandbank outside the River Crouch, despondent, frightened and feeling very much alone. But soon the rising tide floated us (that's me and the yacht) and a brisk southerly swept us up past Harwich, where I hove-to to sleep a little, secure in the bright sunlight and good visibility. I was rudely awakened by an almighty thump and a horrible scraping alongside. A Dutch fishing boat was none too gently feeling out the possibilities of salvage. I was thankful for some words that I had learned on a previous trip to Holland: '*Sode mieter, op, nurk!*' I yelled furiously, and they sheered off.

Navigation became increasingly a problem as we moved northwards. The hollow, resonant thump of semi-diesels suggested the answer. Ranging alongside a trawler, I called out '*Norge*' and waved a chart. A pair of massive fish came thudding into the cockpit. They were welcome but not what I wanted at all. At length, the Danes got the idea. 'You are in Noord-Ooest Zilver Pit,' they offered. I was little the wiser until they marked the position of the fishing ground on my chart and passed it back. Every fishing boat I stopped was equally helpful.

In about the middle of the North Sea I found unexpected companionship. A pair of carrier pigeons landed in the cockpit and proceeded to make themselves at home. I was glad for their company. When night fell they retired to the cabin, where they balanced side by side at the edge of the chart table, swaying in time with the ship's roll. They accepted and seemed to appreciate breadcrumbs and water. But before long the downside became apparent. I began to understand how birds had constructed whole islands of guano. My pigeons were making a good start. The best I could do was to clean up as we went along and, every so often, pick them up, hold them upside-down and scrub their feet. My charts suffered but at least they remained relatively legible.

Nine days out from the Crouch — I thought the voyage would never end and was exhausted from steering by hand — found me hove-to at dawn off the intimidating approaches to Stavanger Fjord. I was trying to sort out the entrance from a maze of rocks and surf when a freighter passed me to enter the fairway. I thankfully followed her in. The nervous strain must have been more than I realised, because, for the first time since my last parachute jump, I burst into tears, and motored up the fjord sobbing and feeling a complete fool. As I came alongside a wharf in the town to ask where to anchor, there was a flutter of wings and the pigeons flapped noisily out of the cabin right in the face of the startled fisherman who was trying to help me.

For me, an adventure by itself could never be enough. Why? What for? Were there things to be learnt from human reactions to stress in extreme environments? These questions intrigued me and still do. I had become well acquainted with the hallucinations that often attend solitude, monotony and fatigue. On my kayak trip, when paddling or hauling cross-country, I had seen imaginary rivers flowing through bush-clad New Zealand valleys. Blondie Hasler, who I was soon to encounter, described a vivid hallucination during his wartime 'cockleshell' raid on Bordeaux. Sitting one behind the other, the two kayak paddlers were virtually isolated. After five or six hours paddling at night, phantom ships or buoys would appear. One time, Blondie became so annoyed at finding his companion 'reading *The Times*' that he was about to remonstrate forcibly when he realised they were creeping through a pitch-dark night without lights. As the action progressed in deadly earnest, however, no such phenomena occurred.

I, myself, took careful note of my own experiences and recorded them in the College of GPs' newsletter. Being forced to steer by hand for long hours in default of a windvane, this Norway trip provided ample case material. Voices and phantom ships were commonplace, especially in the long dragging hours before dawn. (I should stress that this 'dual reality' was not worrying and hallucinations were dispelled the moment action was called for — changing a head sail, for instance.) At times it would appear that another person was at the helm, while my other 'part personality' was critically observing his actions.

That winter I prudently took evening classes in sextant navigation at the Little Ship Club in London but refrained from sitting the examination for fear of failing, all too conscious that a sterner examination lay ahead. I constructed a windvane self-steering gear on a plan generously provided by fellow competitor Val Howells. During the winter, too, I twice sought the high hills. Once it was to clamber along airy Crib Goch (Red Comb) in Snowdonia which was thickly covered with new snow at the time and almost alpine in character. I was unsteady and unused to the height, for I had not climbed for a long time and was now in my forties, but I had decided that my willpower needed toning up. Life in a big city provides little opportunity to test the nervous system's ability to drive us forward against physical fear. It seemed to me that practice in self-control was needed, and would pay dividends in the months to come.

On the second occasion a group of us crossed over Tryfan (Three Peaks) and Glyder Fawr (Big Lump). When we were descending Twll Du (Devil's Kitchen) — of which my father had often spoken — I untied from the rope, left the others, and kicked steps up into a black cleft laced with monstrous fluted icicles. There I stood alone for a little while looking down the Nantffrancon Valley past Bangor, where my father had lived, to the silver gleam of the Menai Straits and the smudge of the Isle of Anglesy beyond. I felt in communion with my father and imbued with something of the spirit of this ancient land, as if I'd been granted strength from those wild crags which he had loved.

Back in the valley, I found that a slim, auburn-haired South African physical education and dancing instructor was staying at the same cottage as my party. Her name was Fiona and she quite failed to notice that I even existed. I was the more impressed when she and her girlfriend, after a hard day in the mountains in heavy snow, set off gaily to meet friends at Pen-y-Gwryd, ten kilometres away. Ten kilometres! I was aching in every muscle and could hardly move! Undoubtedly this was someone who was not meant for me.

In spite of this, I sought her out in London and, with other friends, she helped paint my boat and sailed as one of the crew from Burnham-on-Crouch to Portsmouth on the first lap of the voyage to Plymouth. She learned how to steer and trim the sheets and climbed the mast with scornful ease, and after recovering from seasickness, she played her guitar. This budding friendship was threatening to disrupt my well-ordered, if pleasantly complex, 'bachelor' existence. But Fiona's feelings towards me remained as enigmatic as ever.

In Plymouth, where Blondie Hasler, Francis Chichester, Val Howells and I were gathering (Jacques Lacombe, who was sailing across the Atlantic from the United States to get to the start, only reached Plymouth later, but still had the guts to turn around and complete the course), we felt more like fellow adventurers than competitors. I, for one, by far the least experienced, was much more concerned with tackling the ocean than with the race as such.

I was now forty-three, far from settling down and embarking on an enterprise for which I was only marginally prepared. Every one of my fellow adventurers was infinitely more experienced in the ways of the sea than I was. I was a tyro having to learn new tricks conventionally acquired in young manhood. This was the first time I had faced the challenge of ageing. But it really worried me very little, for I was already learning to reject conventional limits.

Francis Chichester was by far the most competitive among us and set on winning. As I got to know him better in Plymouth and in London, I came to realise how utterly singleminded he could be when focused on an objective. This was his strong point and his tough-minded wife, Sheila, made a wonderfully loyal assistant. She was a vegetarian and a believer in natural remedies. A few years earlier Francis's lung abscess had been misdiagnosed as probable cancer and the couple made a lot out of the 'cancer's' ultimate disappearance. Francis was not surprisingly plagued with recurrent bronchitis after his lung abscess, at which times he would phone me:

'Is that the world famous Dr Lewis?'

'Come off it, Francis. Do you want some antibiotics again?'

'Yes, please. What about dinner tonight — steaks, maybe?'

'So Sheila's out of town, is she? Okay, then.'

Blondie Hasler was more interested in questions of fear and courage, but there was something almost academic about this, as if, rather like the explorer Bill Tilman, he did not quite realise how easily scared the rest of us were. 'I wouldn't fancy those things,' Blondie remarked, gazing disparagingly at the one-man RAF inflatables we had been offered. 'I think I would just rather drink a bottle of gin and go down with the ship!' While his own ship was sinking under him, I thought, he would be conscientiously noting it all down in his log!

Eleven-year-old Barry was staying aboard with me at Plymouth. He was fascinated above all by Hasler's *Jester*, with its ingenious Chinese junk rig. He was forever on board, full of questions and more questions. I thought: 'Here at last I have my secret weapon against Hasler.' But I had underestimated Blondie. Before five minutes had passed there was an understanding between them. Barry had been rationed to fifty questions to start with, plus five every subsequent hour. Blondie kindly but firmly kept him to this agreement.

In the rare intervals of peace and quiet amidst those feverish preparations, I could not help but ponder on the rationale of it all. Why should I, a staid general practitioner, venture out, at the cost of not inconsiderable discomfort and expense, over a predictably stormy ocean? It seems to me that there must be some outgoing imperative, a sense of wonder at the world around us, a curiosity manifested in research, art, philosophy, or in just the simple urge to find what lies over the ranges, that is an essential part of the human spirit. Indeed, without it *Homo sapiens* could hardly have evolved. In earlier times this urge would have found ready outlet in a generally perilous world, but in the increasingly mechanised and impersonal societies of today, where perspectives tend to become limited to amassing dubiously useful possessions, the free spirit is liable to suffocate. Surely it is no accident that it was only from about the mid nineteenth century that people began to climb mountains, not for the view, but simply because they were there. Men like Joshua Slocum and John Voss did not sail around the world for gold or empire, but simply to fulfil something within themselves.

Blondie Hasler told me he thought that people should take controlled risks from time to time to keep themselves up to scratch and fit to react to sudden emergencies. In my own experience, fully a third of illnesses arise directly from chronic states of anxiety and lack of courage and self-confidence. Uncertainty, dread of nameless disaster, and want of self-respect undermine the psyche. Those who have known physical fear, but have learned to control it, seem less prone to these disorders. Of course, security is necessary but security is only one aspect of life — people must also have things to fight and strive for to maintain their essential dignity.

This, I think, was the real reason we five were in this race. Different as our natures were — our attitudes to life, to the sea and to the race itself— we were essentially driven by much the same force.

For each one of us, the problems of getting away, of expense, of (in my case) mastering essential skills, had appeared insuperable, yet something within us had refused to acknowledge the limits of the practicable and the possible. I do not think that the concept of escapism applies to undertakings that demand so much positive planning and effort.

It has been argued that endeavour and adventure are of no practical value. But is it more useful to devote one's life to amassing money and status, only to end it by a coronary thrombosis brought on by the effort and worry? It is also said that adventurers seek risks. Although there may well be an element of danger in anything new and untried, the challenge is in using one's judgment, knowledge and skill to *avoid* trouble. It is the less-skilled whose adventures are liable to become fraught — as I was to find out.

Something of the spirit of our undertaking can be gauged from the wording of one of the race rules: 'Yachts must be fully independent and capable of carrying out their own emergency repairs at sea. Crews have no right to expect or demand rescue operations to be launched on their behalf.' (Hasler's hand is clearly apparent here.) I still firmly adhere to this principle and had no second thoughts even in the worst moments of *Ice Bird*'s Antarctic troubles. After all, we go to sea for our own pleasure. It seems to me that we have no right to endanger others' lives to get us out of the trouble we ourselves have invited.

Officialdom and a growing number of yachtsmen nowadays seem all too ready to rely on rescue rather than seaworthy craft and prudent seamanship. Technical developments like EPIRB (Emergency Position Indicating Radio Beacon) that can pinpoint a distressed vessel's position by satellite, should be used only as a last resort, and should in no way diminish a mariner's personal responsibility.*

The starting date, awaited with much eagerness by the others and with trepidation by me, at last arrived, and Chichester, Hasler,

---

*In 1999, at the age of eighty-one, I did use EPIRB. The reader can judge if this was justified.

Howells and I faced the starting gun. Lacombe was still in the mid Atlantic and would start later.

Carrying all the sail I could muster, I was soon heeled hard over, not a little overpressed, pounding to windward down the Channel, with the English coastline fast receding into dimness astern. Suddenly, without warning, the overstressed mast shattered at mid-point and went over the side in a tangle of sails and rigging. For a brief few moments I was too stunned to do anything. Then the patent need to bring the wreckage on board before it breached the hull brought me to my senses. By folding over the mainsail and staysail, some sort of jury rig could be fashioned, and before nightfall I was limping back towards Plymouth under jury rig, mightily dispirited but with my racing flag defiantly lashed to the stump of the mast, determined more than ever to start again. My fears had all departed. My blood was up.

Mr Mashford, head of a well-known boatyard at Cremyll across the River Tamar, came aboard in a flapping raincoat, carefully looked over the damage, and then said in his deliberate, West Country way: 'You will be able to leave by, say, Monday midday.' It was then Saturday night, and to be able to sail on Monday was far better than I had dared hope. Yet somehow, this seemingly casual statement inspired more confidence than a thousand flowery promises. Life seemed worth living again.

Barry was back with me, brooding over the unfair 'single-handed' rule that had stopped him accompanying me. I was expecting Anna too, but she had not arrived, so I turned in, exhausted by the events of the day. A voice hailed me from the quayside.

'Is Dr Lewis aboard there?'

'I'm sorry, you have just missed him. He sank half an hour ago,' I replied. I shut the hatchway, only to be stopped by Anna's patient if somewhat exasperated voice.

'Daddy, it's me.'

It was a few minutes before noon on Monday when, true to his word, Mashford's launch pulled us clear, and I struggled into my wet-weather gear and began to make sail. At no time had Mashford or his men indicated that there was anything unusual in their starting work at six o'clock on a Sunday morning or going on until midnight, and then setting-to at daybreak the next day. Meeting these quiet, unassuming men had been a privilege for it taught me a new humility.

In the midst of all the last-minute bustle and confusion as I was casting off, a reporter called out from the pierhead, with what I thought was not the most tactful choice of phrase: 'My readers would like to hear your last words, doctor.' Stung by his words, I shouted back angrily, 'I want to get to New York before those buggers drink all the beer and screw all the women!'

A shocked hush had settled over the water, but the sails were up now, and sheeted in, as *Cardinal Vertue* again headed down Plymouth Sound towards the open sea.

The following story has been told in more detail in my book, *The Ship Would Not Travel Due West*. Suffice it to say here that *Cardinal Vertue* tacked out clear of the western approaches in three days, which were enlivened by my efforts to master sextant navigation (the first position came out rather depressingly in the middle of Ireland). Constant watchfulness and lack of sleep took their toll, so much so that I began to hallucinate, once having the distinct impression of sailing along the top of a hill while watching two freighters in the valley down below. The hallucinations, though vivid, were not disturbing, for I knew them to be unreal, and after a few hours sleep, once we had cleared the traffic and had sea room, they departed and did not recur. This was in stark contrast to the previous year's Norway adventure — an improvement I could attribute to the windvane self-steering gear.

We (the yacht and I) encountered the typical North Atlantic weather sequence of a rainy south-wester with falling barometer and rising wind, sometimes to gale force, of the depression's warm front, followed by a squally cold front north-wester with clearing skies. Reefing, unreefing and changing headsails, occasionally lying-to in gales, was our portion. But all things must pass. The time came when the pale green waters of the Labrador Current replaced the blue North Atlantic Drift, the fog shut down and the long-dormant echo sounder registered thirty fathoms. We were over the Grand Banks of Newfoundland and the open Atlantic was behind us. There was still a very long way to go, for this race finished at New York, rather than at Newport, Rhode Island, as subsequent ones would.

The fog persisted, concealing the unseen menace of the icebergs that could be expected in this part of the Atlantic and which had sunk the *Titanic*. It also hid the rock-bound coast of Nova Scotia, on which I very nearly came to grief when lack of sleep had dulled my senses. Fog came to be succeeded by calms over Georges Bank, and we were flicked by the tail of an off-season hurricane before I cut through Pollock Rip Channel into sheltered Martha's Vineyard. This shortcut (banned in later races) did me no good, for relieved at having passed all the dangers, I fell asleep and woke to find *Cardinal Vertue* nosing the sand in Woods Hole, where we had no business to be. Fortunately the tide was rising, so a chastened skipper resumed course to New York. It was fifty-four days from Plymouth when the Manhattan skyscrapers hove into view and I learnt I had come third behind Chichester and Hasler. The real surprise was finding Fiona waiting for me in New York.

The race had presented a 'controlled' situation, where several loners had faced parallel, and predictably stressful, conditions in mutual isolation. What could be learned, I had wondered, from this situation? The focus of my medical interests had by this time tilted away from clinical practice towards research. I had therefore approached the National Council for Medical Research prior to the race, which drew up daily diaries for us to fill in. Questions as to sleep patterns, meals and mood had to be answered — an irritating chore, but one that led to a paper entitled 'Voluntary Solitude' in *The Lancet* and much interest from NASA's space station people, who had descended upon us like friendly locusts the moment we docked at Staten Island. Hasler, Howells and I completed the questionnaires — Francis had no time for any such distractions from racing. Lacombe was still in the mid Atlantic, so could not be contacted. Some of the findings were interesting. It was found before the race that each of us had his own distinct sleeping and eating pattern. Hasler, for instance, functioned on a rigid military schedule; Howells, then a farmer, was up even before the lark; I could not sleep before midnight, when house calls declined. This was only to be expected, but what was surprising was that after some days of disruption, these individual patterns re-established themselves and persisted. There was a lighter side to this chore. In his answer to a question about mood on his first day at sea — 'Do you feel sexy?' — Val Howells said it all: 'Not bloody likely.'

Fiona sailed back with me as far as St Johns, Newfoundland, from where I rode the autumn storms under the cold, flickering Northern Lights in a wild ride to Lerwick in the Shetland Islands. Here Tom Moncrief, who I had met the previous year in Stavanger on his schooner *Loki*, took charge of *Cardinal Vertue* for the winter while I flew back to East Ham and the practice.

With the subsequent publication of *The Ship Would Not Travel Due West*, I had begun to realise a cherished ambition — to write. Save for some minor medical articles, I had hardly put pen to paper since my Otago climbing days. My approach to writing the book was simple. I read and re-read all the voyaging accounts I could lay my hands on, noting the good and bad points of each. Thus, poor maps and confused dates were of no use, as were pages of unrelieved technical detail. The details were relevant enough, but I resolved to split them up. A note on medical kit, for instance, was best inserted when I cracked my head on the spinnaker boom; on cooking when I had run short of matches.

In the summer of 1961 Fiona, now my wife, and I retrieved *Cardinal Vertue* from Lerwick and set about exploring the Norwegian fjords, going climbing near Alesund, and then working our way south towards Bergen and Stavanger. It took us some time to realise that Fiona's apparently worsening seasickness was nothing of the sort. She was pregnant, and duly flew back to England, while twelve-year-old Barry joined me for the return trip to Burnham-on-Crouch. He was already a veteran of a trip we had made to Holland but hungered after bigger things. 'I do hope we have a gale, Daddy,' he remarked. Unwisely, as it proved, for a force 9 gale soon had the poor boy pale green and vomiting, rolling from side to side in his sopping bunk. It was as we were nosing up the River Crouch that he made one of the most touching statements of all time: 'Daddy, for a little time during that gale I *almost* didn't like sailing!'

After all this it was inevitable, I suppose, that the call of distant seas should become irresistible. *Rehu Moana* ('Ocean Spray' in Maori), probably the most seaworthy catamaran ever built (and because of her heavy construction, the slowest), was designed by Colin Mudie and built by Prout Bros at the cost of all my savings. The excessive outlay was not their doing; it resulted from my trying to incorporate too much that was experimental and which all too often turned out a failure. Thus, the heavy ballasted keels, that were scrapped soon thereafter, and the double mast, that collapsed off Iceland, were expensive diversions but not fatal ones. A less spectacular but ultimately more serious fault was the narrowness of the hulls for such a heavy craft, which meant she could never carry the weight of a proper engine without wallowing like a raft.

While *Rehu Moana* was being built there was much more going on; mountaineering trips to North Wales, for instance, since Fiona was an expert rock-climber. We visited Val Howells, too, and I spoke once at a village gathering that he had addressed earlier. The very first question from an earnest lady in the audience nearly floored me.

'How did you keep off the man-eating sharks that attacked your vessel, like they did Mr Howells's?'

'Val, you b . . . !'

'This is Wales, David . . . you must give them their money's worth!'

It was in December 1961 that my second daughter, Susie, was born. Not that the event restrained the athletic Fiona, for the day before she had been rock-climbing on Harrisons Rocks, near London. 'Just like a little doll!' exclaimed the entranced Barry as he touched Susie's tiny fingers.

Around this time we got to know one of the most remarkable figures of the twentieth century, Major Bill Tilman, a man with an exalted place in the story of British arms, letters, mountaineering, and seagoing exploration. I certainly did not impress him on our first encounter. We were driving to the Welsh mountains through the rain in my MG. The canvas hood had worn away from carrying a dinghy on top, but I confidently explained that if we went fast enough, the rain would pass harmlessly over the windscreen. Regrettably, I had not allowed for the serpentine Welsh mountain roads that kept our speed down. 'Don't think much of your theory,' grunted the soaked Tilman, with considerable restraint.

'You can be leader,' he informed Fiona as we approached the crags the next day.

'I can't lead someone who was leader of the 1938 *Everest* attempt!' she exclaimed, appalled at the suggestion. But Tilman was not one to argue with. Eventually, Fiona did lead us up one of the routes on Tryfan. Bill's old-fashioned nailed boots scrabbled for holds, with sparks flying. Then his large hands would clamp down on the rock with the adhesion of an octopus. On the summit, he recited a short prayer in Tibetan as a tribute to the mountain we had climbed, not 'conquered' — an abhorrent notion to him and to me equally.

Our climbs earned Fiona the disapproval of some fellow members of the women-only Pinnacle Club, which regarded Tilman as something of a devil incarnate. Partly this was because of his shyness with women. After all, he had left an all-male school at seventeen to serve for four years as a gunner in the First World War, so he had had scant opportunities to meet any members of the opposite sex in his formative years. Partly, too, because he never realised how much his caustic tongue could wound. 'I was about to put a belay round a moss-covered boulder,' he explained to me once, 'when I realised just in time that it was a senior member of the Pinnacle club.' This anecdote hardly endeared him to Fiona's colleagues.

Tilman had been growing coffee in Kenya after the First World War when, deciding to visit England, he bicycled across Central Africa and the Sahara, living on mealy meal and bananas. His account caught the attention of veteran mountaineer Eric Shipton, who was looking for simpler alternatives to the classic Himalayan expeditions with their hundreds of porters. Tilman sounded like just the man he needed. They thereupon made the ascent of all the peaks of the previously unclimbed and difficult Mount Kenya. This was the start of a notable Himalayan partnership that culminated for Tilman in the first ascent of India's 7817-metre Nanda Devi and his leadership of the 1938 Everest attempt, when they reached over 8000 metres in the icy conditions of an early monsoon, wearing tweed jackets and nailed boots — primitive clothing by modern standards.

Tilman must have been more formal in those days before sailing corrupted him, for the story goes that the more liberal Shipton suggested, 'Now that we have been climbing together in the Himalayas for six seasons, Tilman, perhaps I should call you Bill and you call me Eric?'

Tilman puffed his pipe while he considered the matter: 'But Eric sounds so bloody silly.'

The Second World War found Tilman being parachuted into Albania and Northern Italy. Incidentally, there is a Tilman Day in Belluno, where he made his headquarters on the top floor of the Gestapo building, and whence the partisans smuggled him out in a coffin when he was found out.

When peace returned, experience soon showed Tilman that he could no longer climb over 6000 metres, so he bought the pilot cutter *Mischief* to sail to remote mountains that he was capable of climbing. His maiden effort resulted in a noteworthy voyage, the first crossing of the Patagonian ice cap, and *Mischief in Patagonia*, a wonderful book, scholarly as always and suffused with the dry humour that was his hallmark. He went on to make expeditions to Greenland (on several occasions), Baffin Island, Spitzbergen, the sub-Antarctic islands and Antarctica itself.

I was recently asked what impelled me towards the wildernesses of the sea and the ice. A hard question, for it is never easy, and not always even possible, to discover the wellspring of one's own motivations. Of course, I had been born with restless wanderlust and had perhaps imbibed something of the spirit of my forebears — my father and my Uncle Arthur, Aunt Nora, my great-grandfather Lewis Palestine, the restless Dr Jack O'Neill, and Jim O'Neill, a South Seas naval hero. I am a hopeless romantic, too, so that the word 'explorer' has always set my spirit singing. I do remember it came as something of a revelation when I read Wilfred Noyce's *Springs of Adventure* around the time of my Iceland adventure to find that, with one exception, I had read every one of the accounts of adventuring he cited. Noyce was a member of the successful 1953 Everest Expedition, and his book sought to find common ground between such folk as pioneer airmen, climbers, explorers and the like. I never did meet Noyce, though I very much wanted to. We had arranged to meet on his return from the Russian–British Pamirs Expedition in Central Asia, but this was not to be. In a tragic accident, Noyce and a young Scottish climber fell to their deaths.

Planning for a distant voyage as we were, it seemed desirable that Susie should have a companion. It was in April 1963 that Vicky was born, and the little family was complete.

At last *Rehu Moana* was launched with an invocation by Fiona to Tane, the Polynesian god of forests and craftsmen. The time had come to try her out rigorously. The Arctic Circle seemed a reasonable objective for a cruising catamaran, so six of us put to sea in 1963, helped in no small measure by an English newspaper, the *Manchester Guardian*. The first casualty was crewmember Tony Jennett's dentures when he was seasick, an occasion unkindly immortalised at dinner time by fellow crewmember Axel Pedersen: 'We are going to have our stew and Tony his spew!' The next was the experimental mast. Axel was at the helm. I was plotting our position on the chart (we were about 130 miles off Iceland) when a huge sea broke fair across our beam and swept us. The catamaran hove-over momentarily, to be snapped back violently upright by her enormous stability. The 'whip' aloft must have been monstrous. As the spray cleared, Axel leapt to his feet, swearing in Danish. Then he shouted, 'The bloody masts is gone!' One leg of the experimental A-shaped mast had broken and the whole structure had crashed across to port and lay athwart the deck and twelve metres overside, in one tangled mass of coiling wire, sails, half a mile of rope and splintered wreckage. Dismasting was becoming far too much of a habit.

The dreary business of retrieving the wreckage and raising the 22-foot gaff as a jury mast took nearly two days. The only light relief was when we rigged a jury antenna and made our bi-weekly report to the long-suffering *Guardian*. It was all routine, until journalist John Fairhall asked the question we had been waiting for.

'Hasn't anything else been happening?'

'Well, as a matter of fact we have been dismasted. It is not an emergency, repeat, not an emergency. No assistance is needed. We are setting up a jury rig and making for Seydisfjordur in north-east Iceland.'

John, understandably, never quite trusted us again, and always began on the radio–telephone with 'Any important events?'.

A better jury rig, though not much better, was constructed in the bleak, treeless sub-arctic port of Seydisfjordur. The work was enlivened by the *silde* (herring) girls, young women flown in from Reykjavik to work in the herring factories; some were spectacularly beautiful, though few spoke English. An exception in regard to language but not to looks was Ragna. Slender and hazel-eyed, she was not my idea of a Norse Valkyrie at all, but was nevertheless a typical Icelandic woman.

'We get our green eyes from the Irish who settled at Vestmannaeyjar,' she explained, 'and our fair hair from our other ancestors, the Norwegians. We Icelanders are very phlegmatic and *never* show our feelings. But people think we live like polar bears. Yet today it's warmer than in England.' I hastily agreed, though new snow was down to 150 metres and the wind was piercing. 'You can take me to the dance tomorrow night,' Ragna announced magnanimously. 'It begins at about ten at night. Bring us some brandy and carry your fighting knife.'

'Why the knife?' I queried, alarmed and puzzled.

'Because around two o'clock in the morning the Finlanders will be drunk and start fighting with knives. You will have to protect me.'

Despite my concern, the dance proceeded with noisy good fellowship until, true to prediction, the early hours of the 'White Night' were enlivened by cries of anger as hulking Finnish fishermen drew knives from the backs of their belts and lunged at each other. Fortunately, they were too drunk to see straight; the main danger was being trampled underfoot.

Our makeshift mast stepped, we continued on to the Arctic Circle, or very near it, then returned to Seydisfjordur for further modifications. A proper spar was waiting for us in Stornoway in the Hebrides, the engine had died of corrosion, and the crew's leave was running out. Axel and I would have to sail the crippled vessel to Stornoway. Mist was eddying among the savage crags and snowfields, the fjord lay still; only the arrowhead ripple of a swimming seal broke the surface of the icy water. It was hard to say goodbye, above all to Ragna: '*Bless, elskan mín!* [Farewell, my love!]' Yes, it was more than time to be gone!

The passage to the Hebrides under our dubious rig was enlivened by gales, so it was ten days before Tiumpan Head was abeam and we were stemming an adverse tide. We had radioed for a tow up the firth to Stornoway and could now relax. We caught and cooked a number of mackerel and whiled away the tedium of waiting by opening the last of our wine.

'Lock up your wives and your daughters,' proclaimed Axel, waving a bottle, 'because the Vikings is coming.' That is the last I remember, for the 'Vikings' went to sleep and we very nearly missed our tow altogether.

Fiona and the children (Vicky in a carrycot) joined us in Stornoway, as did the second-hand aluminium mast. Dr (later Sir) Charles Evans, Vicky's godfather, was there in his yacht. He had been deputy leader of the Hillary–Tenzing Everest epic and leader of the 1955 Mount Kanchenjunga climb in Sikkim, a very different effort in which such brilliant non-establishment climbers as Manchester plumber Joe Brown and Don Whillans made their mark on the world's third-highest mountain. Charles held my grandfather's old post as principal of Bangor University. Sadly, he had recently been diagnosed as having multiple sclerosis. He hoped to sail a little longer, though he suspected his climbing days were numbered. Indeed, it so proved, and while Fiona and I later climbed with his wife Denise and her mother, the great Nea Morin, Charles's days on the crags were over.

Fiona did manage to afford Charles some light relief, however. On Sundays, the Stornoway population divided into two portions: one part in sober black raiment, the other happily drunk. One of the latter rushed to help the perfectly competent Fiona off the long ladder at the dockside, grasping her firmly enough to make her lose her balance, then forgot what he was doing and let her go without warning. Fiona managed to grab on. Charles, though not Fiona, found the show vastly entertaining.

Leaving Stornoway, and still in the company of Axel, we duly traversed the Irish Sea to Plymouth. Many lessons had been learned at no small cost, and we set about putting the ship to rights for the role for which she was always intended — to circumnavigate through stormy waters. Through it all, and for the subsequent circumnavigation, the *Guardian* continued to support us loyally. I still profoundly regret that on the very last leg I allowed my then-agent to ditch the *Guardian* for another paper, which was offering a better contract. No matter how persuasive he had been, the fact is I had sold my integrity. My action was unforgivable and I am deeply ashamed.

On a happier note, Axel was to sail with me again, this time to Alaska, twenty-five years later. Our very first contact had been his letter to me via the *Guardian* applying for the Iceland voyage. 'I have not done much sailing,' he wrote, 'only the single-handed passage from New Zealand to Denmark.' Only! Indeed, he had known nothing of sailing at all when he purchased the classic ketch *Marco Polo* in Auckland. 'The wind came up and I thought I should take down the big sail in the middle,' he reminisced. Certainly, by the time he got to Denmark, he knew no more names of sails but he did know how to use them. I was proud when this remarkable sailor joined me for a second time. He had not changed, even to going barefoot in near-freezing conditions when everyone else was in seaboots and layers of socks.

But back to the catamaran project. She had to be seaworthy. Though entered in the second single-handed transatlantic race of 1964, this was only a curtain-raiser. Her real purpose was to traverse the waters at the 'bottom of the world' — the tip of South America where Tilman had sailed in *Mischief*, wild seas whose romance had always attracted me mightily, perhaps even to Antarctica (a dream that, in the end, had to be postponed). We would then continue on around the world, conducting on the way a trial of ancient Polynesian navigational methods, for I was already enthralled by the subject and, provoked by comments from New Zealand historian Andrew Sharp that the Polynesians had settled the Pacific Islands by 'accident', had written papers about the relative ease of making landfall on 'island blocks' in the early 1960s. Wayfinding and the Antarctic between them bade fair to provide enough projects for a lifetime, as indeed they have so proved!

The fact that Fiona and I had become the parents of two little girls did nothing to alter our plans. This statement needs considerable qualification. In those days, cruising with children was not so common as it is today, and mention of our plans brought headshaking and a chorus of disapproval. Were we taking unjustified risks? Given proper precautions like a strict safety-harness regime, we thought not. My being a doctor probably helped give us confidence, more through awareness of the dangers of dehydration in young children, vitamin requirements and the like, than treatments *per se*. I did not realise at the time that Fiona was a good deal more worried than she let on. I, for my part, am an inveterate worrier anyway.

After some long discussions and not without some trepidation, we proceeded with our plans. In due course, Fiona and I sold our home, handed over the practice to my young partner and, leaving a protesting Barry at school (Perle had custody anyway), set out with Susie, aged two, and Vicky, aged one, free from all encumbrances, including a regular income.

One thing that had concerned me prior to setting out on our journey was my back, which had been playing up before the trip to Iceland, to the extent that I had been having physiotherapy at London Hospital. The sciatic nerve was affected and there was some loss of sensation on the back of my right foot.

'No backpacking,' I was ordered. However, while refitting at Seydisfjordur, a crewmember and I had taken time off to sledge in the mountains and test out army-surplus inflatable mattresses for sleeping on the snow. Regrettably, they deflated and my feet were mildly frostbitten.

Back at the hospital it was found that I had lost sensation in *both* feet and, on admitting to the cold injury, I was discharged with ignominy. The problem did give me pause, however. Was it fair to undertake such a long voyage with such a potentially disabling condition hanging over us?

I need not have worried. The trouble had really lain in my sedentary lifestyle. From the first moment I hauled up the anchor, put my weight on the halyards and squeezed down the hatchway, the pain disappeared. It was the same in 1995, when a recurrence of aches and pains was cured within a day of setting sail on the Maori double-hulled *waka Te Aurere*. The painful contortions required to get into the sleeping stretcher did the trick. The best physiotherapy really does seem to be the constant and decidedly uncomfortable postural adjustments so generously donated free of charge by the unquiet ocean.

Rehu Moana and I did not cover ourselves in glory in the second single-handed transatlantic race. A broken boom in the second week had to be overlapped and bolted, so could only carry the mainsail reefed. The ensuing problem of being undercanvased was much compounded when my only large headsail blew out on the eve of encountering the Gulf of Maine calms. When the wind did return, four of us, who had been drifting helplessly off the Nantucket Light, arrived in Rhode Island in a single day. I was the last of these and seventh overall, having made the passage in thirty-eight days.

Fiona and the children crossed the Atlantic by freighter and were waiting for me in Newport. Two weeks were spent stocking up on food, water, fuel and such essentials as cartons of disposable nappies. Ascorbic acid (vitamin C), one 50 mgm tablet each a day, was instituted at this stage as a preventative measure against scurvy. They were a popular item. 'Vitamin C time, Daddy-David. I feed you one, Vicky.' Then: 'Mummy, Vicky done push it up her nose. Naughty baby sister.' Howls announced that the acid tablet had begun to sting the delicate nasal lining. A moment later, more loud yells burst forth, this time from Susie. 'Fiona-Mummy, mine stuck in *my* nose.' Fortunately the tablets soon dissolved and the experiment was not repeated.

Finally, on 20 July 1964, it was time to set sail if we were to avoid the fury of the West Indies-spawned hurricanes. We were seen off by fellow competitors and by a crowd of female well-wishers, mostly Portuguese in background, descendants of the Azores fishermen who had manned the Yankee whalers in the last days of sail. These warmhearted women wept and showered the little girls with dolls, toys and candies, and Fiona and I with guilt. The Chichesters brought Californian wine. Then we cast off and headed out into the sea mist, feeling suddenly forlorn and not at all venturesome.

Fiona was sick again. Sadly, no matter what remedy we tried over the years, this turned out to be the invariable sequence: a few days' misery, then Fiona could weather any gale with impunity. As short a time as two days ashore and the pattern was repeated. Her determination was amazing, but that dread initial sickness took much of the joy out of sailing for Fiona. Then, she was essentially a mountaineer and learning the way of a ship on the ocean did not come naturally to her. Nor did caring for two lively little girls help matters. What had seemed to be teething troubles increasingly became more of a tedious chore.

I tried to help more with the children, but Fiona was so efficient that I left all too much of it to her and, quite unconsciously, began doing nearly all the nightwatches to give her some relatively unbroken rest, with the result that the glory of the ocean under the stars was hid from her. Nor did she ever experience the fierce joy of battling down a flogging mainsail to tie in a reef on a pitching deck in flying spray — the habitual anxieties and all too rare triumphs of navigation had no appeal for her. We each played our own parts in the enterprise, but not as joyful equal partners. The first wisps of cloud were already darkening the marital horizon.

None of this affected the children. Playing on deck wearing (at all times) their safety harnesses, calling out to the unresponsive storm petrels that danced their delicate spindly feet over the foam, seeing strange new places, hearing alien tongues and eating unfamiliar foods (Vicky's first word was *feijoada*, Brazilian black beans in a peppery sauce which, astonishingly, she loved) provided fodder for their expanding minds. Not that either was ever at a loss for words. 'Hand socks' they christened the gloves they first encountered off Tierra del Fuego. Susie, in particular, was a proper little didactic schoolmistress.

'What that animal is, Susie?'

'That's a *lion*, Vicky,' replied Susie, with confident assurance. It was, in fact, a cow.

For us parents, despite everything, living at such close quarters with young children and watching their intelligence and imagination unfolding day by day with such amazing speed was a rare privilege, especially for me, since few fathers can be home all day and every day with their offspring. The girls felt very secure too. Much as they loved playing with other children ashore and sampling the delights of new lands (especially ice cream, for we had no freezer), the boat was their home. They never once objected when we put to sea. Nor did storms faze them. The first and only time we saw them frightened was in New Zealand, when they rushed out of a cousin's house, terror-stricken and yelling that a monster was after them — it was a vacuum cleaner!

So we sailed on: to the Cape Verde Islands, where Vicky had to re-learn how to walk; to Bahia, Brazil, for two months and to Rio more briefly; then southward again to the Cliff of the Condor and Cape Virgins, that guard the Atlantic entrance to Magellan Strait, Patagonia to the north, and Tierra del Fuego to the south. Despite the blazing gas fires of the oil wells, this desolate land amply deserved the name 'Uttermost Part of the Earth'. We spent four months in all in Tierra del Fuego and Chilean Patagonia. The first weeks were spent hauled out on the slip at the bleak city of Punta Arenas, for repairs to our keels and rudders.

Then came hard beating to windward along the rest of the strait itself, where rolling pampas quickly gave way to snow-capped mountains and dark forests of Antarctic beech, and then up the magnificent Patagonian Channels. The 4 h.p. Seagull outboard, our only mechanical propulsion, was less than adequate in these conditions. The pain in our chilled hands as we tended the sheets for constant tacking was almost unbearable.

'You and your bloody boat,' Fiona sobbed once, almost at the end of her tether.

'Remember Tilman's comments at the Cruising Association about cold hands in Arctic sailing?' I asked. Fiona forced a reluctant smile.

'I regret,' he had admitted with embarrassment, 'that some of my crew adopted the unseamanlike habit of wearing gloves at the helm!' We, of course, were made of much lesser stuff, and eagerly embraced the 'unseamanlike habit' inasmuch as our torn and tattered gloves would allow. Through it all, Susie and Vicky stayed warm as toast, endlessly entranced by steamer ducks, kelp geese, whales, fur seals and otters, and by excursions into the wild forests ashore, where tiny green hummingbirds flitted unafraid through the howling desolation.

At Puerto Edén, the only human habitation for five hundred miles, we met the pathetically few survivors of the Alacalufe Indians, who had once paddled their beech-bark canoes to Cape Horn Island itself. There were wonderful wooded anchorages, where we sheltered from the incessant storms. Though it was high summer, new snow lay a hundred or so metres up the wooded slopes. In Canal Wide we eased our way past icebergs, some as big as freighters, that had been spawned by the Hielo Continental, the southern ice cap of Patagonia, which Tilman had been first to cross.

Out in the Pacific, our troubles should have been over, but both rudders broke within hours of each other, so that we eventually limped into Valparaiso steering by odd-looking wooden contraptions. They may have looked funny but they had taken some fitting, for the waters of the Humboldt Current are cold and we had no wetsuits.

'Why is Daddy such a funny colour?' queried Vicky, with interest. 'He's gone pink.'

'No, Vicky. He's blue!'

'Get out of the way you little monsters!' I thundered as I clambered aboard. 'Fiona, is there any rum left?'

Once again we had to call on the services of the *Armada de Chile* to effect repairs, this time in steel, and permanent.

Kindly acquaintances took us sightseeing, once to an exceedingly grand open-air restaurant in Santiago in the shadow of the high Andes. Because the children, especially Vicky, were so messy, it had become the rule for them to undress for meals.

'No, Vicky, you don't have to. Keep your clothes on,' we begged her.

The little girl took no notice, stripped to the skin, and calmly addressed her lunch. It was not all that warm. The other diners were appalled.

'*Crueles los ingleses* — !*bárbaros*!'

In Santiago, Fiona and I were pleasantly surprised to get a letter from Tilman, whose charts we were using. It was in a characteristic vein, laudatory for him: 'I congratulate you on a good trip in a most unsuitable vessel, with a crew that nobody could call strong.'

The rigours of the Patagonian passage while caring for the girls made us realise that we really needed another adult on board, for what we had been doing amounted to one sailing the boat while the other ran a day nursery. The brunt of the child care had been borne by Fiona. With the confined space and constant motion, it was far more demanding than on land. Meanwhile, I had been having most of the fun. Priscilla Cairns, a friend from England, was the keenest sailor we knew. We invited her to join us, and she arrived at Valparaiso in due course, travelling by sea to Buenos Aires, and then by train across the Andes.

Though Priscilla would ultimately do more than her share of child-minding, her very enthusiasm and competence as a sailor rather inhibited Fiona. In personality the two women were quite different. Fiona, from a wealthy Scottish-South African family, was the more widely travelled and cosmopolitan; Priscilla, daughter of High Court Judge (and later Lord Chief Justice of England) Sir David Cairns, had always been over-pressured to achieve academically, something at odds with her main interests of sailing, skiing and outdoor education. Fiona taught physical education and dancing, and Priscilla specialised in teaching 'outward bound' activities, so their interests should have been complementary, but somehow they never really became friends.

All this was in the future when we left Valparaiso before a fitful breeze, escorted all through the first night by the loud clacking of the beaks of a throng of swimming pelicans. A stay on the archipelago of Juan Fernandez, where Alexander Selkirk, real-life model for Daniel Defoe's Robinson Crusoe, had been marooned, was followed weeks later by a few memorable days in Easter Island, where the *moai* or, as the little girls called them, 'stone man heads' mightily impressed us all, and where a gift of a carved wooden figure, of particularly malignant mien, was inappropriately christened by the girls as 'Baby Doll Moai'. Later, we stopped at Mangaréva, where the officiousness of the port gendarme was only matched by the friendliness of the islanders, and then suffered a similar experience in Tahiti, where one particular official was as obstructive as the gendarme in Mangaréva.

'What shall I do?' I was at my wits' end.

'You say "bugger heem", David.' So advised Bernard Moitessier, who was stifling aboard his steel *Joshua* in windless Papeete Harbour.

Fortunately, I did not need to take his advice, since unexpectedly, the chief of police came on side and cut the red tape. Bernard, who was then preparing for Cape Horn, was a steel-boat enthusiast: 'A chimpanzee can do it. You tell heem "chip rust and paint", that is all.' The famous voyager was also exceptionally charming, so much so that I was rather relieved at still having an intact crew when the time came to leave.

four

Heirs of Tane

In Tahiti my insatiable curiosity brought my long-cherished project on Pacific settlement to the point of a practical sea trial. From the outliers of Asia across the ocean to Easter Island in the very shadow of the Andes, from Hawaii in the north to New Zealand in the south, the great canoes had reached every speck of land. What part had been played by conscious navigation? To me this seemed to be the key question.

The subject of just *how* the islanders accomplished their unique maritime achievement had recently become a matter of hot debate, spearheaded by New Zealand academic Andrew Sharp, who I alluded to earlier. He effectively debunked the earlier uncritical acceptance of traditions, often edited, that had ancient Polynesians quartering the Pacific like jet aircraft. Unfortunately, in their place he substituted the assertion that the Polynesians had hardly navigated with deliberate intent at all, but had made their longer landfalls by accident. This theory made good sense to many

anthropologists and historians, who were all too ready to doubt
the nautical expertise of pre-literate Stone Age, native people.
But Sharp's glaring misuse of book-derived nautical data made
no sense at all to Pacific small-boat sailors or, indeed, to anyone
personally acquainted with the islands of the South Seas.

One important issue, that of accuracy without instruments,
I had already addressed in theory well before I left England. With
invaluable help from Professor Harry Maude of the Australian
National University, who was visiting England, I had written papers
in the *Journal of the Polynesian Society* and the *Journal of the Royal
Institute of Navigation*, demonstrating how relatively easy it was to
target any of the huge Pacific archipelagos or 'blocks' of islands, and
then to use pointers like clouds, deflected waves and homing birds
to locate individual islands, which would generally not be very
far apart. It was only several years later, in 1968 and 1969, that this
speculation was dramatically confirmed by the navigators of the
Pacific themselves. 'You steer,' explained Hipour, my Polowat
mentor in the Carolines, 'towards the *screen* of homing birds, clouds,
deep reefs, disturbed waves and islands that stretch across your
pathway.' He then proceeded to demonstrate the process both ways
across 450 miles of unbroken ocean. Similarly, the Hon. Ve'ehala, a
senior member of the Tuita Navigator Clan of Tonga, revealed this
telling saying from their secret lore: 'You do not aim towards an
individual *puko* tree but towards a *grove* of *puko* trees — only then
do you look for your particular tree.'

Here I must tread a delicate line: I have written a good deal
about Polynesian navigation, and the newly revised edition of my
book, *We, the Navigators*, is in print and doing well.* But, as far as
Polynesian navigation is concerned, this book is not the place for a
detailed treatise.

What was clearly timely back in Tahiti in 1964 was to subject
my theories to a sea trial. We therefore resolved to navigate

*We, the Navigators: The Ancient Art of Landfinding in the Pacific, 2nd ed., University of Hawaii Press, 1994.

Tahiti–Huahine–Rarotonga–New Zealand in the manner of the navigator-priests of old. We would follow the directions of Kupe, legendary discoverer of New Zealand, to steer a little to the left of the setting sun in early November. No instruments, neither compass, nor clock, nor sextant, would be used to navigate the vessel. However, for safety and for the record, Priscilla would log our true positions but would not reveal them, except in an emergency, until journey's end. The stars and the sun would be our compass; stars arching overhead in the zenith and the Southern Cross sweeping the horizon our sextant; wave forms, birds and clouds our warnings of land.

The first leg to Huahine in the Society Islands of French Polynesia went well, and there I met Curt Ashford, who was to become a lifelong friend. Curt and his wife Jenny's little schooner *Sea Wyfe* had lost her rudder and been swept over the reef. The couple had built a *kikau* shack on the beach and spent a year making repairs. Their three-year-old son Eric spoke only Tahitian and their daughter Ngaire was about to be born. We were to renew the family's acquaintance a decade later in Hawaii in dramatic and tragic circumstances.

Our course for the next 500 miles through the Lower Cooks was indeed arrow-straight, but we overshot the islands through my ignorance of patent bird clues, and Priscilla had to break her silence. The last 1600 miles from Rarotonga to New Zealand culminated in a landfall only twenty-five miles south of my estimate.

But our arrival in New Zealand is jumping the gun a little, for we paused a while in Rarotonga, for me so redolent with childhood memories. Rarotonga is mountainous, though the spectacular jungle-clad peaks are no more than 600 metres high. But so wild is the cloud forest inland that Rarotonga seems far larger than its thirty-two-kilometre circumference. A coastal plain encircles the island, luxuriantly clothed in breadfruit, hibiscus, tiare, papaya and groves of citrus, while everywhere tall coconut palms lean before the tradewind. This lowland rim is, in its turn, enclosed by shallow lagoons and a reef. Together with my cousin George Cowan and led by Fiona, we climbed a rock pinnacle called The Needle or, more colourfully in Maori, 'Tangaroa's Penis'. (Tangaroa, I should explain, is god of the ocean; his counterpart Tane is god of forests and canoe builders.) Together with Priscilla and George, I also spent another day crossing the island over the then nearly trackless mountains.*

When it came time to leave, our flower-bedecked little girls shed tears. They cried too on reaching New Zealand, when we passed by uninhabited Cuvier Island off the entrance to Hauraki Gulf: 'We thought we were going to stop in New Zealand,' they wailed. But by the time we were approaching Auckland, escorted by a fleet of multihulls that had come out to meet us, they were reassured.

'This was where Daddy lived when he was a little baby boy,' explained Fiona.

'When Daddy was a little baby boy, where were we?'

There was no ready answer.

We stayed half a year in New Zealand, spending Christmas 1964 and New Year 1965 with O'Neill and Cowan relatives and with old friends going back to my early schooldays. While the rest of us were enjoying the comforts of the land, Priscilla, not having enough of the sea, promptly set off to cruise the Hauraki Gulf for two weeks in a local yacht. I, for one, was only too glad to be ashore for a change. *Rehu Moana* was hauled out on the slip at Westhaven, where she received much needed attention. Fixed skegs under the after part of the hulls were substituted for the unsatisfactory keels. I also used my time off to write *Daughters of the Wind*.

There was one particularly embarrassing occasion in Auckland that did nothing to enhance my reputation as a navigator. I was to take the chair at a public meeting at Auckland University for Thor Heyerdahl of *Kon-Tiki* fame. I thought I knew the way to the university from years before, but toiling up streets that had become somehow unfamiliar, sweating with anxiety as the time got later and

---

*I sailed back to Rarotonga from New Zealand in 1996 in *Southern Seas II*, thirty years on. Small girls who had played with Susie and Vicky had children of their own but still remembered their old playmates. Tourist facilities now are everywhere, but Rarotonga remains essentially unspoilt.

later, I knew I had let down the distinguished audience and the eminent speaker. When I eventually arrived very late in the piece, Heyerdahl, far from showing irritation, went out of his way most graciously to put me at my ease.

Regardless of Heyerdahl's theories of Polynesian origins from South America (disproved by excavation, carbon-dating, linguistics, even by the discovery of the bones of *kiori*, Polynesian canoe rats, on Easter Island), the Norwegian explorer did demonstrate dramatically how the oceans were potential pathways, rather than necessarily barriers, to the simple craft of yesterday — a truly revolutionary change in perspective. I encountered Heyerdahl again in Hobart, Tasmania, where we were both speaking at a diving conference. Subsequently, he provided invaluable introductions to people in Russia, particularly to Yuri Senkevich, the doctor on his *Ra* and *Tigris* voyages.

To make up a little for the debacle in Auckland, I was awarded the Bernard Fergusson Trophy as 1965 New Zealand 'Yachtsman of the Year' at a ceremony attended by George Cowan from Rarotonga and the only authentic war hero in the family, Jim O'Neill. By coincidence, he had met George at Mauke in the Cook Islands, home of their common ancestress Mary O'Neill, when the lusty Jim was the rather unlikely captain of a missionary ship.

'You were only a grasshopper then,' he greeted his younger relative.

Jim's wartime exploit had been on the minesweeper *Kiwi*, of which he was first mate. They were sneaking through 'The Slot' off Guadalcanal under cover of darkness, when a six-thousand-ton Japanese troop-carrying submarine surfaced ahead of them. Before its six-inch gun could be manned — it would have blown the fragile little ship out of the water — Jim signalled the engine room.

'Flank speed; stand by to ram.'

'What does that mean?' asked the startled engineer.

'Don't know, never done it before,' replied Jim, as the stem sliced open the submarine and sank it, while the severely damaged *Kiwi* limped on her way.

Once the 1965 cyclone season in the tropical South Pacific was over we continued on our way round the world. The first stop was Tongatapu, the main island of the ancient Kingdom of Tonga, after which we planned to visit Nomuka, Captain Bligh's last landfall before the mutiny.

'You steer two hands' breadths to the left of that star rising in the north-east,' explained *eikevaka* (cutter captain) Koloni Kienga, pointing to the star. He was giving me directions for our passage through the archipelago. I could hardly believe my ears. The 'extinct' art was alive!

'When that star rises too high for convenience, follow the next in line, directly or at an angle. This is called the *Kaveinga* or Star Path. You follow the succession of stars till dawn,' Koloni continued. 'Yes, I do have a compass. It is in the bilge somewhere. I never use it.' He explained how the long ocean swell lines were distorted by land, being bent on each side of an island and ultimately joining beyond it in a complex interlocking pattern. On the windward side a back swell was reflected. 'If you know what to look for these swells can be interpreted twenty miles from the smallest atoll, and you yourself know well enough that an atoll's palms can only be seen ten miles away from a boat.'

If you know what to look for. That was the rub. There must be other Kolonis. How could I find them?

Fiji, Vanuatu, Papua New Guinea! Everywhere we came upon fragments of the old knowledge, and tantalising rumours of active, living star-path navigators in the Carolines, Kiribati and elsewhere. It was in Port Moresby that it all came to a head. I had been holding forth to Ron Crocombe, then head of the New Guinea Research Unit of the Australian National University and married to a Rarotongan 'sister' of mine, about the need for someone to make a systematic Pacific-wide search for these navigators, go to sea with them and record their methods before it was too late. But how?

'Apply for a research fellowship from the ANU, why don't you?' Ron suggested.

'I'm not an anthropologist, nor a historian,' I objected. 'They would never appoint me.'

'Give it a go,' said my fellow New Zealander, characteristically. So, fuelled by rum toddies, we drew up an application that very night and Ron put it into acceptable academic form. It was in the post before we sailed, but neither Ron nor I gave it much chance of success, and I thought no more about it.

All considerations of star-path navigation were eclipsed by a new problem: Fiona contracted hepatitis. After some debate, we decided to make forthwith for the tropical Australian city of Darwin, where good hospital facilities would be available and a decision, based on blood tests, could be taken as to Fiona's fitness to cross the Indian Ocean. The passage through Torres Strait and along the Arnhem Land coast was an easy one, though intolerably hot for Fiona. The Darwin hospital's decision was definite: Fiona must not risk the crossing by yacht. She must fly to South Africa, where her mother lived, and await us there. This was doubly unfortunate, because Fiona at long last had been coming to actively enjoy the sailing, and it seemed only too possible that this enforced absence would reverse the process and tip the balance the wrong way. Sadly, this is exactly what happened.

Months later, Fiona was fit again. *Rehu Moana* had traversed the Indian Ocean via the Cocos Islands to Durban. We had entered the port at night with makeshift red and green navigation lights made up of coloured panties wrapped around torches, our fixed lights having long since corroded. We had been under the misapprehension that the port authorities had seen our lights and signalled us to enter, until a freighter, towering up astern, sent us scuttling to the edge of the narrow channel. Somewhat shaken by this incident, we gave up looking for the Point Yacht Club and brought up at the nearest sandbank.

'Big, big birds!' was how the girls greeted three flamingos that were stalking the sandbank next morning. Flamingos were not going to get us to the club wharf against a tide too strong for our Seagull outboard, however. Here, Robin Knox-Johnston in his newly built William Atkins-designed 'Eric', *Suhaili,* came to our aid.

Robin was en route to England with one companion. He was helpfulness personified, and towed us to the yacht club. The children subsequently did their best to repay him by 'helping' with his cans of food. The bilgewater-vulnerable labels were being stripped off and painted symbols substituted. The girls proceeded to remove labels so enthusiastically that the painters were left far behind, and must have had reason to curse their young helpers for the ensuing confusion. In 1969, Robin won the famous round-the-world single-handed race in which Donald Crowhurst committed suicide and Moitessier, who had been leading, broke off to return to his beloved Tahiti. Robin was later knighted.

It was January 1967 before we rounded the Cape of Good Hope, only having to lay-to twice in southwest gales, and prepared to sail from Cape Town. I was glad to be leaving South Africa, where *apartheid* was in full swing and distasteful racist myths were very much in vogue, even among people who should have known better. Rather than take the usual (and more sensible) route up the South Atlantic, we decided it would be more interesting to follow the coast northward, calling at South-West Africa (Namibia), Angola and Zaire (Democratic Republic of the Congo), before rounding the great bulge of West Africa.

So it came about that we were in Walvis Bay in South-West Africa when the news arrived: I had been appointed to a four-year Research Fellowship at the Australian National University, with the terms of reference Ron and I had proposed. Australia! Our lives were about to take an abrupt about-turn.

There was only one problem, or two, to be exact.

In the first place our ship was, literally, beached. We were in the thick of reconstruction work, knee-deep in plywood, fibreglass and glue, when the message came through. I quote from a transcript of a recorded film interview, without apology for the rather intemperate language: 'Near Walvis Bay we got rammed by a tug, skippered by an Afrikaner moron who had been demoted from every job in the bloody harbour. Skippering a tug was the lowest job a white person could do. They should have shot him. That was *apartheid* in practice.

A sudden nor-wester came up and just about all the boats had to shift, and this tug crushed us against the sea wall. We had to run up on the beach or sink. We did a deal with the harbour board that we wouldn't make a fuss if they helped us with repairs.'

A kindly harbour pilot and his wife took in the little girls, for their bridge deck cabin had been destroyed. They attended the local kindergarten, apparently not disconcerted at finding the teachers spoke only Afrikaans and German. '*Eins, zwei, drei, eisenbahn, alle kinder waschen sie*,' they learned to chant, while marching in line to wash their hands. For years thereafter Susie and Vicky insisted they had been to school in Germany.

The second problem was that the faithful *Rehu Moana* would not be the most suitable craft for the proposed journey. What would be needed was a 'motorsailer' with a range under power substantial enough to seek out navigators in obscure islands without having to worry too much about fair winds. *Rehu Moana*'s narrow hulls would never take a heavy motor or the necessary fuel. This all meant that we had to complete our circumnavigation, and sail from England to Australia in another boat.

The repairs at Walvis Bay were eventually completed and we continued up the vast West African coastline to Lobito and San Antonio do Zaire in civil war-torn Angola. Crossing the Congo River to Banana in what is now the Democratic Republic of the Congo presented something of a problem since the two countries were theoretically at war. They were, however, happily trading Congolese chickens for Portuguese wine and agreed to let us cross the closed river frontier unmolested. Both sides treated us with the utmost kindness.

Susie had been playing with a group of Congolese children, none apparently worried at the language difference, when something seemed to strike her.

'Daddy, why are some girls brown?'

A significant question, indeed. I still think the answer that flashed into my mind was probably correct: 'People who lived many thousands of years in Europe where there is not much sun have faded.'

Our next landfall was Sierra Leone, today sadly racked with civil war, then the Azores and, ultimately, England. Back in Plymouth, after completing the first multihull voyage round the world, *Rehu Moana* was put up for sale and I started negotiating for a very different kind of craft — the gaff ketch *Isbjorn*, a Scottish trawler-type double-ender, thirty-nine feet long and crossing a square yard on the foremast. The engine was a Burgius-Kelvin semi-diesel, an antique monstrosity. Only my son Barry's skill kept it running for as long as it did. The ship's name, meaning 'polar bear' in Norwegian, was a reminder of the Arctic voyages she had made under Professor Jackson, her previous owner.

Selling the catamaran was a good deal like betraying a friend, especially so considering its purchaser. He had heard about the boat accidentally and not through an agent, he assured me. Only after the transaction was completed did he smugly admit he had lied. I felt morally obliged to remit the commission to the defrauded broker, and was unexpectedly rewarded with a case of Guinness in return. Fortunately, *Rehu Moana* was soon resold.*

We spent nearly six months in England, swapping boats, writing to contacts all over the Pacific, soothing the understandably impatient university in Australia and equipping the new ship. A £500 prize from the London *Daily Telegraph* was most welcome. This was when I first met the author and yachtsman Ralph Hammond Innes, who was on the prize committee. He put me up for the Royal Cruising Club, which Tilman, Hasler and Chichester had recently been invited to join (I was awarded their Seamanship Medal jointly with Chichester, and after the later *Ice Bird* voyage, the medal on my own). Hammond Innes guided me through the publishing jungle as well, steering me to literary agency Curtis Brown and their Australian representative Tim Curnow, who

---

*Twenty years on, a family bought *Rehu Moana*, intending to repeat our voyage. They duly set out, but returned the next day for steering adjustments and made the mistake of anchoring *outside* Plymouth Sound in an open bay. Now, this is what you must *not* do on the Atlantic coasts of Britain that face the prevailing westerly gales. It was just such a sudden south-west gale that blew up that night and drove them ashore. The family reached land safely but the catamaran was a total loss.

My grandparents, Sir Henry and Lady Annie Lewis, pictured on a trip to India.

My father, Trevor Lewis, and mother, Carinna O'Neill, walk under the crossed swords of the Royal Welch Fusiliers after their wedding ceremony at St Margarets, Westminster, during the First World War.

Me, aged three, at Orua Bay, Manukau Harbour, New Zealand …

… and as a wiry seventeen-year-old school graduate, pictured with the kayak that I paddled 430 miles between Wanganui and Takapuna, Auckland.

Riding naked with a fellow guide on the Fox Glacier floodplain after a spot of gelignite fishing.

With Doug Dick after losing our car in a flash flood. We had just made the first ascent of the west face of La Perouse with fellow climber Arch J. Scott.

My mother, Carinna, on Mount
Ruapehu, c.1936, in snowshoes
I had made at school.

On Mount Aspiring.

Approaching Mount Aspiring before making the first ascent of the south-east ridge and
first traverse in 1937. *From left:* Harry Stevenson, me, and Doug Dick.

My father, Trevor, at New Monklands, Jamaica, 1938. He was to die nine years later.

With fellow field ambulance personnel in Egypt, 1945. I am seated third from the left.

Cardinal Vertue, 1960.

The proud owner.

My first two children, Barry and Anna.

secured me a timely book advance. I realised something of Hammond Innes's thoroughness subsequently, when I enquired about Western Australian desert tracks on his behalf. In the end the long-suffering National Mapping official exclaimed: 'He is researching this like an academic for a PhD, not a novel writer. He knows all we do and more!'

My old university, Leeds, awarded me an honorary MSc. The zoology professor, who kindly put us up, was ill-served for his hospitality. During the ceremony, Susie and Vicky were left in the laboratory, where they could watch tadpoles and keep out of trouble. The tadpoles were contained in two big tanks, one lot being fed experimental growth chemicals, the other being controls. No one dreamed the bored children might be able to catch the tadpoles, but they did, busily scooping up handfuls from one tank and emptying them into the other. Three months' worth of experiments were in ruins. We were never again asked back to my alma mater.

I said a reluctant goodbye to Priscilla, my best-ever shipmate. Fiona had generously offered to relinquish her place on board to the much keener sailor, but this I felt sure would strain our marriage to breaking point. So Priscilla waved us goodbye as *Isbjorn* motored out of Dover. She eventually returned to teaching, this time at an 'Outward Bound'-oriented school in Wales. Later she skippered an all-woman crew in a tall ship race to Lisbon, and later still she married. She and her husband (a sailor, needless to say) now live in Cornwall.

My seventeen-year-old son Barry had left school by this time and had been instructing in a sailing school on the Orwell in Suffolk. He joined Fiona (ever a gallant voyager, since her seasickness was no nearer being cured), the girls and me for the Pacific. Perle came to see him off. None of us realised at the time that this break with Britain would become permanent. This was also the last time Barry would see his mother, for a few years later she was to die of kidney trouble. For all of us a new chapter in our lives had begun.

Preparations for the voyage were only completed by January 1968, a not very sensible time to brave the Bay of Biscay, but we had delayed too long already. The shipping forecast was good when we departed, taking advantage of a rare favourable wind. Before midnight all had changed. 'Force 8 easterly gales in all sea areas,' said the forecast now. They had got it right this time. *Isbjorn* wallowed through the darkness, the wheelhouse floor awash and perilous underfoot. The contents of a sack of apples and a sack of coal had burst and spilled, and were sloshing about in the water. A squaresail lift parted but Barry succeeded in securing the swinging yard.

A week later we were in a different world of sunshine and fair breezes. 'The sea has no right to be that colour!' exclaimed Barry, gazing over the side at water of an incredible deep indigo he had never before seen in the North Sea or the Channel. We stopped at Horta in the Azores, where the hospitable Peter of Cafe Sport looked after us, as he had done earlier when we called in *Rehu Moana*.*

The north-east trades blew true and sent us rolling across the Atlantic under squaresail and gaff main. And how the ketch did roll! The quick, jerky but level motion of a multihull had made us forget how more conventional craft behaved. The lively little girls were put in charge of the small, triangular mizzen sail, where they could do little harm and might even be useful. I was highly diverted to observe them one day, when Barry was dreamily peeing over the rail, creep up behind him, then suddenly flick his stream into the air. After that, he would peer around furtively to locate his horrid little sisters before committing himself to a natural function. Amusing too for an observer were Fiona's and Barry's conversations. Fiona would say something about the children. Barry would listen courteously then, after acknowledging her remarks, he would describe the topsail he was making. Fiona would listen equally politely, then return to

*Peter (the son now) still sends us postcards.

the subject of her offspring. They were like two parallel railway lines: they ran side by side but never quite intersected.

Our first transatlantic landfall was English Harbour, Antigua, where we moored at the historic Nelson's Dockyard and sampled the fierce local rum punch. Martinique was the next stop, a tropical outpost of French culture and style of living, with its wonderful pavement cafes. We reluctantly sailed after a week, for we had a long way to go.

The next stop was Dominica, to visit our friends Bruce and Ellen Robinson. Bruce had been secretary of the Slocum Society, one of the organisations that had initiated the first transatlantic single-handed race in 1960. Back then, he had been a Madison Avenue advertising executive, stressed to the hilt. Inspired by the single-handers' example, Bruce and Ellen sold up everything and left the hurly burly of New York for the peace of the West Indies in *Picket*, their sixty-year-old cutter. They had settled in Dominica and we looked forward to finding out how they had fared. To our astonished dismay, we found the couple more stressed out than ever. Unable to discard his New York work ethic, Bruce had quickly become the 'chicken king' of the West Indies. Not content with his chicken 'ranches' on Dominica itself, he was flying almost daily to operations throughout the Caribbean. Both Robinsons looked utterly worn out.

In Dominica, we were intrigued to encounter many Carib Indians, who occupy perhaps a fifth of the island, and whose aquiline features and straight black hair stand out among the general population. These descendants of the original inhabitants, who once ranged the length of the Antilles and into South America, have retained over the centuries one striking artefact — the unique shape of the prows of their seagoing canoes.

The great variety of the West Indies never ceased to amaze us. Willemstad, on Curaçao, was a veritable outpost of Holland, set among cacti and oil refineries. Further on, the sight of the walled city of Cartagena in Colombia conjured up thoughts of Sir Francis Drake, who had once taken it by storm. Since leaving Curaçao we had rerigged *Isbjorn* as a kind of squat miniature brig: i.e. the gaff mainsail had been 'put to bed', the big squaresail set on the foremast and a small one on the mizzen, the ensemble being completed with assorted staysails and the jib. I tarried behind at Cartagena yacht club (a one-time fortress, built rather belatedly after Drake had gone) to photograph *Isbjorn* sailing past.

'My God,' exclaimed a startled American yachtsman, 'that's something Columbus left behind!' Nevertheless, though it looked rather odd, this tradewind rig was to serve us, bar an 800-mile fore-and-aft interlude from Panama to the Galapagos Islands, all the way to Fiji.

The San Blas de Cuna Islands off the coast of Panama, jealously controlled by the independent-minded Cuna Indians, were our next stop. A rusted tank-landing craft, pockmarked with bullet holes, was perched on a reef opposite the government building.

'How did it get there?' I asked the customs *jefe*, curiously.

'Colombiano smuggle boat. I shoot like this.' He mimed spraying a machine gun. 'Smuggler duck down so can't see and run up on reef.'

'What was he smuggling?' Colombia! Cocaine at least!

'Potatoes!'

This government post was at that time the only place in the San Blas de Cuna where a Panamanian official was allowed to stay overnight without the permission of the Indian Council, for there had existed an unspoken acceptance of Cuna autonomy within the Republic of Panama ever since a Panamanian expeditionary force had been wiped out in 1925.

The story of the Cuna goes back much further than that. Originally from Colombia, their ancestors had moved in after Columbus's successors had depopulated the Isthmus of Darien (Panama) of over a million Indians. The Cuna drove the Spaniards out of the gold workings in the *cordillera*, or mountain range, which they took over. Their relationship with the English buccaneers and privateers is perhaps best illustrated by the story of Dr Lionel Wafer.

Wafer was with William Dampier, crossing the isthmus from the Pacific to the Atlantic with the Spaniards in hot pursuit, when he was injured in a gunpowder explosion and had to be left behind with the friendly Cuna. Two years later Dampier's same privateers were again in Cuna territory. A lively Indian throng swarmed aboard. Something about the spectacularly painted witchdoctor struck a chord ('Blue and green and yellow, very lovely,' Wafer wrote later in *New Voyage and Description of the Isthmus of Panama*, published in 1699).

'Why, there's our doctor!' exclaimed a startled privateer.

From San Blas we visited Nombre de Dios and Porto Bello. Derelict settlements since the opening of the canal, they had once been vital entrepôts for crossing the Isthmus of Darien.

They were also places where Sir Francis Drake had left his mark. Incidentally, at the time, we were filming background scenes for that story for the West of England BBC. Collina Drake, or Drake Hill, stands as a sentinel outside Porto Bello. Just as we were clambering out of the 'rubber duck' (Fiona was on anchor-watch aboard *Isbjorn*), a metre-long lizard sprang erect on its hind legs and sped away, forelegs pumping. The jungle soon proved too much for the children, so we returned them to the beach, with the stern admonition: 'If you don't behave we will tell the dinosaur.'

The threat must have been worked, for the pair had not so much as moved when Barry and I returned from a fruitless expedition. The vegetation was far too thick to allow us to film anything.

The passage of the Panama Canal was fascinating, but it has perhaps been described by too many yachtsmen already. Even that fairyland, the Galapagos Islands, has become all too familiar. Even so, the islands are so unique I cannot leave them out altogether. Susie and Vicky duly climbed aboard the giant tortoises at the Darwin Research Centre at Academy Bay, but they only settled down with a *whoosh* — as exciting as riding boulders. Uninhabited Fernandina was much better: Susie, dreamy as usual, tripped over a dozing sea lion on the beach; what seemed a frieze of rocks when we first landed at dusk suddenly shifted and revealed itself as a silhouette of hundreds of marine iguanas; busy little penguins waddled imperiously along the foreshore.

A long haul across the eastern Pacific brought us to Taiohae Bay on Nuku Hiva in the Marquesas, where dark rain clouds brooded over great mountain valleys and a three-metre shark cruised by the landing place. Nearby fishermen cleaning their catch, and local children splashing about and swimming, were absolutely undeterred by the formidable shark. We were made of frailer stuff. No swimming for us here, we decided! But Penrhyn Atoll (Tongareva) in the Northern Cooks provided swimming aplenty. From the inflatable moored over coral heads in the huge lagoon, Fiona and I dived for small *pipi*, pearl oysters, two metres down while the girls bobbed about supported by their inflatable armbands. Several two-metre white and black-tipped reef sharks swam past ignoring us.

'The islanders told us they are harmless, so what are you worrying about?' Fiona chided me when I revealed my uneasiness.

'But do the sharks know that?' I replied.

So, to relieve my craven fears, we returned to shore, where we were delighted to find, when we opened the oysters, two little pearls — one for each girl.

At our next stop, Apia in Samoa, we came alongside a dock crowned with lampposts, where we were to tie up to clear Customs. I approached very cautiously, edging in dead slow, but altogether forgetting the square yard on the foremast which, of course, I should have angled. An audible tinkling aloft, repeated as we passed the next lamppost, was a belated reminder. I regret to say that we hurriedly swept up the broken glass before anyone arrived on the scene and admonished us.

Fiji marked the parting of the ways. Barry remained behind to wrestle with *Isbjorn's* antique semi-diesel, which had developed serious corrosion problems, while the rest of us flew to Canberra, where I spent the next three months delving into ANU's library records. Academic research was new to me, and I would not have got very far had it not been for the generosity of my colleagues in the Pacific History Department, who unselfishly alerted me to every navigational reference they had come upon in their own researches. Meanwhile, the multitalented Fiona became happily involved in the more artistic activities of the nation's capital (she later had an exhibition of her silkscreen designs at the opening of the Sydney Opera House) and the children went to school, where they went through a stage of hiding their seagoing past, so anxious were they to appear exactly like their fellows. Their parents were required to conform too.

'Why don't you wear pretty clothes when you go to work like the other daddies do?' asked Vicky, in a justifiable comment on my penchant for informality.

'Seventeen years in London wearing collar and tie is enough for a lifetime,' I replied feelingly.

Leaving Fiji in late 1968, Barry and I set out on a year's systematic investigation of traditional navigation, setting the seal on what, for me, has become a lifelong quest to chronicle humankind's maritime past. The aim was to sail with the traditional Pacific navigators either in their own vessels or, by default, aboard an *Isbjorn* stripped of compass, sextant, timepieces, radios and charts, to learn, in the words of Chief Beiong of Pulusuk, 'the secrets of all the reefs and islands under the stars'. The disciplines of medical research were relevant to my way of thinking, perhaps more so than academic ones. For academic speculations may remain forever unproven in default of objective confirmation, whereas in a medical study, the drug either works or does not; the patient either does or does not get better. It seemed to me that here we had a similar situation. The stern test of landfall would be the criterion of accuracy (in fact, this never failed; the island always appeared where the navigator predicted).

I cannot speak highly enough of the great tradition-bearers Tevake, Hipour and Mau Piailug. Tevake has long returned to the ocean that was his heritage; Hipour, at eighty, is teaching traditional navigation to children in Chuuk; and Mau Piailug (of *Hokule'a* fame) is currently sailing the double canoe *Makali'i*. All three are immortal — cornerstones of the renaissance of ancient star-path navigation that is now sweeping the Pacific.

Tevake's home was Nifiloli, one of the Polynesian-speaking Reef Islands of the isolated Santa Cruz archipelago, whose geographical complexity is only matched by the inaccuracy of the single chart (the Reef Islands are laid down seven miles too far to the west, for instance). While politically it is regarded as the Temotu Province of the Solomon Islands, the Santa Cruz Islands lie north of Vanuatu, with which it has ancient trading links. Indeed, in 1606, when the explorer Pedro Fernandez de Quiros visited Taumako, sixty miles beyond the Reef Islands proper, Chief Tumai told him of seventy islands that he knew. The 60-foot claw-sailed *te puke* outriggers that Quiros saw ranged from Malekula in Vanuatu north to Sikiana, and from Tikopia in the east to Santa Ana and Rennell in the main Solomons chain, more than 500 miles each way. Nor was this voyaging anything new. As long ago as 1100 BC, Lapita pottery makers (ancestral Polynesians) were shipping obsidian for stone adzes 900 miles to Santa Cruz from Talasia in New Britain.

Tevake himself had made two 200-mile *te puke* voyages to Tikopia and another to Vanuatu, as well as everywhere in his own extensive Santa Cruz archipelago. His *te puke* having been wrecked these five years past, our own voyages together were in an *Isbjorn* stripped of instruments.

The best way to appreciate something of the ancient arts to which Tevake was heir, and which date far back over as yet uncounted millennia to when the first seafarer ventured with intent out of sight of land, is to recount an actual passage. One that stands out in my mind was sailing with Tevake on the sixty miles from Nifiloli to Taumako.

We sailed at dusk that December 1968, and the star path was our guide: first, the rising Betelgeuse, then, in turn, Pleides, Castor and Pollux, Procyon; rising either ahead or at a known angle to the course. Just before dawn the navigator picked out the rugged outline of Taumako. The return was in daylight, in blinding rain squalls that blotted out everything. For eight solid hours the lean old man stood on the foredeck, sopping wet lavalava (a wraparound cloth) flapping round his legs, an umbrella palm leaf over his head, gesturing from time to time to one of the young crewmembers, Kaveia*, guided only by the ill-defined 'sea swell' that had travelled a thousand miles from the north-east trades beyond the equator. He only relaxed when the

---

*Chief Kaveia of Taumako, one of the ship's company, is now the senior traditional navigator of Santa Cruz.

dim outline of our destination emerged from the murk half a mile ahead. On a later journey to Vanikoro 100 miles to the south-east, Tevake demonstrated more star-steering, told of wave and current lore, and revealed the strange underwater luminescence called *te lapa*.

The island of Fenualoa in the Santa Cruz Reef Islands, joined by a drying reef to Tevake's Nifiloli, had once been a base for my cousin Charlie Cowan and his trading schooner *Navanora*, and it was with his former bosun Gabriel Paikai that Barry and I spent Christmas 1968 between voyages with Tevake.

'Tell us how Charlie died,' I asked Gabriel. 'It was nonsense to say "sunstroke", as the newspapers wrote — my mother always thought he was poisoned with something like curare.'

'I don't know what bush poison she used.'

'Who was she?'

'His wife from Ndeni, of course.'

'Why did she poison him?' I asked.

Gabriel explained: 'Charlie brought his Polynesian girlfriend back with him from Rennell. I had the sense to leave my *wahine* behind. Ndeni Melanesian women are very moral, very possessive, so his wife poisoned him.'

The lady who had defended the sanctity of marriage so fiercely had since died, I learned. As to the schooner *Navanora*, she had been captured by the Japanese in the war and later sunk by Allied aircraft off Buka in New Guinea.

I was to encounter Gabriel again one last time twenty-three years later in 1992. He had heard I was back in the Santa Cruz Reef Islands and sent a message asking me to visit him. After tying up *Gryphon* and rowing ashore, I found a shrunken 100-year-old man, who was charming as ever but who could not remember who I was nor why he had wanted to see me.

'Do you still make shark magic?' I asked the old village headman on Ulawa.

'No, we have given up such ignorant superstition.' Then, with a twinkle in his eye, he added, 'The sharks know we have stopped. Last year was the first time they took anybody.'

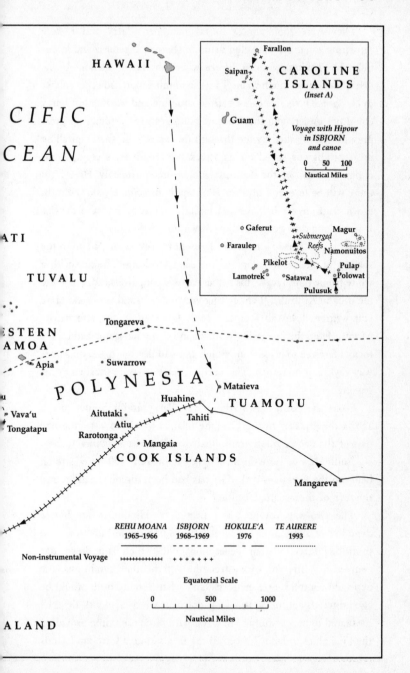

HAWAII

CIFIC

CEAN

ATI

TUVALU

WESTERN
SAMOA

Apia

POLYNESIA

Vava'u

Tongatapu

Suwarrow

Tongareva

Aitutaki
Atiu
Rarotonga

Mataieva

Huahine
Tahiti

TUAMOTU

Mangaia

COOK ISLANDS

Mangareva

CAROLINE
ISLANDS
(Inset A)

Farallon

Saipan

Guam

Voyage with Hipour
in ISBJORN
and canoe

0   50   100
Nautical Miles

Gaferut

Faraulep

Magur

Submerged
Reefs

Namonuitos

Pikelot

Pulap

Lamotrek
Satawal

Polowat

Pulusuk

| | *REHU MOANA* | *ISBJORN* | *HOKULE'A* | *TE AURERE* |
| | 1965–1966 | 1968–1969 | 1976 | 1993 |

Non-instrumental Voyage   ++++++++++++   + + + + + +

Equatorial Scale

0   500   1000
Nautical Miles

ALAND

They were soon almost to take another. Barry and I were returning an empty 44-gallon drum to shore at Pigeon Island in our inflatable, having refuelled *Isbjorn* where she lay at anchor. As the drum took up so much room, I was swimming alongside the 'rubber duck'. Some boys in a canoe started shouting and waving, but Barry could not understand their meaning and gestures. Suddenly a great grey torpedo flashed by me through the water — a shark spiralling in at prodigious speed on its attack pattern. Next second, I was clinging on top of the drum, trembling uncontrollably. How I got there will be forever a mystery. The shark immediately slowed right down, and after a half-hearted circuit, slid away into the depths. It was a long time before I enjoyed swimming after that.

Barry and I bade a reluctant farewell to Tevake on Ndeni in the shadow of the perfect cone of the sacred volcano Tinikula with a white tropic bird, tevake, his namesake, wheeling overhead. He wrote me back in Australia: 'I am getting very old now and very sick. Have you written down all I taught you?' I replied in the affirmative. Months later, the increasingly infirm and dying navigator had bade a formal farewell to his kin on Nifiloli and paddled out to sea on a one-way voyage of no return. The world of seafarers is diminished by his passing.

From the Santa Cruz archipelago Barry and I headed north across the equator to the Caroline Islands in Micronesia, the one part of the Pacific where traditional voyaging was most intact. Even so, sailing-canoe crossings of the unbroken 450-mile stretch between the Carolines and Marianas had been discontinued around the turn of the twentieth century.

The two-way voyage was repeated by Hipour in an *Isbjorn* denuded of navigational aids. All he had to guide him were oral traditions three or four generations old, which laid down star courses for different wind strengths and weather conditions, the expected complex swell patterns, and what homing birds would be encountered. Yet, using this long-dormant word-of-mouth data, he navigated us successfully both ways, with birds each time providing the final clues to land. I received my first tattoo, a Caroline Islands navigator's design, in his honour. We exchanged names and became 'brothers'.

An interesting corollary of our new relationship concerned Hipour's wife, Kamer. It was entirely up to her whether I became her brother or her alternate husband. Though we spoke not a word of each other's language, she quickly satisfied herself that I found her attractive and paid me the compliment of choosing the latter option. Her decision had properly to be communicated by a male clan relative, in default of which she chose a young Peace Corps volunteer. At the time it was still the custom for Polowat women to go topless, though the priest insisted on them wearing dresses in church. Kamer had vastly improved hers by cutting out the front for feeding her baby in church. She came to *Isbjorn*, wearing this magnificent formal garment, accompanied by the blushing young Peace Corps volunteer, who explained on her behalf that I would be her alternate husband and fully responsible for the family whenever Hipour was at sea. Sadly, whenever Hipour was at sea I was at sea with him, so nothing ever came of the arrangement. But what a very civilised way of coping with a voyaging culture, I thought, where men might be away from their families for months. The charming Kamer, indeed, was almost as famous for her liaisons as Hipour was for his voyages!

While writing this book at Herald Island in Auckland a letter arrived from Hipour. It appeared the veteran navigator's English had become remarkably fluent, until a subsequent letter revealed that he was dictating to his son:

Hi there, how are you today? I do hope you are in good mood and as for myself still doing fine ... Please Dave visit me. Will you come back to Polowat someday I want you to join us cause it's been a long long time we are not keep in touch anymore. Oh! my wife says hello. She said she miss you. She just want you to come back to our home island ... Oh: please write to me one sentence will cheer me up as long as I know you are still alive.

What a wonderfully warm message from a very great man. I felt humble at having earned his friendship as I drafted my reply. Can I visit them again? Only the future will tell.

A shorter voyage with Hipour back in 1969, this time to the island of Pulusuk in his own 29-foot sailing outrigger, was only permitted by the powerful Polowat chief and leading navigator, Manipy, on the condition that Barry would take a turtle-hunting party in *Isbjorn* to Pikelot, a hundred miles away. I was to encounter this same Manipy at the South Pacific Arts Festival in Samoa in 1996, where he allowed his 'son', Sosthenes Emwalu, himself a worthy successor to Hipour, to reveal secret navigational lore. Manipy appeared virtually unchanged after a full quarter century.

Barry and I had other mentors — from Ninigo, Tikopia, Kiribati and Tonga — during that eventful year on *Isbjorn*, a year of research and discovery that continued what the *Rehu Moana* test voyage had begun, and which laid the basis of further navigation and route-finding studies in the Pacific and Indonesia, and from the Central Australian deserts to the shores of the Arctic Ocean.

What has been the point of it all? This is the era of electronic navigation, of Global Positioning Systems that have rendered even the sextant a museum piece. Why bother? We should bother, because without those innumerable nameless captains of yesterday who paved the way for us today there would be no GPS; we owe a debt to their memory that we can never repay. Nor were the followers of the 'voyaging stars' limited to the Pacific. There are close parallels with the age-old techniques of the Arabs, Persians, Indians and Chinese, and early European maritime heritage bears similarities with the Polynesian. Here are 1000 AD pre-compass Viking sailing directions from Norway to Greenland:

From Helte Fjord north of Bergen leave the Shetlands just in sight to the south. Go north of the Faroes keeping the sea horizon half way up the mountain slopes. Then sail due west. South of Iceland there will be a multitude of birds but you will not sight the land ...

However, only in the Pacific are such ancient arts still extant to provide a unique window through which we can peer back into the distant maritime past, to which all seagoers are heirs.

Our last island group was Tonga, where we were privileged to be told, in the words of a nineteenth-century navigator from the time when Christianity had demonised the old sea god, Tangaroa, 'secrets that only I and the devil know'. These were, in fact, surviving fragments of the once-closely guarded concepts of the Tuita navigator clan. But this is not the place to detail them, for they are well covered in *We, the Navigators*.

Barry and I left the kingdom most reluctantly, and our reluctance had not a little to do with two young women who had sailed with us to visit relatives on Nomuka. They were named Siulongo, which means 'silent flight of birds', and Uanita, after the film *Juanita*. Our search for the navigators had been a lonely business, during which I constantly had to tell myself that the one thing that mattered was the priceless lore of the navigators. This was a once-in-a-lifetime opportunity to learn from the masters; we were not there to enjoy ourselves. Moreover, Barry and I were in complete accord that the warm-hearted island girls were extremely vulnerable to the blandishments of 'exotic' strangers from the 'great outside' and must not be taken advantage of.

However, these two women firmly took us over. They were less than complimentary about the standard of our 'boatkeeping', Siulongo going so far as to refuse to bring her baby aboard before she had cleaned up, 'in case she catch some sickness'. The upshot was that the two of them went through the ship with such thoroughness that our comfortable, if squalid, bachelor arrangements were completely ruined. Satisfied, at last, they dived overboard fully dressed and gambolled about the yacht.

'Lucky it's not Sunday,' remarked Barry, referring to Tonga's rigid Sabbath laws. And indeed, despite the lifting of earlier bans on dancing or wearing flowers, the hand of fundamentalist Christianity lies heavy on Polynesia, and nowhere more so than in Tonga. This is particularly ironic, since nothing could be further

removed from the doctrine of original sin than the Polynesians'
own conviction that life was meant to be *lived* and that love and
sex enrich its texture — even being sacred in the old religion. But
despite everything, the Polynesian spirit continues to surface.
While swimming or mending your nets on the Sabbath are
forbidden, church service is followed by an *umukai* feast, with
drinking and lovemaking — not exactly what the missionaries
had intended!

Smarting as we were from the disruption of our once well-
organised home, Barry and I could not but concede the right of
Polynesian women to their central place in South Seas legend. Their
independent self-confidence arises from their traditional high
status; in Tonga, for instance, a sister is automatically of higher
rank than her brother. Despite the church's teaching, a girl may
even choose to become what the Tahitians call a 'firebird' or 'free
woman', and eschew formal marriage. This way of life has always
been acceptable in Polynesia.

Not only was *Isbjorn* now so tidy that none of our belongings
could be found anymore, but our privacy had become a thing of the
past. A succession of uninvited visitors kept climbing aboard to look
the yacht over and then, as often as not, would proceed to settle
down and make themselves at home. Provoked beyond measure,
I whispered fiercely to Siulongo, 'Why don't they go ashore? They
have been here for hours, eating everything you cooked for us.
They just sit. When will they be going?'

'But they are our guests!'

'No they are not. We never invited them.'

'Rude, stupid *papalangi* [white person]! What difference does it
make whether we invited them or not? We would not need to be
invited into *their* house. Their food would be ours; we would be
welcome as long as we liked. That would be no more than normal
hospitality and good manners.'

A high standard to live up to, indeed!

Far too soon the time came to leave Tonga for Sydney. Here the
venerable semi-diesel found honourable retirement anchoring

a mooring at the bottom of the harbour and was replaced by a modern Perkins diesel. The Vietnam War was still raging, and Australia, where there was military conscription, was demonstrating its subservience to the United States by spilling the blood of its sons. There was no reason for Barry to contribute. Small trading craft were in demand in Kiribati, where an agreement had been reached for Barry to return and modify the ketch for cargo. When he did arrive at Tarawa, however, the young skipper found the arrangements had fallen through. He was left on his own to study for his local master's certificate, to put *Isbjorn* through commercial survey, and to negotiate cargoes. It is a tribute to his determination and competence that he traded successfully for nearly three years.

I, meanwhile, returned to Canberra to continue library research and ultimately to write the the first version of the book *We, the Navigators*, which was published in Australia and Hawaii in 1972. Unfortunately, by this time, Fiona had become thoroughly disillusioned with me. Her interests were increasingly at variance with mine. But the long and short of it was that I had not been a good husband. As I wrote earlier, I have no intention of wallowing in guilt for past errors. Fiona needed breathing space after our parting so, for the time being, Susie and Vicky made their primary home with me and, as I realised only much later and with some amusement, managed and manipulated me most skilfully. They were unfailingly polite to any adult, but in the most feminine manner would effectively put paid to any potential relationship they did not approve of. 'Are you going to sleep with Daddy like the other lady?' they would ask a dinner guest, with simulated innocence. It was so funny that I hardly regretted the missed opportunities for liaisons. Again, there was the matter of meals. The girls would hurry off to school after eating almost nothing. It was years before I was told that they would repair to a neighbour's, where the kind lady would cook them huge breakfasts.

Once *We, the Navigators* was well in train, my interest in traditional navigation not unnaturally carried over from the ocean to the land. Was there some kind of 'land navigation' whereby Australian desert Aborigines found their way across a featureless waste? Professor Jim Davidson of the Department of Pacific History at ANU generously 'expanded' the bounds of my Oceanic Fellowship so that I could satisfy my curiosity on this point. Later I was granted a fellowship by the Australian Institute of Aboriginal Studies to continue the work.

I have felt an affinity for desert places ever since I first came under their spell in Namibia, during the *Rehu Moana* voyage. The dunes, stretching endlessly rank on rank, the red rock escarpments, the solitude, the vastness of Central Australia, moved me in very much the same way as the ocean. So it was not surprising that the winter of 1971 found the girls and me with Sue Brierley, a Canberra companion, on a train to Adelaide, where we collected a government Landrover and drove north to Oodnadatta. Here we were joined by veteran Arabunna tracker, Wintinna Mick, his wife and their nine-year-old daughter, Ruby. The overloaded vehicle then headed out into the Simpson Desert. The first fact to become apparent was that there was no such thing as a 'featureless' landscape to the eagle eye of this one-time desert nomad. The minutest aspects of the landscape were noted and their significance assessed. 'Land sloping down now,' Mick would announce, as we drove over the apparently dead-level expanse of the Finke floodplain, or 'head towards that high sandhill'.

'But they are all exactly the same height!'

'You bloody blind, whitefella?'

Wintinna Mick would invariably select a high lookout point to pull up for the night, where we would light a campfire with wood collected earlier, boil a billy of tea and make damper in the hot ashes under his instructions, all the while brushing away the flies that swarmed into our eyes, ears and nostrils. Smoothing out the sand around the fire, the old tracker would quickly make imprints with the side of his hand and his knuckles for the three children to identify — *papa* (dingo), *kalia* (emu), *malu* (kangaroo).

'What that one, Ruby?'

'Man.'

'No, no. See the shape, that one a woman. What she doing, Susie?'

'She is standing, I think.'

'No, no, no, she *running*! Look, see how the toes dig in!'

These were precious lessons from the 'book of the bush' for all of us 'townies'. We were learning to use our eyes as never before. Without guidance, we usually didn't know what we were looking at. Straggly grasses and thorny shrubs adorned the desert floor. Yet every few steps Wintinna Mick would stop, bend down and pluck some unlikely looking object: this one gave gum for cementing hooks to *woomeras*; that one could be boiled and eaten; here were *djindi djindi* flowers, a sure sign of water under the sand — you only had to dig.

There were longer desert expeditions; one in 1972, the last in 1974. My mentors were very traditional Pintupi, like Tommy Tjampitjinpa. This cheerful little man of about forty took me to a rock shelter where he had spent nearly a year of his childhood, far to the west of the present Pintupi settlements in south Central Australia. During the time he had spent at the rock shelter, he had not been initiated, so he could not explain the meanings of the faded painted symbols on the rock, but he well remembered pursuing kangaroos with dingo 'hunting dogs' and the chore of grinding wild seeds for damper. The waterhole beside the shelter had dried up. 'When the people leave,' explained Tommy, 'the waters all dry up.' His comment revealed a concept of humans as *part* of the ecosystem, something I was to encounter again in another hunting people, the Siberian Yupik Eskimo.

Another remarkable character, unusual among the Aborigines I have met over the years for his compassion for animals, was the Kukatja Big Peter Jupurrula. I first encountered this splendid man in 1972 when I visited the boys' initiation camp near Yai Yai, where he was officiating. He was not well. A quick examination revealed him to be suffering from congestive heart failure, and prompt admission to the hospital in Alice Springs was arranged. After he was back in circulation, we travelled widely together, sometimes with Susie and Vicky, and became firm friends. We twice drove three days west from Yai Yai over rudimentary tracks to the place of his Dreaming, Muranji Rock Hole, a great vegetation-draped bowl secretly tucked away in the middle of an arid red rock escarpment, where recent excavation has revealed human presence for a span of 25 000 years. Peter painted me a map of Muranji, centred around the legend. If you knew the sacred Dreamtime story, the map would guide you, whereas an uninitiated outsider could well die of thirst before unravelling its secrets to locate the hidden natural reservoir.

This was the first intimation I received that Aboriginal wayfinding, or 'land navigation', is illuminated by *sacred geography*, by sites of supernatural significance and the tracks of the Dreamtime beings that made the land into its present form, tracks indelibly recorded in the sacred chants. I later drove 800 kilometres through the Gibson Desert with a party of Pintupi. Every eighty kilometres or so a different man would be deferred to: we were passing through *his* country; he would now be the one to lead the chants of power; a further eighty kilometres and another would take over. We camped for three nights near the track of the Dreaming of the Great Kangaroo, who had crossed 1600 kilometres of Western Australia, creating mountains and waterholes as he went. Each night around the campfire, with the sonorous cadence of a Gregorian chant, the great poem unfolded. Every riverbed and waterhole had its own memorable incident. I was not allowed to write notes, take photographs or tape-record during the singing. The song was so powerful that it was implicitly believed it would kill any woman or juvenile who accidentally overheard it.

When, on a 1974 journey with the Pintupi Jeffrey Jangalla as my main guide, I asked my companions to point towards places 160 to 320 kilometres distant, checking their bearings with a map and prismatic compass, the directions for secular places were wildly inaccurate but the ones for sacred places were correct within fifteen degrees. This trip was my longest. After laying depots of petrol, we followed old graded tracks and then no tracks at all along the Tropic of Capricorn, 1280 or so kilometres from the Aboriginal reserves beyond Alice Springs to the Canning Stock Route in Western Australia and back again. I never ceased to be amazed at my companions' profound spiritual affinity with their ancient land. They were patient teachers. Rubbish has been written to the effect that Aborigines were ignorant of the role of sex in conception. Of course they weren't. All Aborigines agree that the essence of a person's being comes from his or her Dreaming place. The only contentious issue is whether it comes at conception or at birth. What a tragic irony it is that a people whose very spiritual essence is derived from their country should still have to fight for rights to their land, rights that until very recently were denied altogether.

Since my time in the centre, there has been some progress. Outstations have multiplied, and the Reconciliation process is well underway, with a general recognition of the forcible seizure of the 'stolen generations' of Aboriginal children as the cultural genocide that it was. Nevertheless, the current prime minister refuses to issue an apology, and the continuing state of Aboriginal health and welfare has brought infamy to Australia before the nations of the world.

Jeffrey explained how he kept his bearings. Each time he changed direction in the bush he half-consciously realigned himself, taking mental note of the direction of his base and his objective, or the angle to the sun. I saw what he meant when we were tracking a wounded kangaroo that twisted and turned through near-impenetrable scrub. After it had been shot, Jeffrey made a beeline back to our starting point. At no time had we been able to see beyond the nearest trees. He drew a diagram to explain it all.

Yet when it came to the stars, these same desert people were bewildered. We had to drive east cross-country one night to cut a north-south graded track. By simply keeping the Southern Cross in the right-hand window of the vehicle we could not possibly go wrong. Yet Jeffrey, who was driving, and who had proved himself such a masterly land navigator in daylight, could make nothing of it. I took over the wheel eventually, whereupon the one Christian

Aboriginal in our party, who was at the back of the vehicle, was overheard to exclaim: 'If David can't save us, we must pray to God!'

When there was time for only one more short trip, I drove Big Peter Jupurrula, at his request, from Papunya, where he had his leaky shelter, to stay with friends at an Aboriginal-managed cattle station near Glen Helen. Anywhere was better than Papunya — 800 souls living in makeshift humpies on a cheerless windswept plain. New government houses had been built and more were going up, but they were for white nurses and schoolteachers, who were dedicated people in the main. What hope had the once free-roving Aborigines — living in appalling conditions, prey to boredom and despair, with alcohol their only solace?

Even at Papunya, new initiatives have brought hope, notably the introduction of hardboard painting. Unlike the Arnhem Landers, who had the bark of large trees to paint on, the equally artistic desert people's sacred art was confined to sand sculptures and body painting for ceremonies, both necessarily ephemeral. The use of hardboard and, later, canvas changed all that. Billy Stockman Tjapaltjarri, for instance, who travelled with the children and me and painted the girls a picture of their own Honey Ant Dreaming, is now a world-renowned artist.

Big Peter and I went hunting for our supper after making camp near Glen Helen. 'I shoot bachelor kangaroo, not mother,' announced the gentle hunter, taking aim with his ancient .22. As he fired, the stock came away from the barrel. Peter regarded the two halves of the gun quizzically: 'I think I shoot two *half* kangaroo with these.' We made do on damper that night.

I had missed female companionship in the traditionally sex-segregated Aboriginal communities, so I planned to invite a friend to see something of the desert and then drive back to Canberra with her in my old Holden, which I had left garaged in the Alice. Two equally charming acquaintances had expressed interest, but neither would quite make up her mind. Finally, in exasperation, I sent over the radio identical telegrams to them both: 'Eagerly waiting for you. Will meet you at Alice Springs airport on X flight on Y date.' Of course, I had quite forgotten that radio telegrams were public property and a prime source of entertainment in the Northern Territory. I gathered later that the two ladies were awaited with much interest at the airport (this being Australia, even bets were made!), and everyone but me was disappointed when only one of them turned up.

I should leave the story there with its suggestion of romance, but honesty compels me to tell the unromantic truth. On the first night we camped under a full moon by the picturesque gorge at Glen Helen. I cooked a pair of steaks to perfection over the campfire and there was wine. Then, intending to give my companion a treat, I overdid it. From my wanderings in the Western Desert I had saved some *pitchury* or *minkulpa*, an Aboriginal drug plant whose bitter alkaloids, chewed with the ashes of certain alkaline desert plants, are highly stimulating. My companion trustingly tried it and promptly vomited and passed out. There was no dinner and certainly no romance!

On my return to Canberra I became peripherally involved in a different aspect of Aboriginal experience. This was the 'Aboriginal Embassy', a highly visible tented encampment of activists on the lawn outside Parliament House in Canberra protesting the denial of land rights to Aboriginal Australians. My contribution, however, was limited to the donation of a tent and a kerosene pressure stove, for the Aboriginal participants clearly had their act well in hand. And very effective it was too, and a tribute to the organisers, mostly young urban part-Aboriginals. The conservative government reacted idiotically by bringing in tribal elders from the far north to teach these youngsters how to behave. In the event, the elders saw for the first time that it was possible to stand up to the white man face to face, and they in turn drew their city colleagues back into tribal culture. By the time the government recognised its mistake the damage was done, and Aboriginal communities nationwide had been radicalised. So, after six months, the authorities decided to close the 'embassy' by force.

The Aboriginals were determined to 'go quietly' and not be provoked into violence. I tried to explain this to nine-year-old Vicky, as we arrived for the dismantling.

'Above all, we want a peaceful demonstration,' I explained.

Clearly the point did not get across, for the little girl answered: 'I know Daddy; I will bring my *asegai* [a spear from Angola] and tell the policeman it is to stab Aborigines. Then, when he turns around, I will ram it up his balls!'

'Not *quite* what we mean by non-violence, Vicky,' I countered weakly.

I will now leapfrog some four years for the sake of continuity in my navigation story. Chronologically, Antarctic adventures intervened, but I will come back to them in due course.

In 1975 an invitation arrived to participate in a canoe voyage that could not possibly be refused. The girls and I accordingly flew to Hawaii for me to take up a research fellowship at the East-West Center, Honolulu. I was to go to sea the next year aboard *Hokule'a*, a 65-foot replica of an ancient Hawaiian voyaging double-hulled canoe. *Hokule'a* was built of modern materials, but her underwater proportions (on which performance depends) were based on measurements obtained by Captain James Cook in Tonga and Tahiti. The project had been initiated in the main by Professor Ben Finney, Hawaiian artist Herb Kane and canoeman Tommy Holmes. The idea was to sail the 2500 miles from Hawaii to Tahiti, all of it navigated without instruments by initiated Caroline navigator Mau Piailug of Satawal in the Caroline Islands, neighbour and rival island to Hipour's Polowat. He would be assisted by me for zenith star latitudes south of the equator, and by veteran Tahitian seaman Rodo Williams for local landfall signs.*

From the start there were cultural strains. This is hardly surprising, since at that time the native Hawaiians were at their lowest ebb. They were a minority in their own land, not even included on the census; once proud soldiers of Queen Liliuokalani a mere ninety years earlier were now Waikiki beach boys tinkling ukuleles for

---

*The more technical aspects of this successful venture have been recorded in the latest edition of *We, the Navigators*.

tourists. The art of deep-sea navigation had long since been forgotten and there was profound resentment of outsiders having to be brought in to fill the gap (this understandable prejudice was still apparent in 1996 at the Pacific Arts Festival in Samoa, where I was co-opted into the Cook Islands and New Zealand Maori delegations, but never the Hawaiian). Different Hawaiian factions were at each other's throats back in 1975–76. Crew selection for *Hokule'a* was marred by prejudice — at least two Hawaiian women sailors with more deep-sea experience than any of the men were excluded because of their sex.

A lighter side to this situation — at least to my rather warped sense of humour — surfaced at a committee meeting. A *kahuna* (pagan priest) had laid a curse on the canoe and several alarmed crewmen were resigning. Privately, the *kahuna* had let it be known that he was prepared to withdraw his curse for a payment of $2000.

'Ridiculous,' exclaimed Tommy Holmes. 'Why, I know where I can have him "hit" for one thousand dollars!' This sensible suggestion was overruled on moral grounds and a rival *kahuna* was employed to reverse the curse by blessing the canoe.

My old acquaintances from Huahine a decade earlier, Curt and Jenny Ashford, were in Hawaii, living aboard the new schooner Curt had built. A professional shipwright, and formerly chief instructor at the wooden boatbuilding school in Port Townsend, Washington, Curt had been the foreman shipwright for *Hokule'a*. It had been largely due to him that she was seaworthy at all, so plagued had the project been with self-appointed 'experts'. Curt and Jenny's two children were wild kids. Each had their own sailing dinghy, Ngaire's painted red by her parents to make it easier to spot if she deviated on her way to school to go fishing. She and Vicky soon became friends; they unmercifully teased Ngaire's good-natured elder brother, Eric.

Those carefree days, however, ended in tragedy. Jenny had made a sewing hut on an islet in Keehi Lagoon. One morning, a group of heroin addicts camped on the next islet had threatened her, and were 'seen off' with a shotgun by the independent Jenny. It was with this same shotgun, her own, that they killed her when they returned a few nights later.

Curt would never have been arrested at all if he had had what it takes to obtain justice in America — an expensive lawyer. But most murders are domestic, he was conspicuously un-establishment (to this day he drives without a licence 'on principle'), usually barefooted, and the detective in charge was a fundamentalist Christian with a direct line to God.

'The Lord tells me he is guilty. I can never be mistaken,' the detective assured me. My blood ran cold.

Belatedly, Curt got a lawyer — a singularly unhappy choice, it turned out. Generally impecunious fellow yachtsmen rallied round, and somehow we managed to raise the $1500 the lawyer demanded each day before he would appear in court. On the most crucial day he pocketed his money and sent an uninstructed deputy in his place. Vicky and Eric were called to give evidence — goodness knows what the omnipotent detective had in mind. At any rate, they were both terrified out of their wits, and I am sure that this experience taught Vicky to be afraid, for since then she has tended to turn away from the physical challenges of mountain and sea, and from controversial subjects. She has become, more so than my other daughters, a very witty and charming 'city lady'.

It was a full month before the police realised their mistake and deigned to visit the actual site of the murder. Curt was cleared, but by then the perpetrators had long gone. My relief at his release was all the greater because I could hand over the care of his unruly offspring, not to mention the stray dogs and cats he always collected.*

---

*In 1997 I stayed with Curt aboard *Rat Bag* ('named after my friends, especially you'), a magnificent 45-foot topsail schooner that he built at Mats Mats, Washington, ten years before. A letter I received from Curt while I was delayed in visiting is typical of his bizarre sense of humour: 'You mother! Here we got all geared up and organised for you guys. Bands have been practicing for weeks, so I guess we'll just have to have your party without you. Man, you're missing a feed; we've been collecting roadkill possums for weeks and they're just coming ripe ...' At the time, Curt was anchored in Parekura Bay in the Bay of Islands, for New Zealand, he feels, is his second home. Reminiscing over generous measures of rum, there were many hilarious incidents to recall since the days of *Hokule'a*'s first voyage, for our paths have crossed in Australia, New Zealand and Kauai (where Curt came to my aid after Hurricane Iniki). The tragedy of Keehi Lagoon has not been forgotten but has mercifully receded into the background.

After the drama was over, Susie and Vicky flew to Sydney to be with their mother, Fiona, and *Hokule'a*'s voyage to Tahiti began.

Of course, we were sailing in the opposite direction from the original discoverers of Hawaii, but this was hardly relevant to the navigation involved, nor to the twenty-two plants we carried, all species introduced by the Polynesian seafarers. The plants — including coconut, gourd, sugarcane, sweet potato and yam — were wrapped in moss, matting and tapa cloth, which is made from the inner bark of the paper mulberry tree. All survived and flourished when planted in Tahiti after our arrival.

I will describe only one incident, since it illustrates so well one aspect of Mau Piailug's navigation skills. This was our planned landfall in the Tuamotus after a month at sea. The Tuamotus were deliberately chosen as being upwind and upcurrent of Tahiti itself. Mau Piailug's confident estimates of distance run and observation of the southern stars which now arched overhead showed we were in about the right latitude for the archipelago. One set of ocean swells was rolling in from the north-east and another was coming from the south-east. Towards nightfall the latter swell was abruptly cut off, suggesting the proximity of the extensive Tuamotu atolls in that direction. A pair of large terns, that had been circling the masthead, flew off to the south-east.

'Those *ititahe* never fly more than thirty miles from land and always sleep ashore,' Rodo Williams told us. We altered course to the direction the birds had taken and, shortly before dawn, the silhouette of Mataiva's palms broke the horizon ahead.

In many ways the voyage had been an imperfect enterprise, but the consequences exceeded all expectation. We had hoped that the practical reenactment of a proud tradition would enhance Polynesian self-respect, but I for one was not prepared for the magnitude of the renaissance of far-voyaging that has resulted. The greater part of the credit belongs to a young Hawaiian, Nainoa Thompson, who was trained by Mau Piailug and who has in turn trained a school of young navigators from Hawaii, the Cooks, Tahiti and New Zealand.

In 1979 and 1980 (once again leapfrogging my Antarctic adventures), I spent a total of eighty man days at sea aboard various Indonesian *prahu*, or commercial sailing boats. Why? For a long time I had been intrigued by similarities between Indian Ocean and Pacific Ocean navigation systems. For instance, one recorded Arab 'star compass' and its Caroline Islands equivalent both take the star Altair as their east-west indicator, despite its rising and setting eight and a half degrees out. There are other similarities. Was this mere coincidence? Long-distance passages across the Bay of Bengal and the Arabian Sea were being made thousands of years ago, probably well before the Carolines were even settled circa 1000 BC. If techniques had been transmitted from the Indian Ocean eastward they would have passed through the Malayo-Polynesian heartland of Indonesia, and sizeable Indonesian ships were certainly reaching the Arabian Sea and Madagascar by the dawn of the Christian era. Would any traces of these traditions remain? I set out to look.

My first passage was on the 120-foot Bugis (the name given to one of the peoples of south Sulawesi) *prahu pinesi** *Pantai Harapan*, bound across the Java Sea 250 miles to Belitung Island off Sumatra with a cargo of cement. She was a magnificent ketch-rigged engineless vessel with a bold sheer, triple bowsprit and foremast and twin quarter rudders — a wonderful amalgam of Far Eastern and European nautical traditions. By law she carried a compass, but *juragan* (captain) Andi preferred to use the swells set up by the gentle south-east monsoon, the changing angle of the sun and, at night, the stars for steering. There were no blocks, windlasses or other labour-saving devices aboard.

'*Satu, dua, tiga* [one, two, three] — haul,' chanted the thirteen-man crew as they sweated up the headsails or the heavy anchor. The reason for such a large ship's complement was, I found, to

---

**Pinesi, bago* and *lete lete* are all different types of *prahu*.

handle the cargo. At Belitung I was to watch the crew hauling 100-kilogram sacks up from the hold and staggering with them on their shoulders down the narrow gangway planks — up and down all day in the searing heat and choking cement dust. In contrast to the frenzy of unloading, the actual seagoing was leisurely at four knots or so — the speed reported for the Macassan *prahus* that, in the nineteenth century and earlier, had traded for *trepang* (sea slugs) with the Australian Aborigines of Arnhem Land.

I will not readily forget the kindness of those Bugis seamen to their guest. It was Ramadan at the time, meaning they ate and drank nothing from about half past four in the morning until after the sun had set. I asked to share their fast, requesting only that I be allowed to drink because I was unaccustomed to the great heat. They would not hear of it. To my acute embarrassment, a special fire was lighted, rice and fish were cooked for me, tea was made, and the whole hungry, exhausted crew sat happily watching me while I ate and drank.

The return from Belitung to Java was aboard another Bugis *prahu pinesi* whose *juragan* was exceptionally religious, frequently praying on his mat on the deckhouse. I was puzzled because although Mecca was to the west and a little north of us, he always faced *south* for his devotions. Back in Jakarta, we were asked to a party at the Australian Embassy for two visiting officials of great eminence. Describing our trip, I explained, 'At last I realised where the holy city must be to which the *juragan* was bowing — Canberra.' Stony silence. The ambassador took me aside: 'Don't make jokes about Canberra being a holy city in *my* embassy!' There were no more invitations for me.

On a later occasion I was crossing from Ujung Pandang in Sulawesi to Balikpapan, Kalimantan, in a 50-foot Macassarese *prahu bago*. The course traversed a major shipping route, in which our 'navigation light', a hurricane lamp in a red plastic bucket, was taken for a port-side light and caused not a little confusion to passing vessels. But there could be no ambiguity about our standby for use in close encounters. This was a six-foot bamboo tube stuffed with rags soaked in kerosene. When we did end up lighting it, flames soared up like Krakatoa, and the approaching freighter sheered off abruptly.

Back in Surabaya at a *losmen* (guesthouse) called Bamboo Den, I was invited to join a group of backpackers on a walk up the erupting Mount Bromo. It was about 2 a.m. when we began the ascent. Every few minutes the ground shook, there was a shattering roar and spectacular 'fireworks' blossomed over the ridge ahead. By the time we reached the outer crater the 'fireworks' were revealed to be incandescent lava bombs exploding out of the crater in showers and arching over to land well beyond the inner cone.

'Coming up to the crater?' asked one young man.

'Not on your life,' I replied.

However, I was immediately put to shame by the two French girls who had organised the party: 'Please take us up!'

So, timing the explosions as best I could, I seized one by each hand and ran with them up the steep inner cone to the crater rim. For a moment we gazed down into the fiery inferno. Then I grabbed their hands again: 'Okay. You've seen it — now *run back down*!' With unashamed cowardice I dragged them down again before the next explosion. It was a frightening experience, and a good deal too foolhardy for me, but it was unforgettable, nevertheless.

My longest sea trip during this time in Indonesia was eleven days on a 30-foot *prahu lete lete* from Raas Island (east of Madura, off Java) to Lombok. For my shipmates, this was only the curtain-raiser of a four-month voyage to reefs off Western Australia to collect and smoke *trepang* for the Chinese market. Three *prahu* set off together to the accompaniment of beating gongs, only stopping at one island to fill the big wooden water tanks and at another to cut mangrove wood for the smoke fires. The only on-board supplies for the four-month trip were sacks of rice and salt for preserving the fish they would catch. All through one moonlit night the ghostly outline of the Balinese volcano Mount Agung stood on the starboard bow, with the red spot of its crater glowing near the summit. Next morning a *sampan* landed me in Lombok, and I watched those three gallant little ships tack away against the south-east monsoon. They still had 500 miles to go to their fishing grounds.

What of the study itself? Was the Indonesians' reliance on stars, swell patterns and the rest simply the stock in trade of all men who sail out of sight of land guided by natural signs? I rather think so. Certainly there has been a great deal of cultural ebb and flow in the 5000 years since Malayo-Polynesian speakers first nosed out from their heartland. My idea of tracing the diffusion of techniques was too simplistic to be valid given the complexity of the corridors of prehistory.

five

Antarctic Addiction

I had long been fascinated by Antarctica. There the mountains and glaciers of my youth met the ocean of my mature years. Nor was it just any ocean that lapped up against that remote white land. The Southern Ocean that encircled the globe with its 'roaring forties', 'howling fifties' and 'screaming sixties' was the stormiest on earth. The challenge to brave those waters below Cape Horn was irresistible to a sailor. More than that, no one had sailed alone to Antarctica, nor had many relatively small yachts, even with a crew, made the passage. That whole frozen continent lay virgin, entrenched behind pack ice and bergs. To reach it, relying entirely upon my own resources, was for me the ultimate challenge of the sea.

Certainly others would follow who would make faster passages and better-planned ones, but for me the chosen role was that of trailblazer. There was an aspect of internal discovery too. In confronting Antarctica alone I would learn to really know myself and my limitations. Deprived of all outside support, I would find out what manner of man remained — would there still be a worthwhile person there at all?

Antarctica was no recent objective. Even before setting out in *Rehu Moana* I had obtained charts and the 'Antarctic Pilot' and had sought advice from Bill Tilman and from Sir Vivian Fuchs, the longtime head of the British Antarctic Survey and co-leader of the Commonwealth Trans-Antarctic Expedition, the first to cross Antarctica. I had met him at an exploration medicine conference in London, and been impressed by his no-nonsense attitude after we had listened to a spate of wordy waffle about Polaroid sunglasses. When the chairman called on Sir Vivian he looked embarrassed and admitted, 'As a matter of fact, I just go to Woolworths and buy some dark glasses.'

Back in 1964–65 the damaged keels and rudders that plagued *Rehu Moana* in Magellan Strait had aborted these tentative Antarctic ambitions. Now, in 1972, at the end of my four-year ANU research fellowship, a new window of opportunity had opened: Barry would be bringing *Isbjorn* back to Sydney for me to fit her out for the venture. He was, in fact, on his way from Tuvalu with one companion when a storm breached the old ship's timbers, and she sprang an uncontrollable leak. Mercifully, Barry and his companion, after first refusing assistance, finally bowed to the inevitable and agreed to be taken off by a freighter before the ketch foundered. Barry was devastated. He blamed himself, quite unjustifiably. It had been my own decision to postpone the needed refit until Sydney. Barry had done everything to save the vessel, to the extent of delaying abandoning ship far longer than was prudent. The loss meant nothing beside the fact that my son and his friend were safe.

Nevertheless, there was a major financial problem. *Isbjorn*'s commercial insurance as a trading vessel had expired a week before the sinking (the decision to gamble on letting it lapse had again been my own). Funds were thus strictly limited for a replacement. The 32-foot steel cutter *Ice Bird* was the best available for the price. I strengthened her as best I could — ⅛-inch steel shutters over the portholes, for instance. In view of what later happened and how narrowly this compact steel vessel survived, I cannot help but believe that the earlier loss of the older wooden *Isbjorn*, whose planks and fastenings must have deteriorated over the years, probably saved my life.

Amid the turmoil of preparation there were distractions. Undeterred by the evidence in the recently published *We, the Navigators*, Andrew Sharp kept reiterating, in combative terms, the theories he termed his 'stock in trade as a writer'. Despite my preoccupation, I was at last stung to answer him in a paper entitled 'The Gospel According to St Andrew', which particularly incensed him. On the eve of my departure in *Ice Bird*, when I was worried sick about the coming voyage and fully occupied with last-minute planning, I had no patience with yet another vituperative letter, so I simply scrawled across it 'Bullshit Andrew!' and sent it back. Poor man, he was probably ill then, because he died before I was home again.

The voyage that began on 19 October 1972 in *Ice Bird*, one month into my fifty-sixth year, is the subject of my book of the same name. Looking back now over a quarter of a century, I can feel again the stomach-churning apprehension as I sailed out past the Sydney Heads that sunny October day. I suffered painful doubts about every aspect of the preparations; I dreaded the prospect of venturing into the unknown, unsupported and far from any hope of aid. But it was too late for second thoughts now — the die was cast. And through all those doubts and fears, I can still recall the beginning of a tiny surge and sparkle of excitement. There never would be another adventure like this one.

Indeed there would not. The voyage more than fulfilled my worst forebodings. In retrospect, I started the 6000-mile trip (a quarter of the earth's circumference) from Sydney to the Antarctic Peninsula via Stewart Island, New Zealand, far too early in the season (for all practical purposes it was still winter in the Antarctic) and took a course along the 60th parallel much too far south. Even so, the series of hurricane-force storms that engulfed *Ice Bird* midway were exceptional.

By 27 November repeated severe gales were beginning to get me down. I was running 'downhill' along the 60th parallel in mid ocean under the tiny storm jib, steered by the self-steering gear, aided at times by tiller lines led below. The main water tank in the keel had frozen, but there was more water stored in plastic cans; wet snow filled the cockpit and plastered the rigging. Was I using the right strategy? I had no way of knowing. My whole body was battered and bruised — I could hardly remember when my storm clothes had last been removed. Standing in squelching boots had become habitual; lack of sleep and exhaustion were taking their toll. Sometimes I drifted altogether out of reality into hallucination. In my exhausted state the wild irregular seas that were tossing *Ice Bird* around like a cork were only half comprehended. I jotted down in the log that everything was an effort — there were constant mistakes in my sight workings and twice I recorded, with scientific detachment, hearing voices. Such was my mental state on the eve of disaster.

Next day the bottom fell out of the barometer. The pointer moved right off the scale and continued downwards to about 28 inches or 950 kp. This was for real. The waves increased in height with unbelievable rapidity. Nothing in my previous experience had prepared me for this. By evening the wind had reached hurricane intensity; the seas were conservatively twelve or fifteen metres high and growing taller — great hollow rollers, whose wind-torn crests thundered over and broke with awful violence.

Came a roar, as of an approaching express train. Higher yet tilted the stern; *Ice Bird* picked up speed and hurtled forward, surfing on her nose, then slewed uncontrollably to starboard. A moment later the teetering breaker exploded right over us, smashing the yacht down on her port side. The galley shelves tore loose from their fastenings and crashed down in a cascade of jars, mugs, cooking equipment and splintered wood. I clawed my way to the companionway and into the cockpit. The self-steering vane was gone, its gearing shattered beyond repair, the stainless steel shaft twisted and cog wheels and worm gear missing altogether.

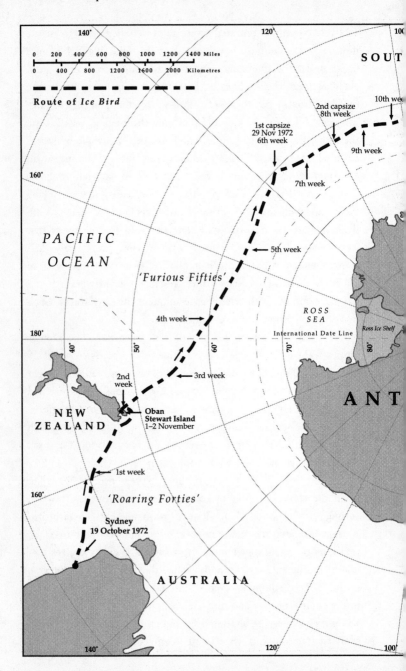

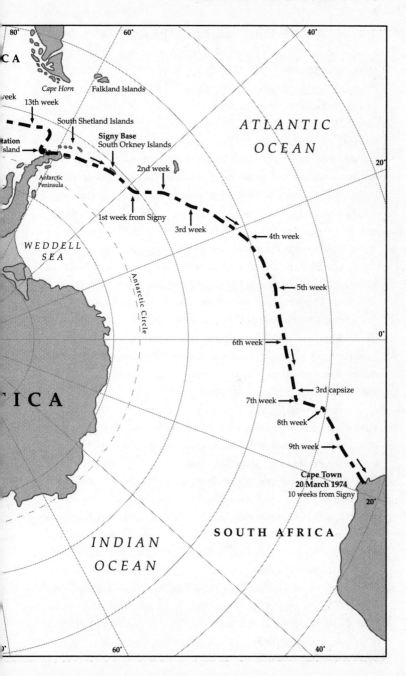

The double-lashed liferaft was gone. The stout canvas dodger round the cockpit was torn and flogging with such intensity that its outlines blurred. Then the two stainless steel wires supporting it parted, and in a flash they were gone. The heavy new storm jib had torn right across. Securing the remains of the sail, I was repeatedly unseated from the jerking foredeck, half-blinded by stinging spray and sleet, having to turn away my head to gulp for the air being sucked past me by the screaming wind. Then, lying on my stomach and grasping handholds like a rock climber, I inched my way back to the companionway and into the cabin.

Hauling on the tiller lines, I tried to persuade the yacht to run off under bare pole, but she repeatedly wallowed helplessly, becalmed in the valleys between the waves. And still the wind kept on increasing. It rose until, for the first time in all my years of seagoing, I heard the awful high scream of force 13 and 14 hurricane winds rising beyond 80 knots. The whole sea was white now. My hallucinations, which had kept the awful reality of my situation partially at bay, faded into the background. Veritable cascades of white water were thundering past on every side, like breakers monstrously enlarged to perhaps fifteen metres crashing down on a surf beach. Sooner or later one must burst fairly over us. What then?

I wedged myself more securely in the lee bunk, clutching the virtually useless tiller lines, my stomach hollow with fear. The short sub-Antarctic night was over. It was now about 2 a.m.

My heart stopped. My whole world reared up, plucked by an irresistible force, to spin upside down through giddy darkness, then to smash down into daylight again. Daylight, I saw with horror as I pushed aside the cabin table that had come down on my head, was streaming through the gaping opening where the forehatch had been! Water slopped about my knees as I stumbled over rolling cans, felt the parallel rules crunch underfoot and pushed aside the flotsam of clothes, mattress, sleeping bag, splintered wood fragments and charts. The remains of the Tilley lamp hung askew above my head. The stove remained upside down, wedged in its twisted gimbals. The mast was gone, pounding and screeching alongside as the hulk wallowed. Two and a half metres of the starboard side of the ⅛-inch steel cabin trunk had been dented in, longitudinally, as if by a steam hammer. A fifteen-centimetre vertical split between the windows spurted water at every roll.

Ice Bird had been picked up bodily, hurled upside down onto her starboard (lee) side, rolled through a full 360 degrees and righted, thanks to her heavy lead keel, all in about a second. Everything had changed in that moment of capsize in 60 degrees 04' S, 3600 miles out from Sydney, 2500 miles from the Antarctic Peninsula. Not only had things changed; everything was probably coming to a end. The proud, if battered, yacht of minutes before had become a wreck: high adventure had suddenly turned into an apparently doomed struggle to survive.

Dazed, I did my best to secure the gaping openings, and like an automaton, I bailed. For something like ten hours I was at it, then collapsed exhausted. But the crashing of the broken mast against the hull soon drove me on deck, where I laboured half stupid with fatigue to secure the wreckage, heedless of the gashes in my numb hands that did not bleed. I was too fatigued to realise they were frostbitten.

In a second hurricane a fortnight later, *Ice Bird* was capsized again, this time bending down the two-inch steel pipe framework over the companionway so that I could barely get the hatch open.

It was another two weeks before I could work out a practicable makeshift rig, during which time there seemed absolutely no hope at all of survival. I was somewhere near the point charted rather depressingly as the 'furthest point from land in any ocean'. My frostbitten fingers were agonising when outside on the snow-plastered deck and little better in my soaked sleeping bag below. The cooking stove was ruined, the ship was leaking, and the radio had been, of course, destroyed.

There was ample time to reflect on my past life. The sense of having let down my children was the most palpable. There was so much living yet to do! Looking at my blackened, swollen fingers, now beginning to exude blood and pus, I could not believe I would ever feel a woman again, even if I did somehow manage to survive. Never having been religious, I could not in decency seek solace in prayer. A deity, if one existed, surely would not look kindly on someone who only moaned for help in time of trouble. Rather, to keep on striving till the last seemed more dignified.

In the end my efforts paid off. The boom was a stout spar that all along had been the obvious jury mast. It was the problem of winching it vertical with a supporting system of ropes that floored me and took so long to resolve. Finally the boom was erected by transferring the main sheet with its blocks to the bow and leading the tail to a sheet winch. Hope returned once more.

There were two grim months still to go, steering manually hour after hour, inching along far south of Cape Horn. My hands ached so dreadfully that all through one gale I shirked the agony of going out into the driving sleet to lower a loose flapping jib, and instead cowered sobbing in the cabin while the sail, one of the few remaining, flogged itself to pieces.

Then, just as those two interminable months drew towards a close, and shortly after two whales that had kept me company the preceding week had sheered off, I awoke one morning to a fairyland of sugar-icing bergs, and that evening at long last saw land — crevassed icefields, broken by stark rock buttresses, soaring into the clouds. The pain in my hands was forgotten as the tension drained away, and my awe at the wild beauty laid out before me began to heal the scars on my soul. A few days later, on 29 January 1973, after threading grounded bergs and shoals, I reached what had been my objective all along — the American Antarctic base of Palmer. The tough little yacht had come 6100 nautical miles from Sydney in fourteen and a half weeks, 2500 of those miles since her dismasting more than eight weeks before.

There was an amusing aspect to my arrival off the wharf at Palmer in the half light of 4 a.m. A motor vessel was moored alongside, which I recognised from photographs as *Calypso*, the oceanographic ship that belonged to Jacques Cousteau. Skua gulls were circling, penguins porpoising and small ice floes grinding past but nobody in the base or the ship was stirring. I dropped anchor, but it repeatedly dragged across the ice-smoothed rock bottom. The wharf was occupied, so I hauled *Ice Bird* alongside the silent vessel and knocked on the hull.

'Anybody awake? Mind if I tie up alongside?' A startled Frenchman appeared at a porthole. 'Did you buy *Calypso* from Cousteau?' I asked idiotically, then immediately felt an utter fool when I realised that this was the famous oceanographer himself.

I was taken aboard, treated with the utmost hospitality (hot coffee! I had almost forgotten what it tasted like) and later filmed communicating by their radio with my children. Cousteau was careful to point his movie camera away from the wharf and the base behind, I noticed. He did not quite say it, but the commentary did tend to suggest that *he* had rescued *me*, rather than *me* finding *him* in a port (of a kind) fast asleep!

The Americans in Palmer were just as hospitable as *Calypso*'s French crew had been. Kindly mechanics began to overhaul the engine, stove and forehatch, and to weld the gaping split in the side of the cabin. I searched among assorted station stores for wooden beams out of which to construct a mast. In the event we glued together a short one. Meanwhile, the station doctor treated my hands and feet — cortisone to reduce swelling, antibiotics to control infection. Actually, my fingers were much better already and ultimately were to heal almost completely.

But what of my emotions, my very character? The prolonged ordeal had shaken me to the core. I had experienced long drawn-out fear as never before. But, as Blondie Hasler once said, you cannot keep being frightened all the time. I discovered in myself a stubborn determination that had hitherto been unknown to me and except for the very worst periods of my journey, a certain wry sense of humour.

Unexpectedly, while I was trying to make the best use of the short Antarctic summer to repair the yacht, *National Geographic* radioed to ask me to postpone the voyage till next season so that I could fly to the tropical Pacific to write about the navigators.

A tourist liner would take me to South America, and I would be returned to Antarctica on the first British expedition ship the following spring. What about *Ice Bird* while I was away? Palmer base solved that. They crane-lifted the battered sloop out of the water and built a cradle to prop her up for the winter.

It was something of a culture shock, though a pleasant one, to board the luxurious *Lindblad Explorer* for the trip to Argentine Patagonia. The handsome woman seated next to me at dinner was aloof and I felt tongue-tied and socially inept, but gradually we both thawed out until, to our surprise, we found ourselves the only guests left in the dining room. Anne Ryan was an older woman, to my mind far more attractive than magazine clippings showed her to have been as a young society beauty in San Francisco. The friendship that subsequently developed between us was something very special for me and did much to heal the wounds left by the *Ice Bird* ordeal. We remained close friends for several years until at length, each of us living in different hemispheres, we drifted apart.

From Argentina I flew to Washington D.C., where for a time I felt more at sea in the headquarters of *National Geographic* than I had on the Southern Ocean.* It was equally disorienting to revisit Hipour and the other Micronesian navigators, and to find myself typing up the first chapters of my Antarctic story in blazing heat, with sweat soaking the paper. The expedition had to be cut short when a shark savaged my colleague, the photographer Bill Curtsinger, in West Fayu lagoon. Happily, he recovered completely and, with great courage, continued his career as a distinguished underwater wildlife photographer.

The southern hemisphere spring of 1973 found me returning to Palmer. As the Boeing 747 lifted over Sydney, and first Botany Bay,

---

*The connection with *National Geographic* was a big help financially, with the story about Polynesian/Micronesian navigation and two articles covering the *Ice Bird* voyage. There were to be three more articles subsequently, the last in 1984.

then the sunlit southern beaches passed by beneath us, my heart sank. Would I ever see them again? I am basically timid though venturesome, and the prospect of another encounter with icy hurricanes filled me with dread. Now that I knew just what the Antarctic Ocean could do, going back there felt a little too much like putting my head back into the lion's mouth. But whatever happened, I was resolved not to back down. Nevertheless, facing Antarctica alone once more was one of the hardest things I have ever had to do.

The long flight took me via San Francisco to Montevideo in Uruguay, where I boarded a British expedition ship back to the Antarctic Peninsula, carrying with me a new self-steering gear. With the generous help of the Americans at Palmer I refitted the yacht as best I could with what materials were available and, when the ice had cleared somewhat, set off again heading southward. Southward, because my hard-won Antarctic goal merited more than a fleeting visit. So it was that two days after leaving Palmer, I threaded the breathtaking Le Maire Strait, one of the most spectacular defiles anywhere. Thirty miles on we came to a full stop, beset by impenetrable pack ice in Penola Strait, within sight of the British base of Faraday. The pack eventually began moving back northward. So, not having any say in the matter, did I. To help things along I poled with a boathook and even stepped down on the ice astern and pushed. The day was cloudless and so warm that I was in shirtsleeves. Ideal conditions for a photograph, I thought. Grabbing a camera, I jumped down on to a floe, quite forgetting that 'action and reaction are equal and opposite'. Away shot the floe, carrying me with it and leaving me to contemplate with some dismay the six metres of frigid water between me and *Ice Bird*. How to get back? While puzzling about the problem, I thought I might as well take the photograph anyway. That done, I thought a little longer, then lay down carefully so as not to upset the delicate balance of the ice floe, broke off a fragment and paddled the unwieldy craft gingerly back to the sloop. I never again stepped down on the ice without a very firm grip on the rail!

Once the pack had released us, I resumed the voyage eastward, calling at Argentine and Chilean bases on the Peninsula, and sailed close by Shackleton's desolate Elephant Island before landing at the British base at Signy in the South Orkneys, nosing ashore through rafts of numberless *pintados* (cape petrels) that stretched as far as the eye could see. The incredible numbers of the fauna of the southern seas and skies and their complete lack of interest in intruders into their private realm is one of the wonders of Antarctica.

Beyond the South Orkney Islands the berg fields drifting north from the Weddell Sea exacted their toll. The replacement wind vane self-steering gear I had fitted at Palmer was smashed by ice in a gale. This was vastly depressing but of necessity acceptable (after all, had I not hand-steered for months the season before?). The incident of my iceberg photograph came as light relief. This extreme close-up of a berg was to earn me commendations on my dedication as a photographer. The truth was otherwise. *National Geographic* had provided me with Nikonis underwater cameras that were clamped on the rails. I was down below and had not seen the monster at all when it suddenly loomed up nearly touching the porthole. I immediately rushed to the tiller, inadvertently tripping over the string shutter release in my panic.

Weeks later the bergs were behind us. But just as I was congratulating myself that we had passed the worst storm zones, I was proved wrong. The gale was not as violent as the previous year's, but it was enough to capsize and dismast the long-suffering yacht. I took my own picture with a deck-mounted camera as I scrabbled among the wreckage on deck. An amusing contrast in American and British styles showed up when the photo was later published. *National Geographic* published the photo with the caption: 'His face a mirror of the bitter fight for survival, Lewis strives to overcome discouragement as he hauls in wreckage of the mast. For three days he works to improvise a mast out of his boom. Raising it, he heads for Cape Town, South Africa, 800 miles to the north. His gamble to be the first man to circumnavigate Antarctica by himself is lost, but not his determination to become the first man to sail there and return single-handed.' The London *Observer* captioned the very same shot, 'Dr Lewis at the Helm!'.

As I was now getting better at setting up jury rigs, I decided to seek refuge in Cape Town. This time I managed to get the motor running too, albeit erratically, and on 20 March 1974 motored up to the swanky Cape Yacht Club, where smartly turned-out yachtsmen and women were tending immaculate vessels. A hush fell on the marina as I approached, and in dead silence I motored alongside and was thrown a line. At length someone broke the silence.

'Where have you come from?'

'West Antarctica.'

I had had enough. What courage I might have possessed had been completely drained away. I phoned Tim Curnow in Sydney to ask for my son Barry's telephone number.

Barry, who had until recently been staying with Tim and his wife, had himself lost all confidence having lost *Isbjorn* and, by his own admission, was 'smoking about 100 cigarettes a day'. Yet he did not hesitate when I begged for his help.

'I'll bring *Ice Bird* home if you like,' he offered. I knew this would involve a major voyage, far more demanding than an Atlantic crossing, round the 'Cape of Storms' and across the whole Indian Ocean and the Great Australian Bight, and that Barry must be understandably nervous. But I was too thankful to do anything other than gratefully accept his offer. Barry flew to Cape Town, repaired the battered yacht, and sailed her single-handed to Sydney — 6000 miles in eighty-six lonely days. I, meanwhile, returned to Central Australia to get as far away from the ocean as possible — an experience that culminated, as we have seen, in that 'unromantic dinner'.

Tim met Barry as he arrived at Watsons Bay Pilot Station.

'I have never seen someone so changed and full of confidence as Barry on that occasion,' he wrote me. 'Bringing *Ice Bird* back was a rite of passage, clearly the voyage was important — the first big solo expedition like yours across the Atlantic.' True enough, except that the Atlantic was only half as far.

I have already speculated a little on the deeper effects of the *Ice Bird* voyage on my psyche. The experience of being alone and afraid and faced with the infinite should have changed me. I should have become someone calmer, more confident, and thankful for the richness of life. I had hoped that would happen, that I would attain a more balanced sense of proportion, and I think to some extent I have. So too has Barry, I believe. As for myself, I do think I am more in tune with what is and what is not important, and have a greater appreciation of my own insignificance in the grand scheme of things. But this is not always consciously apparent; to maintain it I have to sit back and reflect at times, lest something as incomprehensible and irritating as an income tax return should come to loom too large and way out of proportion.

After my visit to Central Australia my rapidly growing daughters and I embarked on a 'double life' in Canberra. We had been offered the rent-free use of a 100-year-old shearer's cottage at Michelago eighty kilometres outside Canberra, provided I could make it habitable. The whole idea was, of course, ridiculous and impractical. For one thing, the distance from school was much too great. Then, even when I had boarded over the holes in the floor, replaced the window panes and installed a fresh water tank and electricity, the place was still primitive in the extreme. We had to collect firewood from the nearby bush for the ancient wood stove and huge open fireplace. Our bath was a choice between a stream full of leeches or a dam full of leeches *and* yabbies (a native freshwater crayfish).

Of course, we took it on. A small paddock was fenced off for Susie's horse and a supposedly secure compound constructed for Vicky's collie, Guppy. Mercifully, Myrtle the Turtle, an aquatic tortoise found by the roadside and adopted by Vicky, escaped into the creek. Both of the remaining animals were endlessly aggravating. When Guppy had been left for the day, apparently securely penned up, we would return to find him sitting demurely in his kennel ('I've been so good and lonely here all day'), but covered from head to toe in mud and burrs, sure signs that he had broken out his sister on the farm three kilometres away and they had been chasing the landlord's pedigree ducks or his prize bulls. We didn't really want to know. The horse, meanwhile, jealous of Guppy's in-house privileges, would have done her darnedest to squeeze indoors and eat the dog's dinner. A hired caravan in town helped with the driving-to-school and work logistics.

However, despite everything, we loved the crazy, impractical tumbledown cottage, the rolling pastures, the bush-clad rocky hills of the Tindery Range behind. For the housewarming party my friend Ulu Fusitu'a, High Chief of 'Tin Can Island' in Tonga, directed us in constructing a magnificent *umu*, an earth oven in which a whole pig and many vegetables were cooked to perfection on hot stones.

The toilet was a tilted-over ruin out in the field. Known affectionately as the 'ladies' powder room', its name was inspired by a very proper American lady visitor who asked the girls, 'Where is the ladies' powder room?' Susie and Vicky had never heard of such a thing and were tongue-tied. I had to come to the rescue and explain.

A less amusing incident while we were living at the cottage was a detached retina in my left (and best) eye. Possibly it was a legacy from the *Ice Bird* voyage, more likely just spontaneous. At any rate, the results of surgery were less than perfect, leaving me with double vision for two years and slightly impaired eyesight thereafter. I still remember the feeling of accomplishment when I began to drive again and, a little later, to ski. We did, in fact, manage a good deal of outdoor living: camping on the coast, where the shy kangaroos would venture out of the bush at dusk to beg slices of bread, and in the Snowy Mountains, before great campfires below the treeline. The girls very quickly left me behind at skiing, both downhill and cross-country, though that was not very difficult.

An unexpected and welcome interlude was a free trip to London to receive the Gold Medal of the Royal Institute of Navigation, and to Washington to receive the Superior Achievement Award of its American counterpart. I was touched when Bill Tilman drove all the way from Wales for the award ceremony and dinner in London. True to form, he did not linger for the socialising but returned home that night. Before he left, he confided in me his ambition to climb the spectacular ice cone of Smith Island in the Antarctic before he was eighty. 'It's not the danger so much as the likely wording of the obituaries,' he said drily. 'Since I'm known as a bit of a misogynist, it would look rather bad if Major Tilman was killed trying to get up Lady Percy Smith!' Sadly, this was what all too nearly happened.

Later, the Australian Institute of Navigation awarded me an Honorary Fellowship and their Gold Medal, also remitting a heavy annual subscription. The Royal Cruising Club were equally generous, bestowing upon me Honorary Membership after awarding me their Seamanship Medal.

At this time I still had an honorary appointment in the Department of Anthropology at ANU, but my grant from the Australian Institute of Aboriginal Studies had run out. The desert report in *Oceania* had still to be written, so I returned to medicine to earn a living. My first job was in student health and sports medicine at ANU. This led to some amusing incidents. For some six years I had been a familiar figure in either Pacific History or Anthropology and was not unnaturally assumed to be an 'academic' doctor (I had, indeed, been considered for a staff PhD, but the idea was rejected because there was no one who knew enough about Polynesian navigation to supervise me!), so it was disconcerting for patients to find me wearing a white coat and sporting a stethoscope. I always asked them if they would prefer to see someone else, but they invariably — perhaps foolishly — declined.

As I detailed earlier, these ties with Canberra were severed by the *Hokule'a* voyage of 1975–76. Afterwards, Susie's and Vicky's primary home came to be, by everyone's consent, with their mother

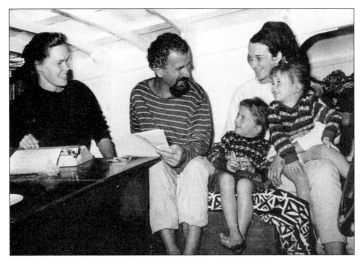

On our way around the world aboard *Rehu Moana*. The journey was to take three years.
From left: Priscilla Cairns, me, Susie, my second wife Fiona Lewis, and Vicky.

Rehu Moana.

Susie with young seal, both equally curious, Fernandina, Galapagos Islands, 1968.

Barry and me aboard *Isbjorn*.

BARRY LEWIS

The great navigator Tevake aboard *Isbjorn*, off Nifiloli, Santa Cruz Reef Islands, late 1968.

Barry inspecting a 52-foot ocean-going outrigger canoe, Ninigo, Papua New Guinea, 1969.

The majestic double canoe *Hokule'a* in Hawaii before its groundbreaking star-path voyage to Tahiti.

With Vicky and Susie before leaving Sydney in *Ice Bird*, October 1972.

Aboard *Ice Bird*, 1973.

Ice Bird beset in pack ice in the Penola Strait, Antarctica, 1974.

Arriving in Cape Town
after the *Ice Bird*
adventure, 1974.

Susie with Big Peter Jupurrula and dead brush turkey in the Western Desert region of Central Australia, 1974.

JUTTA MALNIC

Solo leaving Circular Quay, Sydney, for Antarctica, December 1977.

TED RAYMENT

Approaching Antarctica in *Solo*, 1978.

TED RAYMENT

Aboard *Solo*. I was often required to take sextant shots whenever the sun peeped through the clouds, hence the absence of my clothes. Peter Donaldson is at the helm.

Fiona in Sydney.* I moved to picturesque Dangar Island on the Hawkesbury River forty-seven kilometres north of Sydney, where *Ice Bird* at anchor was visible from the house I shared with a young Canadian woman called Yvonne Liechti. Yvonne was instrumental in helping to organise the *Solo* Expedition of 1977–78, but we had very few interests in common, and I knew it. This was simply an occasion when my heart ruled my head, so I fully deserved the debacle that inevitably ensued.

Medical locums were not just a financial necessity, they provided endless glimpses of Australian rural life. In any case, medicine had been far too long a part of my life to be given up altogether. I had not really believed in the stereotype of tough outback Aussie farmers until I saw some in action at a hospital barbecue one Christmas in arid western New South Wales. The temperature was touching 40°C when no less than three separate lightning strikes started wildfires on one guest's property. Each time the imperturbable farmer and his sons left the barbecue hurriedly but without fuss, to return in due course smoke-blackened, laconic and primed for cold beers.

One day, while I was doing my stint at the hospital, a fourteen-year-old boy rode up on his motorcycle. He had been setting out fishing lines in a billabong on the Murrumbidgee River when he had been bitten by a black snake. I promptly admitted him into intensive care and administered antivenin with the usual precautions against allergic shock. We then heard the full story. The boy had killed the snake, cut it up and used it to bait his lines. Only then had he got on his motorbike and coolly ridden to the hospital.

In the course of time, my courage began to seep back after the *Ice Bird* venture, and I began to turn my eyes towards the Antarctic once again. By 1975 or so I was starting to cast about for ways of obtaining

---

*At the time, Fiona was working in the rag trade. Later, perhaps surprisingly for someone so artistic, she became a zoologist, and has made a name for herself with her research on woodlice.

a somewhat bigger vessel for relatively inexpensive scientific expeditions to Antarctica. Surely there was a niche, I reasoned, for low-technology studies of birds, whales, seals, weather, ice, the interactions of small groups in intimate contact with the polar environment and much more? Intimate contact with the environment, that was what had distinguished the expeditions of the classic explorers from the government enterprises of today. I must stress here, because I have at times been grossly misrepresented, that the *most* small private parties can do is to fill niches. While minor in the overall scale of Antarctic research, these niches are not inconsiderable. Heavy-handed rules seem inseparable from government enterprises, and the flexibility and low cost of small-scale ventures can pay handsome dividends. Secondly, official expeditioners tend to be effectively sealed off from their surroundings in little enclaves of transplanted America, Russia, Australia or wherever, that cut them off from the vast continent around them. Scientific activities apart, they have little opportunity to engage and live *with* the environment.

So together with a number of fellow Australians and New Zealanders, I decided to revive some of the simpler polar techniques of earlier times and see what we could usefully do. Everything would hinge around a ship, of course, and this would involve funding on what would be, for us at least, a massive scale. So we set up a non-profit organisation, ultimately called the Oceanic Research Foundation (ORF). The basic structure of the organisation was worked out for us by a wealthy developer, who then abruptly abandoned the project on the not-unreasonable grounds that I did not have a forceful enough personality to impress business tycoons.

A firm specialising in environmental concerns next showed interest. By then I was going through legal hoops to have the foundation registered as non-profit, and pushing ahead with expedition preparations even though we had not officially received confirmation of the support we required. At least we could count on the use of the firm's stout steel 60-foot motor sailor, and that was the main thing.

It was a devastating blow, therefore, when the firm announced its conditions: it would give us the use of the vessel, but its lawyers and accountants alone would set the terms for leasing it and, in effect, control the finances of the foundation itself. This was obviously legally incompatible with the non-profit status of the fledgling organisation, and was promptly rejected. This left us without a boat.

The planning of ORF's first expedition, however, was already well underway: there was partial financing from the Australian Broadcasting Commission, later the Australian Broadcasting Corporation, which would make a film and publish a book of the journey. Fundraising activities were in train — everything from day cruises to raffles.*

Still, for all our efforts, there was nothing like enough money to purchase a suitable boat. Yet we had to 'go for broke' or lose all the momentum and credibility we had built up. We had a superb crew, favourable publicity was building, and we had not a little general support. But for a proposed seaborne expedition, that would have to cross 2000 miles of exceptionally inclement ocean, a suitable boat was the utmost priority. Time was advancing — there was only a narrow Antarctic weather slot of three months. There was only one thing to do: if we couldn't afford a suitable boat, an *unsuitable* one would have to do!

The boat we bought in the end was the old racing yacht *Solo*, twice a Sydney to Hobart winner and a circumnavigation veteran. She was strongly built of steel. She would be seaworthy. These were the essentials. The downside, apart from the old worn sails that we could not afford to replace, was the lack of comfort. The most we could squeeze in was six berths and there would be eight of us! *Solo*

---

*Essential to the expedition were the 'backroom' men and women. They were far too numerous to name individually, but Yvonne Liechti stood out as an organiser and fundraiser. The dynamic young electronics millionaire Dick Smith acted as our financial adviser. I knew him from having been a compere on two of his Antarctic overflights (one passenger had been very annoyed with me because I would not announce that he had seen a polar bear — from 3000 metres, and in the wrong hemisphere!). New Zealand mountaineer and sailor Colin Putt (who had been with Tilman on Heard Island in the Antarctic and in West Greenland) advised us too.

was also low in the water and would be very wet in Antarctic seas, and there was no shelter in the cockpit.

'This will be the first submarine voyage to Antarctica,' remarked expedition member Fritz Schaumberg lightheartedly. He did not know how true this would be. However, everyone cheerfully put up with a good deal of discomfort, and the scientific results justified their efforts.

It was 15 December 1977 when we pulled out of Sydney Cove and headed southward. It seemed I had at last come to terms with Antarctica, for there was none of the apprehension that had marked the start of each leg of the *Ice Bird* voyage. Of course, the conditions were far different, with a vessel four times the displacement and with a strong crew. There was a change of focus, too, away from pure adventure towards scientific curiosity.

The book that ultimately resulted from our endeavours, *Voyage to the Ice*, told of how seven men and one woman made the first-ever seaborne landing on thirty-two-kilometre-long Sturge Island, largest of the Antarctic Balleny Islands, from which our two scientists obtained geomagnetic rock samples and other data; how we were holed in the ice and repaired the leak with Neoprene from a wetsuit and cement, which had prudently been carried for the purpose; and the visits to Cape Adare at the tip of the Ross Sea and Macquarie Island. So I will not dwell on it all again. Navigation had not then become electronic, and since I was the only one able to use a sextant, there were many occasions when we had to seize any available opportunity to get a shot in a rare moment when the sun peeped through. I would have to drop everything and rush on deck at the lookout's call.

What would otherwise have been a triumphant return to Sydney was marred by ominous news — the seemingly immortal Tilman was missing. He had been aboard the powerful steel vessel of the experienced young Arctic explorer, Simon Richardson, heading for that same Smith Island mountain he was hoping to assault by his eightieth birthday. The ship was sound, the party a strong one. They were due to pick up two New Zealand climbers at Port

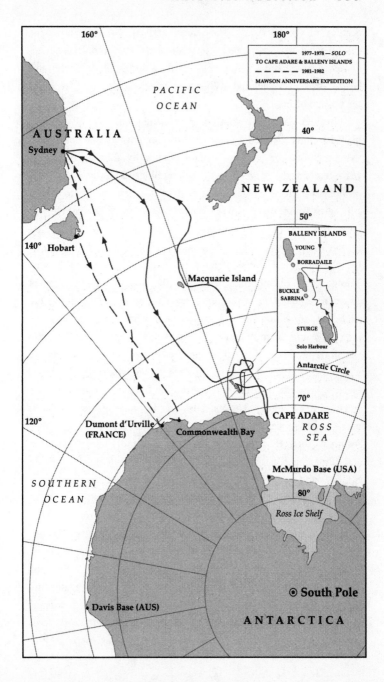

Stanley in the Falklands; they never arrived. No one knows for certain what happened, but a lone shepherd later reported having glimpsed in a storm a sailing vessel strike a distant offshore reef and be instantly overwhelmed. When the gale wrack cleared he could see no sign of her.

This reef was not far south of Port Stanley, but was only too well placed to have claimed a vessel making for port in gale conditions that precluded the use of a sextant. Tragically, this was but a few years before the development of satellite navigation that can pinpoint a position whatever the weather. It is tempting to say there will never be another Tilman. This is nonsense, of course. He will long be an inspiration to others, as indeed he was to the ill-fated Simon Richardson, and to mountaineer-explorers of the calibre of Colin Putt and Greg Mortimer of Mount Everest and Mount Minto fame. The Tilman Medal of the Royal Cruising Club is awarded annually for continuing feats of polar seamanship. One such feat, of which the old master would have been proud, was New Zealand ornithologist Gerry Clark's amazing Antarctic circumnavigation in his tiny bilge-keeled research yacht *Totorore*, which he completed despite capsizes and dismastings. In 1999, Gerry's luck ran out. He was continuing his avian studies off the stormy and dangerous Antipodes Islands, far south of New Zealand, when he disappeared. Only wreckage of the *Totorore* was found. Another Antarctic feat was when New Zealander Greg Landreth and Canadian Keri Pashuk succeeded in climbing the formidable Smith Island peak of Mount Foster from their yacht *Northanger*.

In the midst of my own multifarious activities — medical locums, new ORF expedition plans, the Indonesian project — my son Barry was having his own fair share of adventures. Before retrieving *Ice Bird* he had been sharing a house with a group of trainee teachers, one of whom, vivacious auburn-haired Ros, became his girlfriend. Before long Barry was away north again, this time to Rabaul in Papua New Guinea as skipper of a coaster. Undaunted, Ros borrowed *Ice Bird* and set out with two companions to join him. Despite her lack of sea experience the intrepid Ros took on the responsibility of leading the team and the trio reached Rabaul safely. There Ros and Barry were married. While Barry skippered his coaster, Ros continued to sail. A local newspaper clipping a few months later, reporting her second place in a race to Kavieng in New Ireland, showed she was not resting on her laurels: 'Ros Lewis and *Ice Bird* strike a blow for Women's Lib'. She has since skippered two Sydney to Hobart races.

In due course Barry and Ros sailed *Ice Bird* back to Sydney, where they started a navigation and sailing school. All went well for a time. But expenses multiplied after Jacqui and, later, Maxie were born. Moreover, Barry shuns publicity, and this does not help promote a business venture. For instance, with four companions in the 47-foot *Requita*, he reached Cape Hallett in the Ross Sea, still the furthest south a yacht has penetrated the Antarctic.

'Do you know why we went so far?' one of their crew explained only last year. 'It was because Barry said, "We must go one better than the old bugger!"'

It was not a particularly bad ice year in the Ross Sea, though two well-found expedition ships came to grief — the 'Footsteps of Scott' Expedition's ice-strengthened Icelandic trawler was crushed and sunk and the Greenpeace vessel was damaged. By a judicious choice of route and timing, *Requita* escaped unscathed. But on his return to Sydney, Barry deliberately dodged the media when some publicity would have materially helped the sailing school. I, on the other hand, despite acute embarrassments at debacles after 'talking big' (like the less than brilliant Iceland voyage of *Rehu Moana*) have accepted the role of the media in getting things done.

In the end, the sailing school's financial problems became unmanageable. Barry and Ros reluctantly 'swallowed the anchor' and built a house at Empire Bay on a waterway off Brisbane Water eighty kilometres north of Sydney, she to teach, he to become a computer engineer. I, by this time, 1979, was fully embroiled with ORF plans for purchasing and outfitting the 65-foot steel *Explorer* (at this time *Dick Smith Explorer*) for further expeditions to Antarctica. Neither Barry nor I could afford to keep *Ice Bird* in condition, so we donated her to the Powerhouse Museum in Sydney — and there she sits forlornly in a distant shed, not deteriorating further, it is true, but no nearer being put on view as originally promised.

An unexpected event around this time was an appearance on a prime-time television program. Dick Smith got me to the studio with a tale of a half-price fundraising short film, which sounded plausible enough. So I duly spoke my lines in all innocence until a man came on the stage beaming, and said: 'You are on national television. This is your life.'

Since I had no television of my own I had no idea who he was or what he was talking about. 'Oh!' I said, bewildered. After it had been explained to me by the rather put-out host that I was on a TV show called *This Is Your Life*, I found the whole experience very warmhearted and kindly, though at times I wondered who would be sprung on me next. There was Merton, one of the *Rehu Moana* crew from Iceland, an American from Palmer Antarctic base, and an old skiing mate from New Zealand, Jim McComish.

'Why does he do these things?' he was asked.

'Because he's mad.'

'You can't say that,' said the host in shocked tones.

'Yes, I can. He's mad.'

The purchase and deployment of *Explorer* was a milestone for ORF. Colin Putt, I think, first realised the potential of this heavily built steel boat that was lying at a mooring in Lavender Bay under the shadow of the Sydney Harbour Bridge. She was a Herreshoff 'Marco Polo' design, expanded by a fifth in all dimensions. There was no mast. We followed the designer's plans and rigged her as a three-masted schooner, in retrospect a mistake for Antarctic work, where the less windage aloft the better. There was a lot to be done — the fish-hold converted into a four-berth cabin, for instance. However, for all her rather poor sailing qualities, *Explorer* was to serve us well.

It is time to introduce Mimi George into the story. She was a graduate student in anthropology at the University of Virginia and an experienced sailor when, having read *We, the Navigators*, she wrote me a letter in about 1979. She was going to New Ireland. Had the people there a nautical tradition, she asked me. An interesting correspondence developed, for I was intrigued by the young woman's lively intelligence and individuality. In time the letters became more personal — a photograph revealed her dark, athletic beauty; it turned out she was shockingly young — only thirty to my sixty-five.

'What age difference?' she wrote. 'You are only the same age as my father!' She would stop over in Sydney, she announced, on her next field trip to New Ireland in 1981.

The timing was not ideal. I had recently had a hip, damaged in a skiing accident, replaced by a steel and plastic prosthesis, and was still using two sticks and in a good deal of pain besides. This would not do at all so, driving to the airport to meet her, I threw the sticks into the Hawkesbury River and had reason to regret my rashness as I stood in great pain waiting for the passengers to emerge from Customs. But the discomfort was soon forgotten. The urgent warmth of Mimi's embrace in the airport carpark made it abundantly clear that our relationship was not going to be platonic for very long.

Yvonne was at this time visiting Canada. In essence our relationship had long been dead. Or dead as far as I was concerned. However, so involved were we in a shared house and the ORF that time was needed to disentangle our affairs. We were finished, and I was sure that Yvonne recognised this too, but I was never honest enough to make my feelings clear, so that when I suddenly abandoned her for Mimi, it must have come as a complete surprise.

Mimi paid me a much longer second visit on her way back from fieldwork. We sailed together in *Ice Bird* and took part in the first trials of *Explorer*. The plans for the 1981–82 Mawson Anniversary Expedition were already in train, with the more ambitious 1982–84 Winterover Expedition looming in the background. What a great colleague Mimi would make, I thought. She did not need much persuading to take part in the second and longer venture after completing her MA.

Mimi was back in the United States, and I was in the final stages of preparing the Mawson Anniversary Expedition, when an unexpected opportunity arose for us to meet again. Ecotechnics invited me to bring a partner to an Antarctic/Space conference in the south of France. Mimi met me in London. I was well aware that our vast age difference would logically curtail our relationship yet nevertheless I ignored the problem, and was vindicated by many fruitful years together. We stayed briefly with my daughter Anna in Oxford, where she was a lecturer.* Susie, then a dance student in Paris, was able to join us at the conference. Perhaps the most interesting fellow participant was the author Lawrence Durrell. I remarked on his brother Gerald's *My Family and Other Animals*, which portrays an aesthetic younger Lawrence in a not very sympathetic light.

'I always regarded him as a particularly obnoxious small boy,' reminisced Lawrence, adding, with enthusiasm, 'then he went on to write that masterpiece.'

Back to that perennial (and nowadays so fashionable) phrase 'the bottom line'. The ORF's purchase and outfitting of *Explorer* brought us in contact with all the trials and tribulations of the marketplace. Funding exacts a price, and that price is some degree of loss of control. Wealthy sponsors become instant admirals; media giants have their own style and agenda. So it was that the well-intentioned support of a newspaper cost us far more in credibility than the funding it contributed, for it painted us as some kind of super-explorers, denigrating by comparison the real achievements of the Australian Antarctic Division. That this nonsense incurred the wrath of the official explorers was not surprising, but the way news items were later slanted while we, ourselves, were cut off from all communication, helplessly locked in the ice, was no credit to

---

*Later, Anna won her PhD as an historian and ecologist and went on to author several books under her married name, Anna Bramwell. Through it all her late husband, Roy, backed her all the way. Today, she is the European Commission's Principal Administrator (Environment).

whoever was responsible. In the ensuing years the private sector increased its role in the Antarctic, albeit in unexpectedly commercial directions, and better relations now generally prevail.

You lose one, you win another. How sponsors vary! I approached Channel Seven for block-funding for our two expeditions in return for film rights (*National Geographic* already had the contract for still pictures).

'How much do you want?' TV executive Ted Thomas asked bluntly. I was trying to pluck up the courage to suggest $10 000, when he pre-empted my reply. 'Would $200 000 for the two expeditions do?'

I could only goggle speechlessly.

While still on the subject of financing expeditions, perhaps I should add that, like far greater explorers before me, I spent everything I had on these projects. The last of the O'Neill land money from New Zealand came to me at this time — and went straight into ORF expenses.

The Mawson Anniversary Expedition of 1981–82 that was now in train was one of the most successful that ORF ever had. The aims were well within the capacity of a private expedition. 'Home of the Blizzard', Sir Douglas Mawson had named his base at Cape Denison, aptly enough, since it averages 365 gale days a year. Only a handful of explorers had visited the site in the seventy years since Mawson's day. Here then was a unique opportunity to see what had happened in an untouched part of the Antarctic over nearly three quarters of a century. Had the ice advanced or retreated? Had the penguin rookeries declined or grown bigger?

There were twelve of us in the schooner, a tight fit, though not as crowded as *Solo* had been. Men and women and Australians and New Zealanders were equally represented. The team was a strong one: head scientist Dr Harry Keys had got his PhD on the glaciology of Mount Erebus; Karen Williams, who was shortly to become

Harry's wife, was already veteran of three Antarctic seasons; another couple, Paul Ensor and Jeni Bassett, were experienced polar biologists; three more, Dick Heffernan, Margaret Huenerbein, and Dot Smith from the *Solo* Expedition, were climbers; and Don Richards, who would take over leadership of ORF when I followed Mimi to the United States, was an experienced ocean skipper. There was also Channel Seven cameraman/director, Malcolm Hamilton, and a journalist from the Sydney *Sun-Herald*, Barbara Muhvich, with her deputy editor husband Garry Satherley.

Our route south took us over the South Magnetic Pole, which migrates over the years in a great arc and was then about seventy miles offshore. As we came closer our magnetic compass became steadily more sluggish until it stopped functioning altogether when we had still some 700 miles to go. This was before GPS was available, but we did have a satellite navigation system, which gave us positions in an unpredictable and arbitrary manner — sometimes several in a single day, at other times none for three days. To help us keep heading in the right direction between fixes I constructed a diagram showing the angle of the sun every two hours, for its glow could usually be glimpsed through the murk. Like the Polynesians of old, we also made use of wave patterns and the transient winds.

Brilliant but deceptive sunshine welcomed us to the 'Home of the Blizzard'. Immediately, we got to work: 'penguin counting camps' were set up in the rookeries, and a tunnel was dug through clogging snow into Mawson's hut — a veritable timewarp, with the latest (1913) edition of the *Illustrated London News* reporting the *Titanic* disaster, and tins of jam and honey unspoiled after seventy years of bacteria-free deep freeze.

The unseasonable calm did not last, however, and a sudden 70-knot katabatic blizzard whipped our sheltered anchorage into a raging fury. A party pulling themselves ashore in a catamaran clipped on to one of the mooring lines with a rope and snap link were swamped and clung for dear life to the rope, their heads repeatedly immersed by the driving storm waves. Dick and I were in the inflatable in seconds, hauling desperately along the mooring line towards them. Jeni and Margaret were wearing float suits and could pull themselves to safety unaided, but Harry and Karen, in normal Antarctic rig, were in the freezing water and semi-conscious. Dick must have used superhuman strength to pluck them out, for before I knew it, they were bundled on the floor of the inflatable and we were on our way back. Stripped, dried off and put into sleeping bags with hot water bottles and the plumpest ladies on board, the super-fit victims recovered rapidly. But it had been touch and go, something none of us will ever forget.*

Twenty-two photographic comparisons with Frank Hurley's classic pictures of yesteryear showed little change in the rock/ice boundaries, but the great ninety-six-kilometre Mertz Ice Tongue of Sir Douglas Mawson's day now measured barely forty-eight and was fragmented at that, while the Astrolabe Ice Tongue at the neighbouring French base of Dumont d'Urville had disappeared altogether — highly suggestive of global warming. Happily, all the penguin colonies were intact and had even grown larger.

Visiting the French base on our way back, we were given some wonderful meals (with Australian wines) and were allowed to use the station's powerful radio. Not that the reception was all that clear. The nearest I could get to contact with Mimi was to hear her cry of frustration through the static: 'Radio hams suck!'

There was better luck with the ORF in Sydney. Lord Shackleton, son of the famous explorer, who had become our patron, was revisiting Australia. The reception was again extremely garbled.

'What did you say, Eddie — drinking *peaches*?'

'*Teachers*, old boy, Teachers Scotch Whisky. I'm not a fruit fanatic!'

---

*In 1996 I recalled those terrifying moments in Harry and Karen's comfortable living room at Turangi. They are working as scientific advisers and author/publicists for Tongariro National Park, and are as active and enthusiastic as ever. As I was being accompanied at the time by a film producer making a documentary about my life, we tried to locate the point where I had launched my kayak into the Tongariro River so long ago. We weren't very successful, for the river's course had changed. Harry even traitorously tripped me on my skis for the camera. The day we left, Mount Ruapehu erupted, leaving Harry in a scientist's seventh heaven.

While this was going on, Harry was engaged in a program of iceberg studies and measurements. To this end he and Dick succeeded in snaring a small berg that was swirling past before the tide and anchoring it securely alongside. At least they had *hoped* it was secure, for morning revealed it had broken free and was gone. Harry was beside himself and for once temporarily lost his cool.

'Who has stolen my iceberg?' he hollered. 'Which of you bastards stole it!'

The Winterover Expedition that began the next Antarctic season in 1982 and ran until April 1984 was a very mixed bag. Important lessons were to surface — one we have seen about the wrong sort of publicity, others I will come to about choosing personnel and when you should bite the bullet and delay an ill-prepared enterprise for a whole year if necessary. This, in retrospect, is exactly what I should have done.

Antarctica permits seaborne access for some three summer months only when the grip of the pack ice slackens. Outside these limits the frozen sea, impenetrable except by the most powerful atomic icebreakers, extends up to 1130 kilometres out from the coast. As my aim was to winter the ship somewhere in Prydz Bay, which is roughly south of Sri Lanka, there was a very long way for us to go from Sydney, through Bass Strait, across the Great Australian Bight and halfway to Africa, before turning south across 2000 miles of Southern Ocean to reach the Antarctic continent. Timing, therefore, was everything.

The two previous expeditions, *Solo* and the Mawson Anniversary project, had attracted the cream of young polar scientists and experienced explorers (extra crew for *Ice Bird* had been irrelevant). But these had been three-month summer expeditions. Inexcusably, I failed to realise that far fewer people could be away from home and work for thirteen months, not only forfeiting salary, but having themselves to contribute to the cost of the venture.

Not surprisingly, therefore, suitably qualified volunteers proved to be thin on the ground.

I was not entirely irresponsible. A trial trip was organised to Hobart, Tasmania, with the specific object of crew selection, under the auspices of Dr Carl Edmonds, an Australian psychiatrist, world-class underwater medical expert, and a very good friend. A series of mischances frustrated this endeavour: Carl could only sail on one leg of the trip, so missed meeting with and assessing an applicant who was accepted on face value when the first choice had to drop out for domestic reasons. On the plus side in Hobart, Rod Ledingham, then equipment officer for the Australian Antarctic Division, lent us polar tents and other useful equipment, and several collaborative research projects were initiated.

This all sounds reasonable, but it wasn't. I have no wish to apportion any blame. The positive and negative aspects of this expedition have been aired sufficiently in *Icebound in Antarctica*. Blame there was, but it was my own. As leader of the expedition the decisions and consequent misjudgments were mine alone. The fact that polar challenges proved too much for two of the party was not their fault so much as mine for subjecting them to stresses beyond their capacity. As to contributory factors, deputy leader Mimi's insistence that everyone live up to her own high standard of performance and reliability, while eminently desirable, was a little unreal in the circumstances. Later, she acknowledged this failing.

Explorer's departure from Sydney was on time. Nevertheless, we should never have left at all, but should have put off the expedition for a year — whatever the cost.

The Winterover Expedition was more successful than my stubborn precipitancy merited. Four of the six participants got through a remarkable number of projects during the sea passages and the winter in the ice, while the others did the best they could. Much of our success was due to the unfailing friendliness and helpfulness of the Australian Davis Base expeditioners and the Australian Antarctic Division scientists in Hobart, with whom we mounted a number of joint research projects.

It was well into March 1982 and getting much too near freeze-up when, after much searching among the grounded bergs, rocky islets and ice cliffs of the Antarctic coastline for a secure winter haven, we settled on a protected shallow cove in the Rauer Islands and moored to boulders ashore (we later christened it 'Winterover Bay', though National Mapping got it wrong and misapplied our name to a nearby strait). This was unfortunately some distance away from our main scene of operations, the Larsemann Hills further south, where we had failed to locate a protected wintering spot. There was only time to establish ashore a depot of emergency food, tents and equipment in case of fire or other disaster to the ship, when in a single day the sea froze. Before two weeks were out, we were cautiously feeling our way across it on skis with man-haul sledges. In light of what Mimi and I were to later learn from the Bering Sea Eskimos, we had been far too hasty and were lucky to have got away with it on such dangerously thin ice. But as the days drew in for five sunless winter weeks and the sea ice thickened to a metre or more, we began systematically sledging supplies to lay a depot on the southernmost island in preparation for spring journeys south past the ice cliffs. It was breaking camp in the dark in −35°C and repitching the tent again that night after manhauling through sunless twilight hours that I found particularly trying; my fingers, no better for the *Ice Bird* experience, and face were particularly susceptible to frostbite. Mimi was far and away tougher. I wrote wryly in my journal that 'the best men in the party are the women'.

A three-week winter journey, undertaken by four of us, Gill Cracknell, Mimi, Jannik Schou and myself, was an up and down affair. So chilled did I become after scouting the ice fields before departure in a freezing wind that I became confused and disoriented, and ultimately collapsed unconscious with hypothermia. Only Mimi's promptness — hurried camp, sleeping bag, makeshift hot

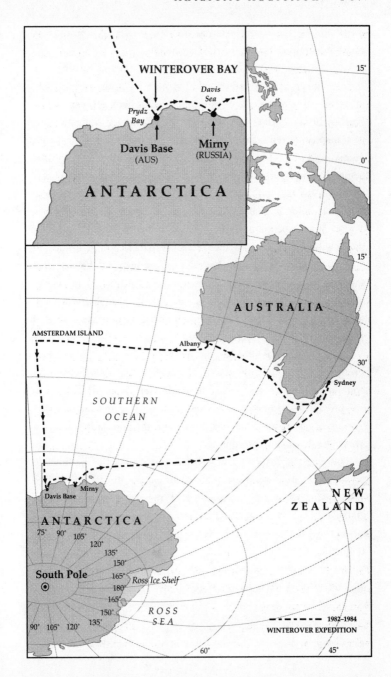

water bottles, and so on — saved the day. We carried on but very rough ice stopped us short of the Larsemanns.

We did much better with the same party in the early spring. In fact, this proved the undoubted high point of the expedition, both in terms of scientific accomplishment and personal experience. During those fifty days we covered some 580 kilometres, manhauling or transporting tents and supplies with our one small snowmobile. Jannik and Gill between them tagged 344 seals, a procedure demanding both a stealthy approach to the tail flippers to quickly clamp on the tag and considerable agility to escape the sharp teeth of the affronted animal. We followed the fifty-two-kilometre march of the emperor penguins to the ice edge, and witnessed the return of the squabbling Adélies to their rookeries (there was a headcount of 4100 on one islet alone). We observed the birth of Weddell seals and watched as the reluctant pups learned to swim. Storm petrels, fulmars, Antarctic petrels, snow petrels, skuas, Weddell and leopard seals arrived daily in unimaginable numbers, so that the shores of Antarctica throbbed with renewed life.*

In the spring of 1984, as the ice began breaking up, the first strengthened supply ships reached Davis Base and their helicopters brought us some much-welcome mail. Curt Ashford, who was building *Rat Bag* in rain-soaked Washington, wrote characteristically: 'It does my heart good to think of you and the poor lady living in a worse bloody climate than this one!'

Unfortunately, these all-too-brief contacts with the outside world at a time when we were still locked in the ice had a destabilising effect on one member of the party, who had to be evacuated via Davis. Shortly thereafter, the ice let us go, and we set off on the 4000-mile return to Sydney, via Davis and the Soviet base at Mirny.

What were the research projects that justified all the effort and discomfort of the Winterover Expedition? Seal-tagging (performed

*I was back in the Larsemanns in January 1998 and again in 1999 as a lecturer aboard an Australian-chartered Russian icebreaker. Now there is a small Australian, a Russian, and a much larger Chinese base, though the mountains, the fjords and the ice cap beyond have not changed.

jointly with Davis Base); seal vocalisation (with the Scripps Institution of Oceanography, San Diego); penguins' diet (we made the poor things vomit); fish stomach contents; lichens and mosses; endless bird counts; ice observations; and Mimi's human interaction diaries (still being referred to by NASA's space station people) to name just a few.

Increased appreciation of the potential of private expeditions has also resulted. The Australian government gave support to the tune of $20 000 to ORF's 1984–85 and 1985–86 Project Blizzard, a survey of Mawson's historic hut and a study of how best to save it. This was a far cry from 1978, when an identical ORF proposal led to us being sternly warned off. But these expeditions are someone else's story. By the time they were mounted Mimi and I were in the United States and *Explorer* and ORF were in other capable hands — notably those of Don Richards, Colin Putt and Peter Gill.

six

Crossroads of Continents

In late 1984, Mimi returned to the University of Virginia to complete her PhD. I went with her, or rather *followed* her, after storing my belongings with Barry and Ros and with Carl and Cindy Edmonds. I then waited anxiously for *National Geographic*'s editors to make up their minds whether to accept the Mawson Anniversary Expedition story and send me an airline ticket, for the Winterover Expedition had effectively drained my funds and Mimi was a typical debt-ridden American graduate student. When no decision was forthcoming, Mimi sold her beloved BMW to pay my fare. An undesirable visitor to the United States, the Customs official in Los Angeles thought me.

'How much money are you carrying?'

'Two hundred dollars.'

'What will you live on?' he asked suspiciously.

'My girlfriend.'

He stamped my passport with a very bad grace, muttering under his breath, but all too audibly: 'We don't want your sort in America!'

So I flew on to Washington D.C., where I landed at Dulles Airport early one morning to find Mimi waiting for me with a woman friend in her station wagon. They had spent the night together 'making Mimi ready for you, David' — a little startling, but no matter. They had prepared a bed in the back of the station wagon, so Mimi and I could become reacquainted in the best possible way on the 180-kilometre drive to Charlottesville. It was springtime. All along the way the dogwoods were blooming. What a wonderful introduction to this engagement with America! For this is what it was for me — a new compartment in my life. I was leaving behind my Pacific homeland to follow the woman I was deeply in love with. 'Wherever you go, I will go; and wherever you lodge, I will lodge; your people shall be my people, and your God, my God.'*

The University of Virginia at Charlottesville was designed by America's third president, Thomas Jefferson, and retains its neo-classical charm. We lived in a tiny one-roomed cottage in the garden of a high-spirited and delightfully opinionated elderly widow named Miz Mayo.

'The old lady over the road, she died aged ninety-five, remembered as a girl seeing Mr Jefferson and the general going into the coffee house that used to stand over there,' she told me, pointing down the street.

'What general?' I asked.

'General Washington, of course!' Miz Mayo had no time for foolish questions.

Mimi and I took great pleasure in watching the news on Miz Mayo's television. Her comments were unpredictable and always entertaining. One particular remark delighted us: 'Can't abide that Ronald Reagan. He's got no sex appeal. And ah know sex appeal when ah see it!'

---

*Ruth 1:16

Mimi's PhD topic on small-group interaction in the Antarctic
regretfully had to be jettisoned as a dissertation subject, for both the
chairman Victor Turner and another member of her committee
had died of coronaries in the preceding year. She had perforce to
change to a Papua New Guinea theme, at the cost of nearly two
extra years at the university. While she knuckled down to this
onerous realignment, I was appointed a Scholar-in-Residence in
Anthropology, an undemanding honorary assignment that left
ample time for boredom. The charm of Charlottesville, a lovely
town so redolent of those highly cultured, albeit slave-owning first
presidents who had drafted a unique constitution, was not enough
to occupy me. There were hikes in the Blue Ridge Mountains and
the historic Shanandoah Valley, and sailing on Chesapeake Bay.
Mimi played basketball with pick-up town and university teams,
and we were flattered when black teammates came to call her
'sister', an unheard of compliment to a white woman in the south.
The *National Geographic* piece (they had accepted my story after
all) and other articles had to be written but these were only stop-
gaps. I needed to get my teeth into worthwhile projects again. So it
was that I became focused on the Arctic, particularly on that
mysterious part of the Russian Far East that lies opposite Alaska,
the region known as Chukotka. For the native Chukchi people used
all the polar technologies — skis and snowshoes, sled dogs and
draft reindeer. Their tundra 'navigation' embraced concepts, not
only of compass points, but of zenith and nadir as well. Moreover,
in the eighteenth century the Chukchi had won their freedom after
battling against Cossack armies, and had only been recolonised in
the nineteenth century. In the end my impatience would be
detrimental to Mimi's career and sow the seeds of her well-merited
resentment of me. It seemed I had learned nothing from that
rushed Winterover Expedition.

The Arctic, however, strongly attracted Mimi too. We recalled
with a shudder our perilous ignorance of the state of the thin, flexing
new sea ice in Antarctica. Who better to learn from than people who
had lived 40 000 years in the similar Arctic environment? Where else

but in the Arctic could our mutual fascination for the ancient wisdom of pre-industrial cultures be combined with our polar addiction? As if this were not enough, an offshoot project began to take form — to help reunite Bering Sea Eskimo families sundered by the iniquitous Cold War.

These Arctic plans were temporarily put on hold in 1985 when we were invited to participate in the Australian National University's Lapita Homeland Project. The venue was the Bismarck Sea, whose sheltered waters wash the north coast of Papua New Guinea and the islands of New Britain, New Ireland and Manus. In this region, upwards of 3500 years ago, the beautiful incised Lapita pots were made by ancestral Polynesians (probably by the women) and traded all the way down the Solomon Islands chain and eventually across the vast emptiness of the far Pacific.* Mimi's study was on contemporary ceremonial trade cycles, involving pigs, shell money and women. Mine was sea routes.

Our old ship *Explorer* had been chartered by the university, and it was a strange experience to travel aboard her as mere passengers around the Bismarck Sea. During the voyage there were differences with ORF's new leadership, who had need, as in all such transfers of responsibility, to establish their own style. These storms in a teacup have long since been resolved. In fact ORF and *Explorer* have functioned very well indeed after my departure.

We witnessed in New Ireland an example of decision-making by consensus, so characteristic of tribal societies. A man was accused of overlooking his neighbours' gardens with an 'Evil Eye', arousing

---

*Given that the ancestral Polynesians had been skilled pottery-makers, it has been a matter of much speculation why their art died away eastward of Fiji, Tonga and Samoa. It was left to my potter shipmate of later years, Robyn Stewart, to answer the question, at least to my satisfaction. She was back from a pottery workshop in Rarotonga.

'Did you dig your own clay?' I asked.

'No, there is no clay there, nor in Tahiti, nor anywhere else east of the mid ocean Andesite Line; before the Marquesas anyway,' she answered.

No wonder, I thought, the techniques of pottery-making must have been long forgotten by the time Polynesians came to New Zealand, where there is clay in abundance. As so often is the case, it had been left to a practical craftsman to unravel a thorny academic puzzle!

fears of witchcraft. The village council set out to persuade him to mend his ways. For three solid nights the matter was chewed over until the stubborn culprit agreed to keep away from other people's gardens. A fine of one kina was imposed, but this was immaterial — the point was achieving understanding and agreement.

On our return to the United States in early 1986, I had the unexpected pleasure of meeting my old Iceland shipmate Axel Pedersen at the New York Yacht Club, where we were put up prior to my receiving of the Cruising Club of America's necessarily delayed presentation of their 1982 Blue Water Medal. I was more than flattered to receive this honour, well remembering how proud Tilman had been when he showed me his plaque at his sister's home in Wales.

The Arctic plans that Mimi and I were cooking up required two things — a sizeable vessel and Soviet permissions. Neither was going to come easily. A non-profit society similar to ORF would have to be set up to allow for funding of the former; the latter appeared simply impossible and went into the 'too hard' basket for the time being. Then a chance to visit Moscow offered a glimmer of hope. Our only Russian contacts were Thor Heyerdahl's companion Yuri Senkevich and the Chukchi author Yuri Rytheu, whom we had met on one of his visits to the United States. Everyone tried to be helpful, but all were powerless under the weight of a stultifying bureaucracy that was said to number more than the whole collective farm peasantry. We were up against a proverbial brick wall. So we flew back to Charlottesville. There was no alternative but to form our non-profit organisation (which ultimately became known as the Pacific Traditions Society), get hold of a big boat, sail it to Alaska and take it from there, meanwhile pestering the singularly unhelpful US State Department and the equally unresponsive Soviet Embassy to obtain the elusive permission.

There were a few blind alleys we went down which, even though ultimately unproductive, were often fun. For instance, a newspaper magnate, prior to losing interest in our project, took us in his Learjet to Florida and provided us with a berth on his private

Victorian-era railcar from Washington D.C. to Charlottesville. Unknown to the magnate, his secretary had filled the car with a party of Lummi Indians off to lobby Congress. It was a hilarious journey, enlivened by meetings with journalists and politicians. I remember a lively Indian doctor (from the subcontinent) coming aboard and announcing: 'I'm a *real* Indian.' As we trundled through little townships we would gather on the open rear platform to wave condescendingly to the peasantry — feeling and looking for all the world like political candidates on a campaign trail.

Now there is no such thing in the United States, when a boat is donated to a non-profit organisation for a tax write-off, as a 'free' boat. Too many agents are involved for that to be possible. In our case, our backer Mike McCune, a wealthy Californian businessman, stood the costs and commissions of sundry middlemen and eventually took delivery, on our behalf but after minimal consultation with us, of the 80-foot schooner *Hawaiian Tropic Cyrano*. This attractive vessel had been built in Abaco in the Bahamas where the sea is only around two metres deep. She drew five feet and had no real keel. The right-wing publicist who had first owned her, had found time, in the intervals between advocating the nuking of the Soviet Union, to install an ineffective hydraulic steering system, twee little cabins and a piano. Her subsequent owners, Hawaiian Tropic Suntan Oil, had allowed her sails, engine, and instruments to deteriorate to the point of disintegration.

In 1987 Mimi got her PhD, so I rushed her down to Florida and, after a most cursory examination, foolishly accepted *Cyrano*. We forthwith put to sea on the long haul to Alaska. By the second day the shoddily patched-up engine had seized and the first sails had begun blowing out in gentle breezes. By the time we crept into Cristobal at the Atlantic entrance to the Panama Canal, major repairs were needed and our volunteer crew's holiday time had run out, leaving Mimi and me to run the huge vessel alone.

In retrospect, it is hard to credit my crass stupidity. My absurd impatience had landed us with a clumsy, unsuitable motorsailer with a rundown motor and sails. My unseemly rush to get started had not even allowed Mimi time to consolidate her dissertation for publication. I don't think she ever quite forgave me — with good reason.

The details of the subsequent litany of accidents and breakdowns before a major refit in San Diego are best glossed over. But some incidents are worth revisiting. We were creeping along the coast of Nicaragua after another engine breakdown, barely two kilometres offshore where we could catch a breeze, when a gunboat surged alongside and young Sandinistas leapt aboard waving AK–47s; ironically, after explaining the cause of our trouble in the engine room, they piled up their assault weapons beside Mimi on deck and inexpertly began helping with the sails. Then there was the time in El Salvador when we recruited an engineer called Julio. He had no doubts as to who was in charge — no request was valid unless prefixed by the magic words 'Miss Mimi say!'.

'Julio, let's steer 310 degrees now.'

'No, Miss Mimi say steer 270.'

'Miss Mimi say change now to 310.'

'Okay, *bueno*.'

It was in El Salvador, too, that anchored off the town of La Union, I became rather alarmed at the volume of firing that was going on and asked the head of the American military mission if the guerillas were likely to attack.

'No — well, only at weekends.' Noting my look of bemusement, he explained: 'They hold down jobs during the week, of course.'

'Oh yes, of course. Do they work at your base?'

'Oh! I hope not.'

The Central American summer sun beat down on us relentlessly. Mimi, half-Italian and one-eighth Mohawk, and Julio were immune to sunburn. My own fair Celtic skin was not. I overheard this comment on the dockside in San Carlos, Mexico: '*Es un gringo tostado* [a toasted gringo]!'

In due course we limped into San Diego, where the schooner was hauled out. My impatience had gained us nothing. We could go no further till the spring of 1988. Even then I managed to waste much of the winter in Los Angeles by developing a bleeding gastric ulcer. Vicky, who had flown to the United States to see me, unsuspectingly phoned my hosts on arrival.

'He is out of Intensive Care now,' they informed my shocked daughter, who had no idea that I was ill.

Once I was out of hospital, after an operation and fifteen pints of blood to the good, Mimi, Vicky and I stayed on a friend's yacht at Marina del Rey while I convalesced, first walking, then running along the Los Angeles beaches and later camping in the Anza Borego and Mojave deserts. I was fortunate in having no assets at all and in knowing people who could testify to my California residency, for the medical bill, should I have had to pay it, came to $86 000.

When we did at last get moving again in the spring of 1988, Axel Pedersen was with us. We had made no further progress with the thorny issue of Soviet permissions, but decided to go ahead anyway. The couple of thousand kilometres from Southern California up the ironbound coasts of Oregon and Washington to the Strait of Juan de Fuca and the Canadian border in the teeth of relentless, often gale-force, headwinds is as miserable a passage as any in the world. Then, inside Vancouver Island and up the forested waterways, you enter a magic world of orcas, sea otters, and, on occasion, swimming moose. At the Alaskan capital Juneau we were able to present our project to the senators to be endorsed. Fresh crews were recruited, for no one could stay with us very long. Axel flew out from Anchorage, while we waited in Homer for the Bering Sea ice to melt. Our base of operations, we decided, would be St Lawrence Island, a rocky treeless 200-kilometre-long strip of land within sight of the Siberian mountains, and whose thousand or so Yupik Eskimo inhabitants spoke the same Siberian Eskimo language as their forty-year-sundered relatives on the 'other side'.

Our first sight of the island came after six days motoring through fog from the Aleutians, guided by radar. The mists parted, revealing, as one of our party wrote rather unromantically in her diary, 'a lot of cliffs covered with birds and bird shit!'. A two-knot current was running along the coast and the shingle spit fronting the village of Gambell was heaped with grounded floes when we anchored at 1 a.m. on 12 June 1988. The fog had cleared and there was bright daylight, though the sun had not yet risen.

There was a crowd on the shore. A 16-foot aluminium skiff put off and motored out and a stocky Eskimo, who turned out to be Winnie the Mayor, called out to us.

'Seven hunters in two skiffs like this were lost in the fog a week ago. Can you help search? The coastguard cutter is stuck in the ice.'

'Of course. You will have to take charge.'

By 2.15 a.m. we were away again, our crew augmented by Winnie and four other leading hunters. Winnie explained what had happened. The missing hunters, together with several other boats' crews, had been out after walrus in marginal conditions. Walrus meat was the main staple of the Gambell diet and walrus ivory the foundation of the cash economy, with an average of 1000 animals being taken by the village each year. The spring hunt makes or breaks the annual subsistence cycle and some risks have to be taken.

It was Junior Slwooko's second trip of the day. His boat was full of walrus and the pack was beginning to drift westward fast when he joined the rest of the boats heading home. The ice was moving dangerously and the fog was so thick they could not see from one end of the boat to the other. Then Junior made what turned out to be a fateful decision to stop at an ice floe to brew coffee on a pressure stove. By chance Junior's boat, crewed by his two sons and his brother, had pulled up next to a second skiff containing two cousins and a brother-in-law.

Conditions were if anything worse when they set off again half an hour later. But a host of baby auklets on the water showed they were off Gambell spit, and they radioed that they would be home in a few minutes. They would have made it had it not been for a strange mischance. A storekeeper with a recently purchased direction-finding radio had been monitoring the hunters' calls and mistakenly gave Junior the reciprocal of the correct bearing, so that he headed westward out into the empty Bering Sea. A short time later his petrol and radio batteries ran out and he never called again.

The first few days' searching produced nothing. We returned to Gambell to resupply and refuel, and to land the senior Slwooko, Howard, who was patently past it, having recently, we learned belatedly, endured triple-bypass heart surgery. The chimney of a diesel heating stove on the boat that had been installed in Homer was so poorly insulated that at full blast the deck would get red-hot. Regardless of the fire danger, Howard kept turning up the stove to maximum. After repeated warnings, Howard was eventually discovered rubbing his hands together amid the billowing smoke of the burning deck, saying: 'Nice and warm now.'

'A senile skipper is enough without a geriatric crew as well,' I muttered darkly, and turned about for Gambell.

The main dilemma for the searchers was that the hunters had gone astray at about the point where the currents divided, so that they could have been swept northward on either side of the island. West (the Russian side) was the consensus. So we skirted the Soviet coastline as far as the Diomedes at the entrance to the Bering Strait and beyond. Little Diomede on the east side is American, Big Diomede, four kilometres westward is Russian — the nearest the two countries approach each other.

The lost hunters, we learned much later, had hauled up their boats onto a fog-shrouded ice floe. For the first six days there was plenty of walrus meat to eat and old floe ice, which melts down to fresh water, to drink. Then the floe became unstable and broke up just as they were launching the boats. The boats were lashed together with walrus-hide ropes, and Junior instituted strict water-rationing and health measures. Socks were wrung out and feet massaged daily, especially the boys'. Birds were shot and their blood drunk, and moisture was licked from spread tarpaulins. Nevertheless, by the end of the second week thirst and exposure were taking their toll, and the boys especially were growing weak.

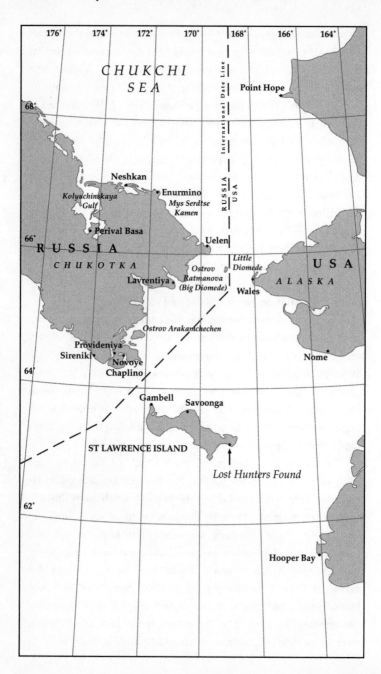

The picturesque township of Inalik on precipitous Little Diomede was rather like an outdoor butcher's shop. Bundles of dead auklets, joints of walrus meat, and pegged-out walrus and polar bear hides festooned the racks outside the brightly painted little houses. Yet in the near-frigid air there was no offensive odour. *Umiaks* (skin boats) and skiffs were drawn up on the rocky foreshore. The Little Diomede hunters, who had already scanned the floes beyond the strait, advised us to try the east (Alaskan) side of St Lawrence Island, where we had not yet been. The ice there was reported to be heavy and I had had about enough of taking this unsheathed wooden vessel into close pack, but there was no help for it. Fog closed in again as we nosed our way cautiously along the leads towards the island's north-east coast.

'We heard something on Diomede about where the hunters might be,' said one of our young Yupik companions, looking at me doubtfully, as if in two minds whether to continue.

'Was it a rumour?' I asked, sensing his dilemma.

'Well, kind of. A shaman from a village near Nome saw those guys in a vision. They were drifting out west of King Island. Should we go look that way?'

'The pack is like a wall there, but we did have a good look west of King Island on our way north. If they are in the middle of that ice jumble they will be on ice floes where they can get water and game too. Better off than drifting at sea where we are heading now.'

At length we cleared the pack, and the fog lifted to reveal the island eight kilometres off. Ungalaq was trying to raise Gambell on the radio when a faint voice came on the air.

'Got any smokes?'

'Who are you?'

'Junior. We are ashore at Sekinak.'

'IT'S THEM; IT'S JUNIOR SLWOOKO! THEY'RE ALIVE!'

The castaways had landed that morning, lit a campfire and warmed their radio batteries. Three of the seven were like zombies and could barely walk. But their three-week ordeal was over now. Within minutes a National Guard helicopter was on its way.

Minor frostbite and dehydration were but temporary sequelae. None of the men sustained permanent damage.

We were left with a final thought as we ploughed through a rising gale towards Gambell — while the Nome shaman had not been all that accurate, his prediction had been several hundred kilometres nearer the mark than the US Coast Guard's estimate had been.

Back to the 'drawing board'. Still no Soviet permission, though now we had a Soviet sponsor, Gennady Alferenko, who was striving manfully in Moscow. Meanwhile the villagers met to decide just who should go to Siberia on the schooner. This was a thorny question since, of course, everyone wanted to go. Should the more senior villagers have priority? What about the youngsters? The issues were argued patiently and reasonably back and forth until, bit by bit, consensus emerged, and the eleven vacant slots were filled. This patient, long-winded process of achieving a generally acceptable solution was reminiscent of the marathon 'Evil Eye' discussions we had earlier been privy to in New Ireland, half a world away. Timely reminders, Mimi and I thought, of the age-old wisdom of our forebears.

There was no permanently protected anchorage at Gambell. With little warning the wind would swing round and strengthen, rollers quickly building up and crashing onto the shingle. *Cyrano* would pitch and roll wildly, the anchor chain bar taut as she plunged, her stern no more than a hundred metres from the breakers. At such times we stood not on the order of our going but sought refuge down the coast at Tiflighak Bay. This was about seven kilometres from Gambell, up over Sevuokuk Mountain and across open heath, which one of our party, after being shown how this tundra was a treasure house of edible and medicinal plants, likened to 'walking over a salad bowl'.

It was not salad that was on my mind this particular evening. I was making the trek at dusk as I had many times before, when I became prey to fanciful forebodings. Every boulder looming through the mist took on, in my imagination, the fearsome shape of a polar bear. Now, these animals are most uncommon on the island in summer, and my fear was about as logical as dreading sharks in an indoor swimming pool. Aboard the schooner we laughed at my inexplicable phantom terrors. That was until the next morning, when Darlene Apangalook, on her three-wheeler, came upon huge pugmarks that a polar bear had made the night before, right where I had been treading so nervously.

Meanwhile Gennady Alferenko in Moscow and his Foundation for Social Innovations was having less success over our permissions than with his other projects of bringing Vietnam and Afghanistan war veterans together and sponsoring a joint Canadian–Russian trek across the North Pole. No less than thirty-four departments had to approve our visit. He decided in the end to risk his foundation's future. With considerable trepidation, he called the head of the KGB direct.

'Do you realise the coast facing America is the most sensitive defense area in the whole Soviet Union?' was the minister's comment. Then, after a pregnant pause, while Gennady's heartrate soared: 'Why not? We have nothing to hide!'

This broke the log jam. All thirty-four offices signed their assent; the official letter of permission was e-mailed to the San Francisco consulate; and visas were issued in two hours to be carried by Air Alaska and Bering Air pilots to us in Gambell, all in that single August 1988 day.

That same afternoon we were at sea.

'What if they hold a grudge because my parents left there?' worried Esther Koonooka.

'The greatest day of my life!' exclaimed her husband Gerard. As Sevuokuk Mountain shrank to nothing behind us and the foggy silhouette of the Chukotka Mountains became clearer, our eleven passengers were too nervous and excited to eat, but sat around in groups on deck, talking quietly. The misty mountains flanking Bukhta Provideniya (Providence Bay) were looming up in the starlight before our calls on Channel 16 were finally answered.

'Provideniya port control.' Thank goodness they spoke English.

'We will be alongside at 2 a.m. your time.'

'That will be satisfactory. Immigration and pilot will come out to meet you.'

We were duly met and meticulously vetted by immigration officials while we continued towards the dock with the pilot on board and Jim at the helm. At a call from Jim, Mimi hurried on deck to bring the unwieldy schooner alongside. To her horror, there was not nearly enough room to turn and we were going too fast anyway. The choice was between rocks, a freighter and some rotted shore timbers. Our bowsprit impaled the latter with a crash, but fortunately sustained no real damage.

The pilot beamed approval at Mimi: 'This historic moment — first time woman dock a ship at Provideniya!'

The mortified Mimi for once was speechless.

Provideniya is a no-nonsense industrial town, a staging port for Northern Sea Route icebreakers in preparation for their long haul across the top of Siberia to the distant Atlantic. Columns of black smoke from old-fashioned soft coal heating and power stations stretch across the fjord. Of more interest to our passengers was the 550-strong Yupik village of Novoye Chaplino at the head of landlocked Tkachen Bay, nineteen kilometres from the town. It was a beautiful spot, the still waters of the bay reflecting the surrounding mountains, their gullies filled with last winter's snow. Thirty years before, the authorities had relocated the village from an exposed promontory that stood astride the sea mammal migration routes to its present site, which is useless for hunting.

Our companions were quickly accommodated in the village, some immediately finding relatives or fellow clansmen. Often, because of new American or Russian names, tracing relationships took much longer. In fact, our stay was nearly at an end before a young woman in our party, who had been particularly drawn to the oldest man in the village, learned with profound emotion that he was actually her grandfather. The whole party was in tears at that revelation.

Many differences had become apparent in the forty years the Yupik communities had been separated. The American branch had become deeply involved in a cash economy. Hunters had come to rely on sophisticated equipment — high-powered rifles, snow machines, outboard-powered aluminium skiffs, CB radios, and the rest. Their Siberian counterparts had simpler tools, like dog sleds and ancient carbines. In Alaska every man was a hunter, though his need for expensive equipment with little paid employment available encouraged non-traditional and illegal abuses like 'headhunting' walrus for their ivory alone. The Siberians, on the other hand, were restricted by inflexible regulations; one was either a clerk, or a hunter, or a truck driver, but never free to be all of them. It is only fair to say that before we left Chukotka for the last time in May 1990 this rigid almost feudal order was already much relaxed. Should the word 'feudal' be questioned, it had become very clear to us by then that the revolution had changed very little in Russia — the gulag labour camp system, the internal passports, the state heavy industry, the medical service, and the rest were pure unchanged vestiges of the Tsarist era. Ill-digested Marxism had been grafted onto a medieval state, and the changes eternal Mother Russia had suffered were mainly cosmetic.

Despite these outward signs of regression and oppression, our Yupik companions' comments were illuminating.

'While the standard of living is less in Chukotka than Alaska and their public facilities are rougher, the family structure is in relatively good order, and there is a quality of pride within the community that could benefit Alaskan villages,' said Leonard Apangalook.

'When I was a little boy and the Siberians came to Gambell,' said elder John Aningayou, 'they were very poor. Their clothes were shoddy. Now they live very different, in some ways better than us. They have central heating here, good meals very cheap, rent very cheap, electric power very cheap, their clothes are very good now, and the village store is well stocked and things are not expensive at all.'*

Our visit closed with a magnificent dance of celebration. A long row of chanting drummers flanked lines of swaying women in

---

*Sadly, this uneven but real progress has since been aborted and come to nothing.

colourful dancing smocks and leaping hunters who mimicked swooping eagles and ravens and recreated the awesome drama of the polar bear hunt. The vivid scene was framed by a jagged mountain frieze, while little painted clouds moved majestically across a picture book blue sky.

Before we left, Mimi and I were invited to fly back to Chukotka the following spring and spend a whole year in the Yupik and Chukchi villages. There were tears and promises of further reunions when we regretfully sailed out of Tkachen Bay. The weather remained perfect, the reason being, said one old lady: 'The captain has no anger.'

So, after landing our passengers at Gambell, and the fine days now clearly being numbered, *Cyrano* stood south before the stormwinds of autumn, and was already eighty miles away when a 60-knot gale swept over Gambell. Eskimo hunter Roger Antagame was with us, and at False Pass in the Aleutians we picked up another crewman. When Roger had to leave us at Homer, his place was taken by Eric Muegge, stepson of the legendary dog-musher Colonel Norman Vaughan. After threading the Alaskan and British Columbian channels, a last brisk run under full sail brought us to Port Townsend at the end of September 1988. There, after attending to minor repairs, we were able to hand *Cyrano* back to Mike McCune in better condition than when she had left San Diego.

Termination Dust, the first light snow of autumn, was sprinkling the peaks of the Olympic Mountains when Mimi and I received a welcome letter from the University of Alaska. 'You have both been appointed Affiliate Professors of Anthropology by the University of Alaska's Fairbanks and Southeast campuses,' it read. This modest appointment was the highest I ever rose in academia (and particularly noteworthy because I am not an anthropologist!); it was to serve us well in negotiations with status-conscious Russian officials.

There followed an all too brief interlude staying with Norman and Carolyn Vaughan in their cabin at Trapper Creek and trying our hand at dog-mushing. How could one not be smitten! Those eager, intelligent creatures were so anxious to get going that, in the hands of a novice such as myself, they would tangle up their traces inextricably and look back contemptuously at me when I did something wrong. We were only managing five dogs apiece and covering no more than forty kilometres a day, but gliding through the forest, with only the swish of the sled runners and the patter of the dogs' feet to break the silence, was like drifting through an enchanted world.

All too soon, early in 1989, we left the forests behind and flew back to treeless Gambell to make our home for the rest of the winter in a tiny old cabin, whose double-plywood walls enclosed a layer of sealskin, and where we soon had to tunnel down to the doorway through two and a half metres of drifted snow. But we had in our pockets a fulsome invitation from the Provideniya Soviet and Party secretaries, which read in part: 'Dear Friends, Accept our invitation to visit Provideniya for a year.' In our innocence we anticipated no official barriers to our flying back to Chukotka in the spring.

seven

'Magnetic' Polar Bears — Siberia

The spring of 1989 came, the snows melted and the green tundra sprung into life again, but where were our Soviet visas? Held up, apparently, by the very same people who had invited us so cordially. Gennady pulled strings in Moscow and visas were eventually issued, but only for one month. It was at least a start. We flew to Provideniya accompanied by Roger Antagame. Only then did it become clear that the delays were not due to bumbling bureaucracy — the local party secretary and mayor regretted their invitation and had no intention of honouring it. Our Yupik Eskimo friends in Novoye Chaplino had no doubt at all that their paranoid fear of us 'stirring up ethnic unrest' was the reason.

Nothing in Russia should surprise, but even so an encounter with a professor of theology from the monastery centre of Zagorsk did take us aback; we had not realised there were theology professors in the Soviet Union. But when the professor told us he had crossed the nine time zones to Provideniya at the invitation and expense of the KGB to lecture on the 'National Question', our minds simply boggled.

The whole bizarre situation culminated in our being ordered to leave forthwith, despite Moscow having confirmed our year's permission. We refused to go voluntarily.

'Arrest you? Expel you? No, you are good people. We would like you to stay.' The KGB major, perhaps influenced by the theology professor, was very positive, and the shoddy plot collapsed.

Nevertheless, it seemed wise to move to Lavrentiya in Chukotskiy *rayon* (region) further north, where the Chukchi mayor, Yuri Tototto, bade us welcome and meant it, and a cooperative offered to sponsor us. 'Cooperatives' at this transitional time were really private companies. This one unloaded ships by lighter in ports like Lavrentiya where there were no wharves. This cooperative, *Lesh*, was headed by ex-*komsomol* (All-Union Leninist Communist Union of Youth) secretary Sergei Kotchetkoff, who offered to sponsor us and pay our expenses to boot; he asked for nothing in return.*

We travelled widely through Chukotka that summer by coastal steamer, truck and tracked vehicle. Then, when the green tundra had turned red-gold and the first snow had dusted the mountains above Provideniya, we flew in the bi-weekly twenty-seat MI6 helicopter to the coastal village of Sireniki, where we had been invited to join the autumn hunt.

The Bering Sea surf crashed down on a crescent of gravel beach walled in by shaley cliffs and sea stacks. Brooding over the township was a border guard post with its radar, while the ruined redoubts of a past military era crumbled slowly into dust on the stony hillside.

---

*Happily we were later able to arrange productive Alaskan port visits and the gift of a computer.

The hospitality in Chukotka was universally amazing, from Yupiks, Chukchi and Russians alike. The feisty little Providenyia port doctor, Klaudivanna, gave us the keys to her apartment. In Sireniki, Klava, a pretty young Eskimo widow with a six-year-old daughter, Bella, insisted we stay with them in their one-room apartment, and Roger at her mothers, instead of in the hostel where we had booked. The hostel was a place of ill-omen, she insisted. Brooking no argument, she called in a friend to partition her all-purpose room with a curtain and allocated the larger of the two settee beds to Mimi and me. There was a kitchen annex and a snow porch, but no toilet or bathroom. In the snow porch stood a water cask, which was kept filled by a tanker truck that did its rounds daily. A massive steel rubbish sledge, into which we emptied the sanitary bucket, was parked nearby. Waste water was simply tossed out '*na ulitsa*', into the street, where it quickly froze into a lethal skating rink. Heating was from a Russian coal stove.

The household was completed by dog Strelkye and her two well-disciplined pups, who lived in an underground kennel. Strelkye was a very responsible member of the family, who 'had been given a human spirit by mistake', Klava told us. This idea was entirely in line with Eskimo and Chukchi belief, wherein all living things possess their own spiritual essence and the dichotomy between humans and animals is blurred.

In keeping with the mores of Soviet society at this time, when there was an enviably non-mercenary community spirit, Klava would not let us pay a penny for our keep during the two months we stayed with her. The most she would allow us to contribute was some help with paying for food. Shopping and general information-sharing was much facilitated by what Mimi and I christened the 'Women's Telephone Mafia'. Telephone calls cost next to nothing.

'*Etta ya*, it's me,' Klava would begin. 'An icebreaker is bringing in onions today; there are chocolates in Store Two; the government is announcing new *sovkhoz* [state farm] regulations; the militia man is drunk again.' She would hang up abruptly without saying goodbye, and back and forth for the next half hour equally laconic phone calls would be exchanged. Before the week was out Mimi was making her own contribution in understandable, if ungrammatical, Russian. Very few happenings escaped the scrutiny of this female 'internet'.

By this time we had travelled pretty extensively up and down the Siberian Bering Sea coasts facing the United States and would later traverse many hundreds of kilometres of Arctic coastline and interior tundra, so we could testify to the utter absence of sophisticated military establishments. Tumbledown roofless barracks, crumbling one-time gun emplacements on virtually every headland, coastguard radar stations manned by casual soldiers — this was all there was, save only the acres of rusting 44-gallon drums that marked the Red Army's passing. The few airfields, even the military one at Anadyr, had only gravel runways and were far from being all-weather fields. Modern electronic landing and navigation aids were non-existent. All of this must have been fully revealed by American military satellites. We in the West have clearly been victims of one of the greatest confidence tricks of all time — deliberate fabrication of a totally mythical 'Soviet Arctic Menace' — all to ensure fat military contracts.

'Too rough!' declared old Angkana, studying the surf from her bench outside the hunting brigade's shed on a bluff overlooking the breakers. The vastly experienced retired hunters sitting beside her, peering out to sea through slitted old eyes and searching for quarry — walruses, seals, belugas, great whales — were inclined to agree with her. The young hunters politely heard the old lady out while steadfastly ignoring her advice. The 25- to 30-foot *baidaras* (skin boats) were lifted off their storage racks and carried down to the beach. The five *baidara* crews had met at the *sovkhoz* office at seven o'clock that morning to decide the day's program, after which Mimi had accompanied Kostia, the elected head of the hunters, to the border guard office to have us put on his crew register. The gear was put aboard — 35 to 50 h.p. Suzuki or Russian-made outboards that would be lowered into wells, spare fuel, harpoons, rifles, inflated sealskin and plastic floats, walrus-hide line, oars, rudder, Primus stove, food and water, as well as Mimi's carefully wrapped-up video camera, on loan from the University of Alaska.

'These *baidaras*,' Kostia told us while we were waiting for the border guards to give the all-clear, 'are lighter and more seaworthy than whaleboats. Generally we replace the skins every one or two years. Yes, we use three skins for a boat — unblemished female skins [the males tear their skins fighting]. The women split them and then use the outer part, which is a good four centimetres thick. Look how the joins are overlapped; they are stitched from each side so that the stitches go only halfway through to keep the seams watertight. You can see how the skins are lashed to the frames with whale sinew. This is the harpoon whaling line that is cut as a single strip from full-thickness walrus hide, far stronger and more elastic than any synthetic rope.'

The *pagranichni* (border guard) drove down to the beach to check our papers and all was ready for the launch. The boat was pushed down till the bow was afloat and all watched the run of the breakers. Then, at a word, the *baidara* was pushed forward and everyone tumbled helter skelter aboard, thigh boots dripping, while the bowman plied his oar feverishly. Beyond the break of the surf the oars were laid aside, the rudder and outboard engine were shipped, and we headed out to sea, the five *baidaras* fanning out on their preferred search patterns. We could see that all the crews were standing, making a frieze of stick figures, exactly like the prehistoric rock artists of Norway had shown in their carvings. They had been *baidara* hunters too; we know they were because hunters stand in their boats searching the sea, while fishermen stay seated.

There were a couple of false alarms, after which we skirted the cliffs almost to Bukhta Provideniya, seeing nothing but some wild sheep high on a mountainside. At midday we pulled ashore in a tiny cove to gather edible seaweed and to lunch on boiled and raw reindeer, dried walrus meat and succulent orange sea bladders.

Our luck changed that afternoon — a walrus surfaced ahead.

'*Aghah, Aghah*!' Kostia cried and we roared away with ancient carbines blazing. The walrus dived as we raced towards it. Then it was up again, a hit, and as it disappeared our two harpoons went in, the floats were tossed over the side and the harpoon shafts bobbed to the surface. The walrus was held fast. All hands could now relax in the assurance that the animal would not sink or escape. Now and again the inflated seal-skin floats would tug and surge as the stricken creature tried to go deeper. But eventually it had to breathe, and as its whiskery head and tusks broke the surface, the end came in a final head shot.

The *baidara* heeled over as the carcass was hauled alongside and made fast by thongs passed through holes cut in the flippers, and we chugged slowly shoreward, where the walrus was hauled up the shingle by an electric windlass and willing hands ran our boat up from the surf, while the agile crew leapt into the shallows. Not so where I was concerned, because I was cramped and chilled and stayed seated until I could clamber stiffly out onto dry land.

Now that the hunters had brought in their quarry, and carried out their task with keen weapons and good gear, as was the animal's due, it became the prerogative of the women to butcher it, carefully, thoroughly, wasting nothing, thus showing their own respect. For it has been known for millennia that if the creatures that share the world with man are not respected they will cease to come to his spear, and the age-old interdependence of all living things will be broken. The hunter's respect for his quarry is well portrayed in a poem by Canadian Dale De Armond.

> *Oh brave one*
> *Oh strong one,*
> *How beautiful you were*
> *in the water.*
> *You came to my spear,*
> *I mourn your proud death*
> *And I pay you honour and*
> *thanks this night.*

At this time in the Soviet Union the products of the hunt were state property, and as such had to be sold at standard prices. Elders were entitled to ten kilograms of free meat a year, the rest had to be bought — cheaply enough, it is true. However, we were happy to watch the old people staggering off with at least six months' entitlement in their overflowing buckets, so apparently things were being managed with more regard to tradition than the strict letter of the law would indicate.

The ice, and with it the bowhead whales, were slow in coming south that season, and neither had appeared off Sireniki by the time our Provideniya district permits had nearly run out. The time had come, therefore, for Mimi and me to move to Chukotskiy *rayon*, to its capital Lavrentiya, to the Arctic Ocean settlements of Uelen, Enurmino and Neshkan beyond, and to the reindeer tundra. This was traditionally the domain of the 'Reindeer Chukchi', who exchanged reindeer meat and warm reindeer-skin clothing with the 'Beach Chukchi' and Yupiks of the coast for sea mammal fat and waterproof (but not overwarm) seal-skin clothing. We were to find that, largely unknown to the Russians, this exchange network was as strong as ever.

Yupik Eskimo Roger Antagame would not be coming north with us into linguistically foreign Chukchi-speaking territory. He would helicopter from Sireniki to Provideniya, and thence in a Bering Air Piper Navajo home to Gambell. His departure was certainly in style. The dignified little hunter in his large Russian fur hat strode along at the head of a procession bearing gifts his relatives had given him, looking for all the world like a caricature of an African explorer with his bearers. There were boxes and cases containing samovars, brightly decorated crockery, champagne, vodka, children's toys, candies, and much else. But the *pièce de résistance*, balanced on the head of the last porter, was an entire reindeer carcass.

Very soon afterwards we followed suit. Leaving Sireniki, and especially Klava, was a wrench. We embraced and pressed noses, sharing the breath of life, a shamanic ritual identical to the Maori *hongi* of New Zealand. Nevertheless, we could not help but look forward to the coming winter in the Chukchi lands, when the tundra would be transformed under its blanket of snow, and skis, snowmobiles and dog sleds would determine our journeyings.

'Oh, you *krasnaya dedushka* [beautiful grandfather]!' exclaimed a drunken Eskimo crone with no top teeth, throwing her arms around me and kissing me warmly in Provideniya Airport. Mimi's unseemly convulsions of mirth were no help at all. Not that my unsuspected 'beauty' was the only hazard of Soviet travel, for the lunatic Aeroflot schedule decreed that to reach this adjacent centre 160 kilometres away we must fly 645 kilometres via Anadyr, and spend at least one night at the airport there before catching an identical ANT 24 forty-seater turboprop for the rest of the journey. In the event we spent two nights in the Anadyr airport lounge.

'You must realise,' explained an outspoken journalist from the district newspaper *Triumph of Communism*, who met us in Lavrentiya, where the potholed streets were now choked with snow and the children's adventure playground we had earlier dubbed 'Hypothermia Hill' was windier than ever, 'that this system, where communications radiate out like spokes of a wheel from the centre without connections round the periphery, is pure Tsarist. Each district is isolated from the one next door, and visits are discouraged by the travel and residence permits we need.' We were to remember his words when we saw how this centralised arrangement restricted candidate recognition in the March 1990 Russian election.

Lavrentiya was merely a stepping stone. Our main interest lay with the hunters on the shores of the now-frozen Arctic Ocean and the herdsmen of the inland tundra. Our base to begin with would be the coastal centre Neshkan. Living and transport expenses would continue to be met by the generous cooperative *Lesh*.

The 160 kilometres by helicopter to Neshkan was across the neck of the Chukotka Peninsula and was the route from the Bering Sea back to the Arctic Ocean that was favoured in the spring by 'magnetic' polar bears. We coined the term when listening to the old hunter Levite'u.

'When you meet a polar bear on the tundra it is always walking north,' he told us, much to our bemusement. He went on to explain, speaking Chukchi with his nephew translating into Russian, for the old man claimed not to speak it, 'In the early winter, like now, the bears come south into the Bering Sea with the floating ice, but in the spring as the ice melts they come ashore and take a short-cut 100 miles overland back to the Arctic Ocean whence they came.'

Jumbled ice floes were already piled up nine metres high on the beach when we landed at Neshkan and the ocean was frozen as far as the eye could see. We were allotted a little storeroom behind the post office, with just enough space for a bed, a hole-in-the-floor toilet and a hot water tap next door. The rather basic cooking facilities did not matter, thanks to the hospitality of our neighbours in the flats above, who made a shocking fuss over us.

Attracted by the drums of seal oil stored on the outskirts, the great white bears, who were strictly protected by law, were no strangers in the town. Almost nightly the dogs would howl in unison at uninvited visitors. The previous winter, we were told, a massive male bear, attacked by some loose dogs, sat himself down on a snow-covered roof, batting thirty-kilogram huskies like billiard balls. Everyone, except the dead dogs' owners, sided with the bear. The children lose all constraint when a bear comes to town, rushing out from school in defiance of their teachers to follow it around. Recently a half-grown cub was given so much chocolate and candy by the children that it became sick.

Chukotka is a harsh land with a grim history. As far back as 1690 the Chukchi revolted against the extortion and brutality of the Tsar's Cossacks. The Chukchi's main weapons were powerful wooden bows backed by sinew, while their slatted wood or ivory armour and split walrus-hide shields proved more than a match for the Cossack muskets and sabres, so that the Cossack Captain Kusnetsov and all his men were destroyed. From 1729 to 1747 full-scale war raged, until the most brutal and able of the Russian commanders, Captain Pavlutski, was defeated and slain with every man who did not run away. The Russian forts were abandoned, and not until the early nineteenth century was a more peaceful Russian takeover accomplished.

'When we cut open Pavlutski a block of ice fell out.' It was with these words that Ifkiev, Chukchi-elected chairman of Neshkan *sovkhoz*, described this Asiatic version of Little Big Horn. The symbolism of the cruel Pavlutski's lack of heart comes clear across a quarter of a millennium.

Turning to contemporary matters, Ifkiev, a heavily muscled young man with a long Chukchi face and intelligent eyes, explained how the rigid industrial *sovkhoz* structure introduced in 1970 had resulted in a once prosperous *kolkhoz* (collective farm) going steadily downhill as the economy nosedived in the 1980s.

'Did *perestroika* in 1985 help cause the breakdown?' asked Mimi.

'Not really; the last straw perhaps. Now everything is rundown.'

This confirmed what we had already noted in Novoye Chaplino and Sireniki: the people worked hard and efficiently, but the problems were man-made and came from above. Despite its decline, the Neshkan/Enurmino *sovkhoz* was by no means moribund. Ifkiev gave us the figures: '27972 square kilometres of unfenced tundra, 129 kilometres of Arctic sea coast and the ninety-six-kilometre-long Kolyuchinskaya Gulf all full of seal and walrus, and several huge lagoons teeming with fish. We are a many-sided enterprise. We pasture 16000 reindeer (10 per cent privately owned), 5700 blue foxes, seventeen milch cows, 100 pigs (plus 1000 privately owned), with 250 full-time reindeer herdsmen and women. There is a hunting brigade with seven motor whaleboats — they are using seal nets off Enurmino now; a fishing collective; an ivory master carvers' workshop; a sewing collective that makes skin clothes for the herdsmen and hunters; and a kindergarten. Dog teams and snowmobiles are privately owned.' The herdsmen's transmitter-receivers were obsolete, he added; six-wheeled trucks were useless in soft snow and there were only two *visdehods* (tracked vehicles).

'You want to visit Perival Basa, the *aleinevoti* [reindeer herdsmen's base] at the head of the gulf?'

'Yes, please.'

'Well, there should be a *visdehod* going down next week. I will let you know.'

There was plenty to do around the settlement. Nikolai, the blind nephew of the old hunter Levite'u, could still care for his dogs and was generous in allowing us to drive them. On my third morning out it was very cold — in the low –30s°C, and I watched with interest while Nikolai poured boiling water from a kettle onto the upturned sled runners and then smoothed out the rapidly congealing liquid with a piece of polar bear skin.

'*Put, put, put,*' I called, but the wayward dogs swung left instead of right, determined to take advantage of their novice musher and return home. But my Russian companion and I were hard-hearted: '*Tahum, tahum* [go, go],' we shouted, then '*Khe, khe* [left, left],' and the splendid Chukchi dogs, making a virtue of necessity, pulled with a will. After an exhilarating ten-kilometre run, I turned the sledge over and curiously inspected the runners. The surface remained glassy smooth like Teflon, and so cold that it 'burned' my foolishly bared finger. The dogs were each given a well-earned chocolate, for this was how they had been trained — with rewards.

'My uncle Levite'u is the best person to answer all these questions you are asking,' said Nikolai. Navigation/wayfinding was still very much my obsession. 'He knows more than anyone about finding his way on the tundra. Come and meet him with me tonight and I will translate because he doesn't speak Russian.'

Mimi and I already knew what the old hunter had to say about polar bears. He had much more of interest to tell us about finding one's way — the key to Arctic survival.

'I have been an *aleinevot* as well as a sea hunter,' Nikolai translated. 'Stars, winds, *sastrugi* [snowdrifts] formed by the prevailing winds give us direction on the tundra in blizzards. At sea we know the direction of the land in fog by a bird called a *kulek* [snipe] that swims far out and always flies parallel to the shore. In winter, blocks of sea ice develop sloping snowdrifts on their south sides. *Sastrugi* generally lie NNW to SSE. How can anyone get lost?'

'Very easily for us in winter darkness and storm,' Mimi commented drily.

KAREN KEYS

The treacherous Antarctic sea.

BARBARA SATHERLEY

Dick Smith Explorer moored at Cape Denison during the Mawson Anniversary
Expedition, 1981. Mawson's Hut can be seen on the extreme right.

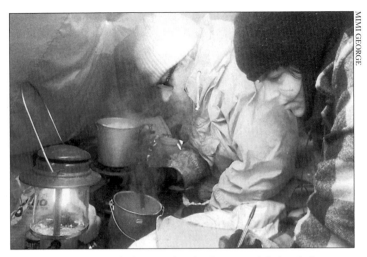

MIMI GEORGE

Mimi George making notes for her research project in our tent pitched on the frozen Antarctic sea, 1983.

Cyrano off Chukotka, 1988. The yacht carried many flags, including the Stars and Stripes, the then-Soviet 'courtesy flag', the Alaskan children's 'friendship flag' and the Australian flag.

Searching for lost walrus hunters, 1988. An eskimo *umiak* (skin boat) carrying floats, harpoons and walrus meat is pulled ashore on the island of Little Diomede, Alaska. Big Diomede, its Russian counterpart, can be seen in the background, barely four kilometres away.

A dance of welcome from the citizenry of Novoye Chaplino to its Alaskan relatives, 1988.

MIMI GEORGE

With reindeer herders in Neshkan, Chukotka, c. 1989. Note my splendid wolfskin hat. To my eternal regret, I later lost it.

DON LOGAN

On Mount Rainier, Washington, 1993.

SALLY ANDREW

Te Aurere in Doubtless Bay, New Zealand, at the end of its voyage from Rarotonga, 1995.

Robyn Stewart, with black eye,
Rarotonga, 1996.

Mary Moos, Avana Harbour,
Rarotonga, 1996.

Hipour of Polowat, 1998.

ERIC METZGAR

The *Kapitan Khlebnikov* crashing through Antarctic pack ice, 1999.

CHERRY ALEXANDER

Aboard *Kapitan Khlebnikov*, 1999.

ERIC METZGAR

'We are whole again.' Handing back the sacred *rokeyok* to Urupiy, senior navigator of Satawal, Yap, 2000.

JO SOLOMON

Aboard *Leander* in Rockhampton.

Levite'u chuckled: 'Not really. Out on the winter tundra you only have to scrape the snow away to see which way the grass is lying. It will have frozen in the direction of the first autumn snowstorm and, of course, you remember which way that was blowing.'

'Of course!' we agreed.

'Don't forget the animals,' the old man adjured us. 'They are smart. Reindeer on their own will head for good feeding grounds they remember from last year; in storms they drift downwind. Wolves hunt upwind.'

'Well, this is just the sort of thing we missed being told in the Antarctic, isn't it?' Mimi remarked. 'But it is all much easier to talk about than to practise!'

I could only agree.

On 20 December 1989 we left Neshkan by *visdehod* for Perival Basa, heading initially towards the first of the *yarangas* (portable framework dwellings) we were to visit en route. All eight of Neshkan's herding brigades were housed in these yurt-like tents that, in order to follow the herds, could be dismantled and taken to new sites on heavy sledges drawn by specially trained draft reindeer. There was but limited visibility, even around midday, here on the Arctic Circle at midwinter at the best of times, but persistent fog reduced visibility to near zero. Since the *yarangas* are of necessity mobile, there can be no permanent roads. As the steel tracks ground over the uneven hummocks, I asked the driver how on earth he was keeping straight.

'By keeping at the right angle to the *sastrugi*, of course,' he replied, stating the obvious.

Even so, he did veer some five degrees off-course that afternoon, landing us with a very cold night 450 metres up in the Innymney Mountains. In the morning, after relieving myself in –40°C air temperature, my hands congealed into lumps of meat that did not belong to me, so that, feeling no end of a fool, I had to call Mimi over to zip me up. What a relief it was to arrive at the Second Brigade *yaranga*! Primus stoves had been lit and ice blocks set melting for tea upon sighting our vehicle. Mimi and I gazed at the great pyramidal tent with interest.

'Teepee, Fenimore Cooper, Last of the Mohicans,' a herdsman offered unexpectedly in English, proving that American classics were no strangers on the tundra. Removing our coats and boots, we gratefully crawled under the curtain of furs into the warmth of the *polog* (inner enclosure), where we reclined luxuriously on fur rugs, and were soon feasting on boiled reindeer (the best meat in the world), tea, bread and New Zealand butter. The latter was so hard frozen it had to be chopped up with a hatchet, whereupon it splintered like glass.

'God damn!' swore Mimi, more startled than hurt, as a sliver of frozen butter sliced a gash in her arm.

'The cow cockie in Taranaki who made this butter would flip his nut if he saw that,' I remarked in some awe.

Yarangas are extraordinarily efficient 'mobile homes'. The walls rise straight up to shoulder height, thence they slope steeply up to the open apex where the poles come together. They are generally made of canvas nowadays, though the Eighth Brigade's one, we saw later, was mostly assorted skins. The main tent is unheated, floored with snow in the winter, and here the cooking is done. On one side the sled dogs find shelter in the worst weather. The inner rectangular *polog*, suspended from the 'rafters', is made from twenty reindeer skins and is floored with split walrus hide (like *baidaras*), over a layer of tundra grasses. It is lit by candles and its only heating is by a homemade kerosene wick lamp (seal oil in the old days), yet even when we experienced –40°C weather and blizzard conditions, we never needed the sleeping bags we had brought with us.

How does this thermal efficiency come about? The occupant's body heat is retained by the *polog*'s walls and roof, while his/her moist breath and sweat transpire through the pores of the reindeer skins to the outside, where it freezes. First thing every morning it falls to the lot of the lady of the house to soundly beat the ice crystals from the outside of the *polog* and many more bucketsful from the inside walls of the *yaranga*. The needs of nature are catered for ingeniously. Chamber pots are placed within easy reach outside the skin curtain, with a large block of fresh snow to empty them into. In the morning the block is carried out into the tundra.

Our hosts told us about an incident at their *yaranga* the previous winter which illustrates the extraordinary efficiency of skin clothing. A near-blind and deaf old lady set out to empty the chamber pot well away from the *yaranga* one morning while a blizzard was raging. She was prudent enough to have donned full double-layered clothing, which was fortunate, because when she turned for home, she could not find it. Neither could anybody find her. For two days she walked about and hunkered down in the blinding storm. Finally the wind eased and the clouds of drift snow settled. The indomitable old lady spotted the *yaranga* and walked in as if nothing had happened — still clutching her chamber pot!

Perival Basa, the 'Base in the Pass', was a stoutly constructed building overlooking the frozen Ioniveyem River that 'mothered' six *yarangas* at distances varying from eight to ninety-six kilometres. The main room past the snow porch centred around a Russian stove that warmed the wall fronting the nine-metre sleeping platform on one side and served as a cooking range on the other. The caretaker couple had separate quarters. A wind generator was backed up by a diesel one, and a large open garage housed snowmobiles and noisy sled dogs.

Originally we were scheduled to return to Neshkan within two weeks, but no sooner had the *visdehod* driven away than storms virtually isolated the tundra, putting all transport on hold. Day after day the 'Northern Master' swept down off the frozen Arctic Ocean, and accelerated down the Kolyuchinskaya Gulf, lifting wind-driven snowclouds fifteen metres into the air that cut visibility to less than a metre. The temperatures were –30 to –40°C, with wind chill as low as –100°C. The smallest exposed area of my skin (though not Mimi's or the Chukchi's) froze within a minute, so that I was never without red and swollen or peeling patches on my face, neck or ears. Nor did my fingers, sensitised by the exposure I had endured on the *Ice Bird* Expedition, stand up very well either.

Nevertheless, brief let-ups through January and early February 1990 allowed us to stay at the nearer *yarangas*, travelling usually on skis, ever-mindful of our route. Once, as I was gliding along, I glimpsed out of the corner of my eye a slender animal coming up on my left. Dog, I thought. To my surprise it was an arctic fox that trotted past me, no more than four metres away, ignoring me completely.

My vulnerable skin was not the only casualty that winter. The splendid video camera, lent to us by the University of Alaska, was no match for bumpy sled travel. It expired and had to be sent back to Anchorage for repairs, which were not completed until after we had left Chukotka. But in the *yarangas* it was warm and cosy. We ate tender boiled reindeer meat old-style from great wooden platters: you take a bite into the meat, then cut it off with your knife, being careful of your nose.

Usually somebody stays with the reindeer twenty-four hours a day, equipped with a lasso wound round his/her waist, knife, biscuits, frozen raw meat or river fish, perhaps a small portable stove, and a pair of small Chukchi snowshoes that are generally preferred to skis on the treeless, wind-blasted Chukotskiy tundra. But the present winter was too severe for such close supervision. One frigid dawn found us with chief reindeer herder Tola Kuttagin cresting a ridge in search of his herd, which had drifted. The reason was soon apparent; a half-eaten carcass lay in the snow before us.

'What do you do about wolves?' I asked.

'The wolves have to eat too,' Tola reminded me, revealing the fundamental difference in attitude between people who live *with* animals and Westerners (an American farmer would call for planes, machine guns and poisoned baits if an unfortunate wolf were sighted within 150 kilometres of his property!). 'If the wolves get too greedy,' Tola continued, 'we go after them with helicopters, but in weather like this they can even help us by culling the weakest animals and keeping in touch with the rest as they scatter.'

Back at the *basa*, old Vala, the caretaker's wife, said rather hesitantly, 'The old people say that the spirits of the wolves and

killer whales are one and the same. When the sea freezes the spirits
of the orcas enter into the wolves. On days like now when the
storms are so terrible we can no longer stay out with the reindeer,
we simply let the wolves act as their guardians — just as the killer
whales are guardians of the walrus.' She gave us a funny look, and
added, 'But, of course, that's just old-fashioned superstition!'

It never ceased to amaze Mimi and me how skilfully *aleinevoti*
picked out particular deer from perhaps two or three thousand
animals and then did their John Wayne act with the lasso. The thirty
or so harness-trained animals among such a herd are similarly
recognised and cut out when needed. They are harnessed up, two
skittish reindeer to each tiny one-man sled. Before you know it they
are off, the sled bouncing, airborne half the time, across tussocks
and *sastrugi*. They are over the horizon in minutes.

The stormbound days dragged by slowly, nevertheless, especially
since our English-language reading matter was limited to one
yachting magazine and Hugo's optimistically entitled *Russian in
Three Months*. So we were relieved when, in early February 1990,
the storms eased enough for a *visdehod* to reach the base with much-
needed supplies. We returned aboard it to Neshkan, riding the
frozen waves of *sastrugi* and pressure ridges down the length of
Kolyuchinskaya Gulf, all too conscious of the three-ton weight of
the vehicle as it lurched along, separated by only a metre or so of ice
from the deep water. Our two-week stay on the tundra had extended
to six.

The Arctic village of Enurmino lies fifty-three kilometres
along the coast from Neshkan. We rode there in sledges behind
snowmobiles, cosy enough in our fur hats, borrowed reindeer skin
clothing, *tarbassa* (moccasins), and mitts. We shared half a house in
Enurmino, rather like Klava's apartment in Sireniki, except for the
fact that we had to break out our freshwater ice from a pond
ourselves and sledge it home, and the complete lack of sanitation.
That problem, however, was handled most efficiently by the sled
dogs, who rushed eagerly to lap up the faeces even before we had
finished tipping out the pail. This penchant of huskies for fresh

human excrement is well known and the subject of many, no doubt apocryphal, Antarctic legends of over-eager sled dogs lurking under latrines, emasculating expeditioners.

The other half of our house was occupied by Oxana, a lovely young herdswoman, and her brother. Soldier's Day in Russia is marked by the presentation of gifts to the men — all veterans, by virtue of universal military service. My package included a bottle of eau de cologne, which Oxana's brother asked to borrow 'as he was seeing his girlfriend'. Whether he saw her or not I do not know, but next morning the bottle was empty, and he had a monumental hangover and smelled like a brothel.

My stay in Enurmino was restricted by a whiplash injury sustained on a bouncing sled, which was then compounded by striking the back of my head in a hard fall on slippery ice which reactivated my old problems with the detached retina. I had to rest a lot and was only once able to join Mimi and the hunting brigade laying seal nets through the ice.

My disabilities clearly illustrated how Mimi and I were beginning to differ. In our earlier seaborne projects I had been the prime mover; Mimi had been overshadowed by my reputation. I had tried (sometimes too hard) to push her forward, but she had resented playing second fiddle. Now in the Arctic, no longer at sea, our roles were reversed. I could not stand up to cold and trauma as well as she could; my poor grasp of language made me a drag; there were some nights now when we did not make love. Neither of us realised it at the time, I think, but fundamental changes in our relationship were taking place.

First in Enurmino, then back in Neshkan, we attended spirited candidates' campaign meetings. We hardly recognised Tola Kuttagin's wife Nina, our formerly fur-clad *yaranga* hostess, as the elegantly dressed young woman in high heels and sheer stockings who mounted the platform.

'We want a school in the tundra, and we want it now — a kindergarten and the first three grades to start with,' she insisted forcefully, wagging her finger under the chairman's nose. 'Yes, Ivan Ivanovitch, our children live at the boarding school. We never see them except in the summer holidays, and that's the only time they get to live in the tundra. Soon, if this goes on, there will be no more *aleinevoti*. They tell us no teachers will go to the tundra, but that is not true. There are two Chukchi teachers in this room who are willing and eager to go. Isn't that so?' There were confirmatory shouts from a man and a woman in the audience. Nina sat down to enthusiastic applause.

At each meeting the candidates were heavily cross-questioned. Repeatedly Mimi and I were asked to give our opinions.

'Go ahead. You speak street Russian like a native now. I don't,' I urged Mimi. Everyone voiced encouragement and the chairman thought she was probably the first *Amerikanka* to participate in a Russian election campaign.

'I explained how we have many similar problems and that all is not well in the native villages in Alaska too,' she told me after she had sat down, for her Russian had been too fast for me to follow. 'Yet I did not want to give the impression of parroting the old Party line that things are worse in America, because most are not — at least it is not a simple comparison. Certainly, indigenous people in both countries could do with more autonomy.'

Questions continued thick and fast. Given the chaotic state of the exchange rates, price comparisons were pretty well impossible to make, and reminded us of the contemporary Russian joke: 'How do you compare the pound, the rouble and the dollar?' The answer: 'A pound of roubles equals one dollar.'

'This is a "last chance" election,' Yuri Tototto had told us in Lavrentiya. 'The USSR Supreme Soviet Deputies were elected two years ago, the bulk of them representing the Party. The economy has crashed. We are a spiritually rudderless people with a vacillating president. It is up to the Russian Republic on its own now — maybe Boris Yeltsin?'

Tototto's sense of urgency was fully shared by the candidates. Sasha, our *visdehod* navigator and reputed shaman, stressed the isolation of districts from each other. He was later elected. So, more significantly, was Boris Yeltsin. To our delight, the two-faced head of Provideniya district was defeated and was mayor no more.

The 'White Spring', the magic time when the returning sun presides over a sparkling snowscape, gave way to the 'Green Spring', when the tundra 'salad bowl' awakens and the poor scuttling field mice lose the snow roofs of their winding tunnels to become ready prey for hawks and falcons. It was time for us to be leaving. We managed to cadge a ride on a militia helicopter directly back to Provideniya without the tedious detour through Anadyr (just how it was arranged we never learned), to await a plane for Alaska. We crossed to Nome in May 1990, after eleven of the most thought-provoking months I have ever spent.

Alaska Airlines took us on to Anchorage, where we rented a flat. Here we managed to entertain not a few of our Russian and Eskimo friends from over the border. We, or rather Mimi, made a pilot video on Chukotka, but while we got some support from corporate donors and the Alaskan Foundation for the Arts, there were not nearly enough funds for a full-scale production employing professionals. The idea was probably doomed from the outset, for we lacked both experience and skills.

In any case, this became a time of great personal tension for me, which was an effective distraction. Being reserved by nature, it is hard for me to write about what happened next. Yet domestic upheavals are nothing but the common lot of us all and there is nothing really for me to be embarrassed about.

While still in Russia, Mimi had frequently questioned women about 'homosexualism', but found mostly disinterest. One particularly beautiful young woman from the North Caucasus, who was scathing about Russian men ('never lift a finger in the home, just drink vodka'), showed no interest in Mimi's hints about an alternative, but simply quoted the Russian saying: 'If you can't get a fish, a crayfish will do.'

It was much different in Anchorage, where there was a thriving lesbian community into which an enthusiastic Mimi was absorbed and promptly fell in love with a woman. We had lived and worked so very closely together (too closely, I suspect) that her newly separate and distinct social life devastated me. The signals of Mimi's bisexuality might well have been apparent early on, though the proportion of her female to male lovers had then been negligible. Still, the homosexual element in her family was remarkably pronounced, no fewer than half her siblings and first cousins being gay. Not that I was averse to sharing intimacy with two women. Quite the opposite. The close bonding that existed between Mimi and me did not preclude mutual relationships with others. The word 'mutual' is the key. Everything had been shared. With Mimi's *separate* and antagonistic love affair the days of our mutual trust were numbered. Never mind that our thirty-five-year age difference had made it likely from the first that the duration of our time together would be limited, I had foolishly come to take our love for granted. There were to be repeated attempts at a compromise, but in the end, only friendship and mutual respect survived in the ashes of what had been a wonderful relationship.

One of my first reactions to the crisis was to stop drinking. I have always been partial to wine, probably to excess, but fearing that I was relying on it as a prop in my distress, I gave up alcohol altogether. This unexpectedly proved to be no hardship at all. But several years later, when all was over and the need for a prop had passed, I saw no reason to forgo a civilised pleasure and began drinking again. In fact, tutored by friends Chianti and Ray Fernandez, I was until recently brewing my own 'château mangrove' in the forepeak of *Southern Seas II* from grape juice concentrate. I even had a label: Mangrove Creek Wines.

I have bidden a very cursory farewell to Chukotka. This has been partly because of the personal turmoil, but also because neither

Mimi nor I commanded *written* Russian, so we inevitably lost touch with people and events. How then can one make sense of a society in the throes of major transition? Virtually everything we saw in Chukotka has since altered out of all recognition and is still changing. One positive reform, at least on paper, was the 1992 granting of economic independence to the region by the Russian government. Today, it is known as the Chukotka Autonomous Okrug, and is a separate entity to the region of Magadan Oblast, of which it was formerly part. The rich harvest of sea and tundra can now, nominally at least, be sold by the producers for market prices. However, as Novesti's *Northern News* commented, after enumerating Chukotka's potential, 'bureaucrats in Magadan are highly reluctant to be denied a piece of Chukotka's cake'. The Chukotkans are well aware of the issues and who stands in their way.

'Get "Big Brother" off our backs and we will manage very well,' *sovkhoz* chairman Ifkiev had told us. They will in the long run, no doubt. The sad reality is that all the good things — free health, education, affordable, if substandard, housing and a notable absence of greed — are being jettisoned; the baby thrown out with the bathwater. The rigid dictatorship of the privileged, no more adaptable than the dinosaurs, is bringing down with it what was once a great power. We were there in its death throes, and the experience has been neither easy to comprehend nor to describe.

One thing at least has changed for the better in the Bering Sea — despite bureaucratic obstacles from both sides, the border has remained relatively open. There is a story a young hunter told me while we were searching for the lost hunters off Gambell. The decimation of the introduced reindeer on St Lawrence Island, he told me, was not, as officially stated, due to a thaw and freeze that coated the tundra in ice so that the reindeer starved, but to a magic wolf sent by a Siberian shaman.

'When the wolf had killed most of our deer,' he said, 'our hunters saw its giant footprints leading out over the ice back to Siberia.'

Uncannily symbolic, therefore, were forty-four Siberian reindeer that materialised out of the winter darkness at Gambell in

December 1989, having traversed almost 100 kilometres of fast-drifting, spinning and dividing ice floes. It was utterly unprecedented.

'The Siberian shamans have sent the deer to us as a gift to make amends for the great wolf, the ill-wisher once sent to destroy our herds,' the St Lawrence Islanders averred. 'Now we and our Siberian kin are one again.'

eight

The Challenges
of Age

For me the break up with Mimi has been a nodal point. In a general way I can date my return to my Pacific roots and my conscious confrontation with age from the events in Anchorage in 1991 and 1992. Was I too old at seventy-five to pick up the pieces and start again? Of course not! But the processes of realignment were long drawn out and far from simple. Unexpectedly, now that the trauma is over, this 'post-Mimi' era is proving to be as full of personal discovery in its own way as was its predecessor, the 'post-*Ice Bird*' era. The resentment, bitterness and self-pity, that puts me to shame when looked back upon, is happily long passed.

Age had already been a factor to consider when at fifty-five I had set out in *Ice Bird*; more so when I embarked on a series of Antarctic expeditions in *Solo* at sixty-one, an age when most explorers are thinking of retiring. I had never expected to be with another woman when living with Mimi, and certainly was not ready for a fresh commitment. But on looking around without the blinkers I had been wearing, it was apparent that there were other very attractive women around. I had managed to this point to ride roughshod over the conventional limitations of advancing age. No doubt there would be a limit somewhere, but I was damned if I had reached it yet! My father once told me, 'David, learn when to cut your losses, recognise when you have to put a failure behind you and move on.' He was right. No more moaning! My blood was up in the face of this challenge, just as it had been with the broken mast at the start of the first single-handed race.

The upshot was that I left Mimi to think things through in Anchorage, and repaired to Port Townsend in Washington, Curt Ashford's old stamping ground, equipped with a borrowed MGB and intent on finding a small boat of my own. The MGB was a joy to drive, weaving in and out among the massive American cars, but frustrating when the windows of drive-through banks and take-away outlets were all out of reach. I eventually found *Gryphon* tied up against a tumbledown wharf at Port Orchard, a ferry ride from Seattle. She was a 32-foot gaff cutter, a William Atkins 'Eric', built of ferro-cement. In every other respect she followed the tradition of her wooden forebears, so much so that the Port Townsend Wooden Boat School (where Curt had once been chief instructor) rigged her in return for my giving lectures and the Wooden Boat Foundation accommodated her on similar terms. My letter of thanks read in part: 'The well-known feat of changing water into wine has been overshadowed by your foundation changing concrete into wood.'

I had intended to take a complete break from Mimi, but things did not turn out that way. Commuting periodically from Alaska, Mimi insisted on helping physically and financially with the fitting out, so that our ill-starred relationship was artificially kept alive with unrealistic hopes on both sides. Mimi's bisexuality was too central an issue to be denied, but neither of us wanted to expunge our decade-long relationship without a struggle. So the misery was prolonged and my clear-cut sea escape became complicated.

Nevertheless, the compromise which eventually emerged did seem sensible enough at the time. This was for me to sail with our kayaker friends to the September 1992 South Pacific Arts Festival in Rarotonga, the theme of which was to be voyaging, and where traditionally navigated double canoes were to gather. Mimi would join the ship in Hawaii and sail on the Rarotonga leg. Then, after the festival, she would fly back to the United States, while the rest of us continued on to New Zealand. All very neat and practicable, and it would have come about as planned had not fate had a terrible rendezvous in store for us.

I will not dwell on the routines of fitting out *Gryphon* for sea, nor the enjoyable sailing trials off Port Townsend and Seattle, and the cruises among the beautiful San Juans and the Gulf Islands of British Columbia in late 1991/early 1992. This was the first boat I could call even partly my own since *Ice Bird*, and I revelled in being my own master and not beholden to temperamental wealthy sponsors. I learned anew the boon of friendship, and of how helpful and supportive the most casual acquaintances often turn out to be. There was Sally Renée, an old flame of Curt's; Kit Africa, who gave me the hospitality of his treehouse; John 'Kiwi' Ferris, who had sailed with Curt from New Zealand back to the United States and has since bought Curt's schooner *Ishmael*; and Jonathan Raban, the English author and sailor, who was living in Seattle — a very nice man indeed, who had extracted part of *We, the Navigators* in the *The Oxford Book of the Sea*.

Then there were the three veterans of a hair-raising Bering Strait kayak crossing, Arlene and Martin Leonard and Don Logan. They reintroduced me to mountain climbing, as I mentioned in the introduction. In 1992 all three crewed on *Gryphon* to Hawaii, a respectable twenty-one-day passage from Port Townsend to Hilo, from where we cruised on down the Hawaiian chain, snorkelling in the warm water and gorging on paw paw and mangoes.

And a great crew they were too. For me it was a relief not to have to cope with the necessarily inflated companies demanded by expeditions. It is a fault of mine, of which I am only too well aware, that my 'sociability factor' is limited by a recurrent need to switch off communication and withdraw into myself for, though I like people, I am essentially introverted. As a result I have all too often evaded my responsibility by not making the effort to keep in close verbal touch with my team. 'Hands-off' leadership is one thing, but I now realise that I have used this as an excuse for avoiding contact, internalising and dodging meaningful conversations. This fault of character was especially harmful during the Mawson Anniversary Expedition and the Winterover Expedition.

For that matter, I readily seek to escape from my own serious thoughts into the realms of light fiction and am even addicted to the unsociable habit of reading during meals. This is a habit my son shares, so that we always get on very well non-communicating together at sea. I know I am rather too prone to spells of escapism and am still oddly shy at times — I avoid unnecessary confrontations. It has taken a long way into this book for these realisations to surface, no doubt because ingrained reticence, even from myself, is so much a part of my nature.

It was perhaps a symptom of these character traits that I came to enjoy the voyage to Hawaii, largely unaware of the interpersonal tensions that were simmering among the party. These had nothing to do with me nor with the voyage, but dictated that each would shortly go his or her separate way. Happily all have remained my very good friends.

There was time to spare in Hawaii during the middle of 1992 before we embarked for the September Rarotonga conference, and it was well spent, mostly on the idyllic western island of Kauai. We tarried first at the lovely summer anchorage of Hanalei Bay, whence we trekked the wild Na Pali coast as far as the deserted vale of Kalalau, then moved to the less picturesque but better protected Nawiliwili Harbour in the south-east. There I met Donna Goodwin, an attractive and adventurous woman, coincidentally exactly the same age as Mimi.

Now, during the decade of living exclusively with Mimi (I was quite content at the expectation of never sleeping with another woman), certain happenings in the outside world had effectively passed me by, particularly the changes in mores brought about by AIDS. Donna and I were already good friends and trusty companions when she invited me to stay over.

'So what is this condom thing?' I asked, puzzled, for condoms belonged to my distant youth. 'Aren't you on the pill?'

I was enlightened with some asperity.

One new activity Donna introduced me to was outrigger canoe paddling. Our scratch crew of six would launch at sunrise and put out to sea. Once we found our rhythm the canoe would come alive and begin to run — an unforgettable experience of harmony between sweating paddlers and the ocean. Donna also took me hiking through the stupendous Waimea Canyon and down the rugged Na Pali coast to Kalalau by kayak. The month we spent together was a truly magic time.

Kalalau is a lonely mist-wreathed valley, backed by 1200 metres of fluted, crumbly cliff-face, that had once been the scene of high drama. Long ago, the leper Koolau, tricked by the authorities into captivity, had shot and killed a deputy sheriff while escaping and took refuge in Kalalau. The story was romanticised by Jack London in his short story 'Koolau the Leper' but the truth is dramatic enough. Besieged by police and soldiers, Koolau was forced into a trap where the head of the valley was walled in by those unscaleable cliffs I mentioned. Or so it seemed, for Koolau climbed them, where none could follow. He disappeared into the almost one-kilometre-deep Waimea Canyon, where he lived and eventually died in solitary freedom.

Something uncanny, some echo of past events perhaps, seems to linger in Kalalau. Each time we hiked or paddled the sixteen kilometres to camp, a valued possession would unaccountably disappear — my best knife, a locket my daughter Susie had given me — as if the spirits of this special place demanded an offering. But then came the strangest occurrence — a gift to us *from* the sea.

Donna and I had kayaked down the coast to Kalalau and slept in a sea cave on the beach. The next bay beyond the rocky headland was completely isolated and strictly forbidden of access, so we naturally determined to go there. Stripping naked and leaving our clothes behind on Kalalau Beach, we swam round the point and landed easily, the current being with us. However, when we made to return some hours later, the trade wind was blowing strongly, propelling a formidable contrary current. Try as I could, I was unable to make it and repeatedly ended back at our starting point. Donna, who is a much stronger swimmer, could have turned the headland but swam back to keep me company. We stood knee-deep in the surf, wondering what on earth to do. Then something washed up against my leg — a mask and snorkel. I lost no time in donning them and, with their aid, just succeeded in making it round the point to Kalalau. I was stumbling ashore when a freak wave rose up from nowhere, whipped the mask and snorkel off my face and washed them away back out to sea. The sea's gift had done its job; now it was time for it to be taken back into the depths.

Gryphon was provisioned and ready to sail and Mimi had flown in to join Don Logan and me for the passage to Rarotonga when the radio began issuing hurricane warnings. Kauai was directly in the path of the storm, which would be with us within days.* Nawiliwili Harbour is doubly protected by outer and inner breakwaters. Two tiers of slips are mounted on concrete piles, and are not floating. There were upwards of fifty yachts and powerboats in the slips plus a number at moorings or at anchor in the inner or outer harbours or alongside the mangroves in the river.

The eve of the storm found Donna and me busily collecting fallen mangoes from our favourite roadside trees. We reasoned,

---

*This may be as good a place as any to explain the rather confusing nomenclature of tropical storms. East of the International Date Line (e.g. the West Indies, Mexico, Tahiti and the Cooks) they are called *hurricanes*; west of the International Date Line and south of the equator (e.g. Samoa, Fiji and Australia) they are *cyclones*; west of the International Date Line and north of the equator they are *typhoons*, which so cruelly devastate south China and Bangladesh. Many names for exactly the same things.

correctly, that very soon there would be no more mangoes on Kauai. Before retiring we did our best to secure Donna's very substantial house.

Next morning, 11 September 1992, I joined Don and Mimi on *Gryphon* in the marina, where increasingly dire radio warnings of the approaching storm had us putting below or lashing and stowing everything moveable and tripling and anti-chafing our mooring warps. We moored bow out, stern to the expected north-easterly initial blow, in order to keep our mast out of sync with the yachts next door. 'If you have to leave the ship take refuge in the toilet block. It is a solid building,' advised a port official. So we duly stowed our dinghy in the women's section ('Probably safer than the men's,' said Mimi, ever loyal to her feminist principles). This was indeed fortunate. When the solid roof eventually blew off, scattering twenty-centimetre-diameter ferro-cement beams like matchsticks, the women's section, though roofless, was intact, while its male counterpart was choked waist-high with debris.

The following is largely from the log:

10.20. Barometer 1006 kp, light ENE wind, drizzle, heavy surf over outer breakwater. Radio reports Iniki moving north at 17 mph and speeding up; high water spring tide 1500.

12.20. Bar 1001 kp, ENE estimate 40 kts; surge.

14.20. Bar 982, est. 70 kts, visibility limited by driving spray; big ketch ashore.

15.30. Well over 100 knots. The Beneteau 30 in the next slip parted its starboard bow warp and mounted our deck, demolishing gallows, stanchions and bulwarks, all with enormous shocks. We could hear nothing above the thunder of the storm. Mimi gallantly but futilely tried to secure the Beneteau, wading through thigh-deep water over the dock, with a line to her safety harness.

The heavy Beneteau next took out a chain plate and smashed our twenty-centimetre-diameter spruce mast at the deck, broke boom, gaff and fife rail, and at last came free to drift ashore to leeward. Meanwhile, the Columbia 20 on our other side came briefly aboard, broke open against the dock, disintegrated, sank alongside and was seen no more, except for three sheet winches on a fragment of deck that Don dived for later.

15.50. Bar 965, wind remains ENE, violent pressure effects hurt ears, the force in the gusts unbelievable; glimpses of flying debris, trees, masts, whole multihulls flying like birds.

16.00. Bar 945. LULL, EYE OF THE STORM. Three 50-footers are piled up on the dock as well as smaller craft.

16.20. Bar 964 rising. Hurricane wind resumes from opposite quarter, WNW, quickly moving to WSW. Yachts ashore break loose, the Beneteau of ill-omen drifting out of the harbour. We suddenly realise that a drifting Freedom 40 is manned; a figure can be glimpsed juggling with three anchors. When he comes within reach ninety minutes later, Mimi and Don, keeping their footing with utmost difficulty, help him secure.

16.55. Bar 971, hurricane force WSW; tornadoes can be glimpsed passing in the storm as visibility is better with wind off the land. Don, trying to secure a sports-fishing cruiser, found our glass skylight (intact) in the cockpit.

18.00. Bar 985; first lull; severe gusts.

19.40. Bar 1000; wind down.

How strong was the wind? Estimates are hard to come by. Most of the island's instruments were destroyed. The crew of the Coast Guard cutter near us were sheltering ashore, so could not monitor their instruments. Actually, they were fortunate, because a large multihull at anchor in the outer harbour became airborne 800 metres away and ended ten metres up on the cutter's bridge, which it demolished. (This was probably a record for an unmanned flight by a catamaran, we thought.) The most authoritative estimates seem to be a sustained strength of 140 knots with gusts of 160.

How had Donna fared ashore? She and a girlfriend had crouched in an inner room, while the house vibrated wildly and tore to pieces; the roof was ripped off and blown away and the adjacent rooms one by one disintegrated. The two women, miraculously unhurt, crawled from the wreckage that evening to find the fragile carport beside the wrecked house had remained quite intact with the two cars not even scratched.

The island was declared a disaster area; there was no electricity or fresh water and not much food. The army flew in and set up camp, then sat around not knowing quite what to do. Meanwhile, municipal employees toiled tirelessly day and night to restore downed power lines and clear roads, while in a bizarre contrast, the local Harbour Board exerted itself mightily writing out marina bills and devising obstructive rules. But such negative attitudes were very rare. The general atmosphere was of mutual helpfulness, determined optimism and good cheer.

The only one who benefited from the debacle was Don Logan. The wooden ketch *Scotty Ann* was underwater, obviously holed, and pressed down beneath a fifty-ton motor-cruiser. Don offered $1000; the owner asked $2000; they compromised on $1500. The gamble paid off. In due course the little ketch was crane-lifted ashore and very much later was replanked, the seams paid, and remasted. It was a whole ship again.

As we surveyed a foreshore festooned with craft in various states of obliteration, we were relieved to be alive, but still in a state of shock, daunted at the extent of our own ship's damage. Like our own, most of the damaged vessels were victims of inadequately secured neighbours breaking loose and ramming them. Apart from that, there did not seem to be an aluminium mast left standing. We could forget Rarotonga. Regrets were pointless; what remained intact had to be salvaged from the wreckage, options had to be explored and repairs got underway as soon as possible. All of us who were uninsured saw things this way and got on with the job as best we could. The minority of yachtsmen who were insured seemed to react quite differently, so taken up with what to include in their claim forms that, more often than not, they sat around doing little more than agonising. Meanwhile we scavenged and traded. For example, I got a mast section to join to our broken spar in return for two six-packs of Budweiser, and in due course had the mast stepped by an off-duty crane driver for $50, instead of the company rate of $250.*

No sooner did Curt Ashford hear of our predicament than he put his own cruising plans on hold and sailed across from Honolulu in *Rat Bag* to help. Working with an adze, he scarfed the mast by eye, repaired the ravaged deck, and in six months had us once again in commission. I had to keep track of his hours myself, otherwise he would have cheated himself out of even the ludicrously inadequate hourly rate we had agreed on.

'What are friends for?' he said. 'The only thing really worthwhile in life is friendship.'

Curt helped the impulsive Don Logan with *Scotty Ann* too. Indeed, he was so helpful that after Don had inadvertently set fire to the yacht and crunched the forefoot against the dock (hence his nickname 'Mad'), Don and his more responsible partner Maureen cruised successfully to and round New Zealand and round Australia. They were last heard from riding out the cyclone season in Fiji.

Our plans had to be radically changed, of course. The Rarotonga festival would be long over before *Gryphon* could hope to sail again. Unfinished navigational 'business' remained for me in the Santa Cruz Islands, where many aspects of Tevake's legacy had yet to be explored. John Koon, a master mariner under sail and an expert on Micronesian canoes, as well as having useful Polynesian language skills, expressed interest in taking part. The plan was for me to then continue on to Australia — alone. I had not sailed single-handed since *Ice Bird* eighteen years earlier, and the question 'Can I still do it?' was increasingly echoing in my thoughts. Was I too old at seventy-six for such an undertaking?

As for Mimi, her plan was to go back to Alaska to complete various projects, then return to Kauai, and possibly sail with me to the Santa Cruz Islands, before returning again to Kauai, an island

---

*Very welcome funding, to the tune of around $2000, eventually came our way from Federal Disaster Relief. But there was no rebate from full marina dues, regardless of the virtual destruction of the marina itself and its facilities.

that increasingly attracted her. Also in the air was the thought of a final attempt to salvage our relationship, stimulated not a little on Mimi's part, I suspected, by a touch of jealousy over Donna, and the possibly coincidental fact that she had broken up with her lover in Anchorage. There was also the new bond forged through our shared storm ordeal.

Unfortunately, Donna had no patience with light relationships. Hers was an all-or-nothing personality. I was not prepared to put aside all that had been shared through the past decade with Mimi and jettison even a faint chance of achieving some *rapprochement*. Certainly, I had very much in common with Donna. In fact, never in my life had I been so happy as during our time together. But we had been living a 'honeymoon idyll', divorced from the cares and responsibilities of the real world, a time out of mind. I was not ready for absolute commitment — in any case, lonely as I was and desperately missing a feminine companion, our attachment would never be as uncritically all-embracing as it had been with Mimi. I thus contrived to handle the situation with matchless tactlessness and ended up mortally affronting Donna. The spark of hope with Mimi, of course, soon proved illusory.

During the months working on *Gryphon* I became intrigued with the songs, rhythms and spiritual connotations of the Hawaiian hula. The hula *halaus* (groups) dedicated their art, I found, to the woodland goddesses Hiiaka, Capo and Laka. It seems a far cry from dance to voyaging, yet the great myths and legends of the gods and heroes of Polynesia that spanned the whole Pacific Ocean were enshrined in the hula, no less than in the wake of the voyaging canoes. Thus Laka, she/he of the ohia flower (which is named rata in New Zealand) and patroness of surfers, is transformed among the sea-girt Santa Cruz Polynesians into a culture hero called Lata the Navigator. His female helper, Hinora, is kin to Hine-Moana, the Ocean Maid of the New Zealand Maori, where Lata's homologue is the navigator Rata.

With 1993 being the hundredth anniversary of the overthrow of Hawaiian Queen Liliuokalani, there were several historic reenactments (during one of which the Stars and Stripes was officially replaced on government buildings for four days with the flag of the old kingdom — Pearl Harbor fairly boiled with the outrage of the military!). The hula *halaus* naturally played an active part in these pageants. In the century since the deposed and imprisoned queen's farewell ode to her country, the haunting 'Aloha Oe', was banned as a revolutionary song, Hawaiian culture had sunk to its lowest ebb. Now it is reviving, and the traditions exemplified in song and dance are not its least manifestation. An amusing incident during the reenactment was when an onlooker singled me out from among the historic figures, and announced satirically, 'Why, there's Captain Cook.'

It was an exciting moment when the now-healed *Gryphon* spread her wings once more. There had been shakedown cruises to make sure all was well again, but this was the real thing, storming along hard-pressed on a beam reach, logging 150 miles a day, we were set fair for the Santa Cruz Islands. There were three of us in the expedition — Mimi, John Koon and I. With Mimi's *tok pisin* and John's rather 'generic' Polynesian, we would be much better armed with language than Barry and I had been a quarter century before. The visit was particularly timely, because the revised and updated edition of *We, the Navigators* was shortly to be published and there was yet time to add new findings, at least as footnotes.

Back in 1969, when Tevake had navigated *Isbjorn* from Taumako by the feel of the swells, a young navigator named Kaveia had been on board. Today this same Kaveia, now Chief of Taumako, has become the most distinguished traditional navigator in the Solomons. In 1980, Kaveia and four companions built a *te puke* voyaging canoe on Taumako, which he then navigated by traditional means (indeed, he knows no other) 100 miles to Ndeni in the Santa Cruz Islands, 150 more to Santa Ana, then along the whole length of the Solomons chain to Vella Lavella. Here, headwinds forced them to turn back at the Papua New Guinea border and return to

Honiara on Guadalcanal, where his historic vessel today lies rotting under a Public Works Department lean-to.

'Up that stream is where Hinora gave Lata the Navigator the tree to build his *te puke*,' explained Kaveia. 'You see how little water there is in it? So Hinora made a flood to float the canoe down to the sea — *te puke* means "the flood".' He went on to show us the rock where a magic eel had nourished the infant Lata, and the lagoon that Hinora had blocked off in a fit of temper, thus denying haven to the navigator.

We were Kaveia's guests in his sago-thatched house in the village of Tahua, which had so impressed Quiros nearly 400 years earlier that he had called it 'Little Venice' because it stood on an artificial island on the fringing reef, surrounded by water at high tide. Here Kaveia taught us the voyaging stars whenever the clouds broke to reveal the heavens — all too rarely to John's intense frustration, for he had moved ashore to Kaveia's house to be ready for breaks in the overcast sky. In the daytime, Kaveia stood over John's prismatic compass, repeatedly indicating the precise points from which the guiding winds blew. He told us, too, about his 1980 voyage.

'The wind was from *teulu*, south-south-east, from the star *Tepapokau* [Canopus] for much of the way. I "killed" the unfavourable winds "long custom",' he claimed confidently. Kaveia had earlier shown us the little totemic structure behind his house that he used to 'kill' bad winds, though he never explained to us its detailed working. An enviable accomplishment, I thought, and one in full accord with beliefs and traditions that span the Pacific Ocean from Papua New Guinea all the way to far Tahiti.

We made no voyages with Kaveia, who was feeling his age a little, but merely took him on a day-trip to demonstrate *Gryphon*'s paces and to move to a secure anchorage after Kaveia had conveniently 'killed' the heavy weather that had made the narrow entrance hazardous. The haven, Kalua, proved to be a bay encircled by the reef and almost totally enclosed at low tide. Within minutes our helpers had deployed anchors bow and stern, and led lines to coral boulders.

13 September 1993 was a red letter day. We were awakened at dawn by Jeffrey Ali, his pregnant wife and their family. It was low tide so heavy canoes could not cross the fringing reef which had dried out. The woman was in labour and well overdue at the maternity clinic beyond Tahua. We struggled to buoy and cast off our five points of attachment as quickly as possible, but it all needed time. Meanwhile, nature took its course. The baby girl was born in the cockpit, the mother-in-law presiding, and we duly motored up the coast to land mother and child somewhat precariously by canoe. All went well and the baby was named 'Mimi' (the name may become something of a handicap, since '*mimi*' universally in the Pacific means 'pee').

One thing I had come to realise about orally transmitted arts was that, without textbooks, no single person, no matter how eminent, knows everything. Each practitioner selects those techniques he finds most useful. Thus Kaveia, while largely taught by Tevake, uses wind directions more and stars less than his mentor. Neither Tevake nor Kaveia, unlike the culturally similar Tikopia people, made use of the overhead or zenith star for latitude. But the navigators' confidence is perhaps less based on specific techniques as such, than on a synthesis of those they like best, cemented by an extraordinary 'ocean-friendly' outlook. Tikopia is in the Santa Cruz voyaging range — Tevake's — and it was a Tikopian navigator named Rafe who best expressed this confidence to me before ever I met Tevake. Rafe had captained canoes from isolated Tikopia 112 miles to Vanikoro and 110 miles to Vanuatu, and was not being obtuse when he failed altogether to understand a question as to why he could not miss tiny Tikopia on the return.

'I know the way my island is,' he said. 'It is my island. It is where I follow the stars where to go — I cannot miss my island.'

Mimi's special interest during the trip was the role of women at sea and as spiritual personifications of the ocean's *mana* (inner power). The late navigator Drummond Vaia of Pileni had been a contemporary of Tevake. His widow Jocelyn Sale and daughter Joanne had been the core members of his *te puke* crew.

'For women to go to sea was unusual but not unknown,' Jocelyn explained. 'Our sons were away at school, so Joanne helped her father. Families were always preferred as crews. If a stranger was included and a fatal accident occurred, it would be grounds for a blood feud.'

Both women claimed, perhaps over-modestly, to have been just 'deckhands', for this was not the general opinion in the Reef Islands. What is certain is that they could have claimed navigator status had they so wished. There were no social barriers against their sex.

Throughout Polynesia and Micronesia, women's inherent spiritual power is perceived as being linked with the ocean. Both are fruitful; are intimately linked with the moon; and share a sea smell. This spiritual power is interpreted in different ways. A Tongan wife must behave decorously while her husband is beyond the reefs, lest the sea in its anger destroy him. In the Carolines, though navigation was traditionally the gift of mythical heroines, fear of women's magic necessitates their seclusion in special huts on the outrigger platforms. By contrast, two centuries ago, the chieftainess Paintapu was sole navigator of a Kiribati war fleet. All in all, the Santa Cruz Polynesians seem to have been pragmatic about women's role at sea.

With the hurricane season approaching, I left our Santa Cruz friends with real regret.

'David is very like Tevake — and he is very old now. You must never let David sail alone any more, because as he gets weaker he might give himself to the ocean like Tevake did,' said Kaveia on the eve of our departure.

'Don't worry, he will always have people with him,' John reassured him in good faith, unaware of my private plan to go solo.

John flew back to Hawaii from Santa Cruz, Mimi from Honiara. She has since been back to Taumako in *Gryphon*, with a female crew, and has raised funds and built two big *te pukes*. She is successfully enriching the Hawaiian voyaging renaissance with input from the unbroken traditions of Santa Cruz. No mean achievement!

Our separation had been so long a-building that I for one was relieved it was over. Moreover, I was thinking of other things now and had no time to be bothered with the past. Thoughts of the coming solo passage filled me with mixed feelings — trepidation, for I had been relying on younger companions at sea ever since *Ice Bird*, but above all with excited anticipation of the new challenges that lay ahead. There was the question of my roots, too. A wanderer like myself, at home almost everywhere, must nevertheless have some primary anchorage. There were new vistas of engagement with New Zealand, Australia and the South Pacific. In a sense, I was coming home. But it was not a return to the past; rather it was an adventure of fresh discovery.

It was 6.30 a.m. on 12 October 1993 when I wrote in the log, 'Honiara *towards* Coffs Harbour' ('towards' never 'to' — fate should not be so tempted) and started the 10 h.p. single-cylinder Saab diesel, already wearing my safety harness as always when alone. It takes time to get used to the different parameters the sea dictates. Everything is a little more difficult than on land. Cooking, for instance, is complicated by your kitchen lurching sideways and simultaneously bouncing two metres, not to mention leaning over at thirty degrees when pounding to windward. These are average conditions on the open ocean. Nor can you ever relax completely, especially when alone, not even at anchor, for sudden squalls can wrench out the anchor, and the beauty of coral reefs is only matched by their uncompromising hardness. Indeed, one could justifiably paraphrase life in a small boat as being 'nasty, brutish and often scary'. Why then subject oneself to such discomfort and anxiety?

The sequence for me when putting to sea has always remained the same and is intensified both positively and negatively when alone. When first detached from land-based supports I feel lost, jittery, over-anxious. Gradually the realisation dawns that the forgotten phone call or the bank manager's unwelcome letter are no longer significant. You have prepared for the voyage as best you could.

Now it is up to the sea. No matter the falling barometer or the tight isobars on the weather fax, there is little you can do to dodge bad weather in a small yacht. Nor is there very much you can do to materially speed your landfall. The wind calls the tune. You are dependent on the forces of nature and your own resources to a degree rarely experienced in other pursuits of the modern world.

After a time you accept this and become deeply content. As Blondie Hasler once remarked to me: 'You can't keep on being frightened forever; you get used to the feeling and come to ignore it.' Instead, you are uplifted by the awesome splendour of the ocean world and feel at one with the ever-changing sea. There is a sense of kinship with your maritime fellows — the ubiquitous wave-skimming shearwaters (how demeaning to call creatures of such exquisite grace 'mutton birds'); the boobies, frigates, terns and the long-tailed tropic birds called *tevake*; the gannets, penguins and albatrosses of New Zealand's waters; and dolphins and whales, if you are fortunate enough to encounter them.

Once we were well clear of land, the yacht got into her stride over longer swells, so that by noon the next day we were 115 nautical miles from Honiara. At midnight, I spotted a ship, and did not expect to encounter another until the Australian coastal shipping lanes. Not that this absolved me from keeping a lookout at every opportunity, for a freighter can come over the horizon and be upon you in a quarter of an hour. Alone, you can only do your best, cat-napping at night, perforce trusting to your navigation lights and the radar reflector. Going off course inadvertently is less of a problem except near land, for a change of angle over the waves alters the yacht's motion and usually awakens you.

Gryphon lay over on the port tack with one reef tied down and plunged into the head seas. I cooked a hefty meal of rice, sweet potatoes, and fried corned beef in spite of the motion and wolfed it down hungrily. I also ate the last of the paw paws. My taste in food at sea is not necessarily admirable or to be recommended: snacks and candies, so essential for nightwatches and bad weather; stews of corned beef, sweet potatoes (*kumara*) and onions, liberally salted;

fruit in quantity when available (I cannot abide too many green vegetables); lashings of butter; red wine; and, sometimes, when my income permits, rum. I shave regularly too; to shave, even if only with a mugful of water, which suffices for a token wash as well, is for me a matter of morale — even more essential when alone.

The end of the first week found me congratulating myself on good progress and having safely weathered the first of the reefs that stud the Coral Sea. It all seemed too good to last. Indeed it was. At 8 a.m. the next morning in calm weather the throat halyard parted without warning and the mainsail came tumbling grotesquely down, suspended only by the peak of the gaff. With some trepidation and difficulty I scrambled up the ratlines and clung to the mast to retrieve the broken rope's end. I was unable, however, to get at the upper blocks to rethread it, nor was the clumsy long splice I produced while swaying about aloft thin enough to go through. In the end I had to content myself with passing the halyard through the lowermost block, knotting it, leading the tail to a sheet winch, and laboriously winching up the sail. The result was an unseamanlike concoction that at least allowed me to sail and to reef, though to lower the mainsail completely I would have to go aloft again and cut it free. I only hoped there would be no one to see it when the time came.

I had something to prove to myself, that I could overcome this 'age challenge', so we kept on our way, and by 25 October, nearly two weeks out from the start of our journey, *Gryphon* was dipping and curtseying over sparkling seas. I could not but revel in the joy of accomplishment, for the dim sunlit line of Australia was unrolling to starboard. Not far to go now. It was all over bar the shouting. Cirrus clouds spreading from the westward and a falling barometer put an end to this foolish optimism. By midnight we were hove-to in torrential rain, thunder and lightning, and a force 8 northerly gale was blowing. Nevertheless, we came through this gale and a second one reasonably enough, I felt, and eventually reached Coffs Harbour, where, as anticipated, I had to cut free the halyard. Thankfully, there was no one about to see. The 1417-mile trip had taken fifteen days, twenty-one hours.

The Customs officials were a little puzzled at an American flag vessel with a naturalised Australian as crew, but were helpful nevertheless. Barry drove up to meet me and, two weeks later, my fifteen-year-old granddaughter Jacqui sailed with me to their home north of Sydney. On the last leg we anchored for the tide and rowed ashore. 'Now we can get some *proper* food,' said Jacqui. Had I been starving the child, I wondered guiltily. No. Jacqui proceeded to stock up with such 'essentials' as chips, chocolate and ice cream.*

In Coffs Harbour, I had time to reflect on the single-handed experience. So far, so good, I thought. At any rate, Kaveia's dire forebodings had not even begun to enter the picture. I could still handle a boat at sea alone. Thus, I began to turn my thoughts towards making a circuit, a reconnaissance as it were, through the South Pacific to find out if it really was my home territory. I had always believed it was, and the sense that I had earned in some measure a modicum of spiritual kinship with the Polynesian navigators of old was increasingly taking hold.

But in 1994 I was to take up medical practice again, both out of interest and for necessary replenishment of funds. I joined a group practice at Booragul on Lake Macquarie, some 120 kilometres north of Sydney. Lake Macquarie is a picturesque twenty-four-kilometre-long bush-fringed saltwater lake that connects with the ocean via a channel spanned by a swing bridge. The work was enjoyable and my colleagues generously helped me to 'catch up'.

I did my best to maintain proper medical decorum in the practice, but I doubt if I ever really looked the part, nor could I hide the conspicuous navigator's tattoo on my hand, a memento of my voyages with Hipour back in 1969. The design depicts dolphins, a shark-bite pattern (symbolising danger) and birds (guides to land). I have another one in a less conspicuous place, but that is irrelevant.

---

*How time accelerates! The generations fly by like the years used to do. A scant four years ago Jacqui was very much a child. Now, at eighteen, she is not only the mother of a baby boy named Cameron, but has gained distinctions in two subjects in her first year at university. I am very proud of her.

'He doesn't look much like a doctor, does he! And whatever are those funny marks on his hand?' a curious patient asked one of the nurses.

'Why, didn't you know, he really is a *witch doctor*.' The patient, I was told, was suitably impressed.

Once the 1994 cyclone season was over I decided to embark with a crew in *Gryphon* on an exploratory survey of this South Pacific 'territory', visiting New Zealand, Rarotonga, Aitutaki, Suwarrow, the two Samoas and Fiji, thence returning to Newcastle/Lake Macquarie. In Auckland we were guests of the National Maritime Museum, a courtesy they extended on subsequent visits for they apparently regarded me, in the rather tongue-in-cheek words of the curator, as a 'living treasure'. The crew Sally Renée, Lara Passfield and Gordon Lewins, while individually the nicest of people, were not at all at ease with each other. Sally, for instance, was an experienced sailor and friend from Port Townsend, who had flown over from the United States to take part. Unexpectedly, she became proprietorial and managing, especially of me, but also of Lara. Gordon, from Newcastle, a meticulous seaman, was a perfectionist, stereotypically 'Germanic', and could not tolerate the relaxed and happy Lara. The irony was that she was German while he was not. 'Sweetie Pie Captain', began a note Lara wrote me once. I was unwise enough to show it around, and have not been allowed to forget it.

After it was over, I knuckled down to medicine again, and after some false starts, was lucky enough to take over a practice in Hornsby, on the upper north shore of Sydney. The only snag was travelling time, since I was staying either with Barry's family some eighty kilometres north of Sydney, or at Lake Macquarie, forty kilometres further afield.

But I was not destined to remain static for very long, for in 1995 I was invited to give a course of lectures on Indigenous Knowledge and Western Science at Auckland University. The airfare was duly provided, but I spent it all on a new boat (I will explain why in a moment), so I had no choice but to cross to New Zealand by sea.

The dates of the lectures, August and September, dictated that the passage should be made in July — midwinter — a notoriously stormy time of year, but there really was no help for it.

The reason for the purchase of the 27-foot fibreglass cutter *Southern Seas II* was that Mimi, as co-owner of *Gryphon*, was due to take the vessel back to Hawaii for her turn. *Southern Seas II* had been designed and built and extensively cruised by Bruce Walker of Sydney. When asked, I describe the yacht as 'the Walker 27'; *the*, not *a*, since she is the only one. Such is the know-it-all nature of yachtsmen, that the invariable comment is, 'Yes, I know all about them' or 'They are good boats' or something like that. No yachtie worth his/her salt would admit to never having heard of it!

The little yacht was sturdy and roomy and was soon to prove an exceptional seaboat. She was slow, however, and her full lines and modest draft of four feet six inches limited her windward performance against the steep head seas of the open ocean. But her small Bermudan mainsail was much easier reefed and stowed than *Gryphon*'s big gaff sail, and her sizeable roller jib was a boon. Down below, there were only three really usable all-weather bunks, the forepeak being impossible at sea. Two were quarter-berths beneath the sides of the cockpit — long, narrow, low-roofed 'caves' into which one wriggled, with convulsive heaves and contortions. The other was sandwiched behind the table on the starboard side, by which the occupant was insecurely kept in place, and most effectively hindered from getting out, by a canvas lee cloth. The engine was a single cylinder 10 h.p. air-cooled Chinese diesel, a model said to power 25 million Chinese tractors and *sampans*, and which must be the noisiest ever made.

Necessary alterations were largely carried out by Lake Macquarie yachtsman Roger Powell, and by Tim Brokenshire and by Barry. I owe them an enormous debt, for I am the least mechanical of men. A liferaft was provided at a quite ridiculous discount by Kiwi Ferris. An EPIRB emergency locator beacon also came with the yacht. I was determined, after the previous year's experience aboard *Gryphon*, either to sail alone, which I now had confidence in doing, or to choose companions more for their personalities than their seagoing experience.

The first candidate, Jenny Middlemiss, was a thirty-year-old documentary film producer. Her idea was to make a documentary of her introduction to the ocean by an old sailor, illustrated by flashbacks of his life. I liked the idea and suggested calling it 'The Senile Sailor'. *My Maiden Voyage* was judged to be a more suitable title when the project was funded by the Australian Film Commission.*

Jenny was a bundle of energy. She showed absolutely no embarrassment when interviewing people, shoving the camcorder into their faces. The technique worked surprisingly well. After a short time one relaxed completely and forgot the camera was there.

Then there was Mary Moos, who I mentioned in the introduction. At the time we met in 1995 she was handling a fiendishly demanding job as a TV film censor. It had left her overstressed and desperate to spread her wings elsewhere — the sea seemed to meet the need.

Mary's disarmingly innocent look — big eyes framed by high cheek bones from under a dark fringe — effectively concealed her strength of character. Nor was her physical toughness at all obvious. In fact, I had no idea what reserves of strength resided in that slight frame until we dragged ashore in a storm in Rarotonga a year later and she handled heavy anchors well beyond her physical scope.

In retrospect, I believe Mary had decided she was going to sail across the Tasman long before I ever thought of asking her. If she had not, my ludicrous performance on her first venture afloat with me would surely have put her off. On the face of it, nothing could possibly go wrong on a fine afternoon on sheltered Lake Macquarie, yet the first thing to happen was that I ran us aground. I was paying so little attention in those familiar placid waters, that I hardly noticed when the yacht glided gently to a halt. The subsequent manoeuvres — going astern with a roaring motor shattering the

*What has happened to the documentary? The sad and untimely death of Jenny's partner, Graham Chase, grounded the project indefinitely.

Sunday peace, leaning the craft over by suspending the crew over the water on the boom, and so on — were ultimately successful. Fortunately, Mary had had the foresight to bring champagne. Thus fortified, we continued our cruise, not noticing the time. I had neglected to take note of the marina's leading lights, and night vision is hardly my strong point. So nightfall found Mary, clasping a torch in the bows, uttering cries of warning as she directed us through the maze of moored craft that obstructed my ill-chosen line of approach. I hardly expected to see her again after this debacle, but she was more hooked on the ocean crossing than ever.

It was 4 July 1995 when Jenny, Mary and I put to sea on our 1100-mile crossing from Newcastle to the Bay of Islands. A brisk south-west wind sped us on our way over a lumpy sea. Since the North Cape of New Zealand lies due east of Newcastle, this wind was a fair one. The day was fine. The barometer stood at 1002 kp. Everyone was in good spirits. Phenergan and ephedrine were doing their job and no one felt seasick.

Mary had the first nightwatch from 8 p.m. till midnight. The wind had fallen so light that the yacht only marginally self-steered. With a hand on the tiller, Mary encountered for the first time the magic of the soft-breathing ocean under the stars. When Jenny's turn came after midnight, the breeze fell away completely, so that by 1.30 a.m. it was flat calm and, after two ships passed by too close for comfort, I ran the motor for an hour. A light breeze then came up, to strengthen with the sun and hold as a good sailing breeze while the fine midwinter day wore on. This was our first full day at sea and Mary decided to make a special effort in the galley. The occasion was not to pass without drama, for she had not quite grasped how the alcohol stove worked and produced a spectacular blaze. Being a meths fire, it was easily doused with water, and Mary went on to cook a splendid stew.

That evening, spreading sheets of cirrus cloud from the south and west and a fall in the barometer gave promise of evil things to come, and by midnight on the 6th we were experiencing our first force 8 gale. *Southern Seas II* jogged along safely if uncomfortably under staysail alone, steered by the wind vane. The violent motion was too much for Jenny, who had barely got her sea legs. Unfortunately she never did get them, and every time the weather worsened, she was laid low again. During the night the gale blew itself out and the glass rose, though the sea continued to run high. The noon-to-noon run, despite the gale, was ninety-five miles, our best so far.

Even a moderate gale is an alarming experience, and no matter how many I experience, the overwhelming power of an ocean in anger never fails to keep me tense and anxious. Yet neither Jenny nor Mary showed the slightest sign of nervousness. I did have a fright once when Mary seemed to have vanished, until I spotted her sea boots projecting out of a quarter berth into which she had dived head-first like a rabbit down its hole.

As the weather eased a little, Mary and Jenny would sit side by side in the cockpit, securely fastened by their safety harnesses, singing songs from 'The Sound of Music' and, perhaps more appropriately in the circumstances, 'Yellow Submarine' to the dark skimming shearwaters and a black-browed albatross they called 'Alby', who circled in our wake. It was coincidence, of course, but whenever Mary was on watch, the great bird would appear; when she went below he glided away out of sight.

A second short-lived westerly gale ushered out our first week at sea — 640 miles, more than halfway. Over the next three days the barometer plunged down to 974 kp and I dreaded the worst. When it did howl down from the north (force 9 gusting 10), however, the yacht hove-to in relative comfort under her small staysail, and the sharp blow was soon past. By the 16th, five days into the second week, according to the Magellan GPS (no sextant sights were possible through the overcast), land was near. The weather was vile — streaming rain and a northerly force 8 gale. We began peering anxiously through the murk. It was Mary, surprisingly, for her eyesight is nearly as bad as mine, who first shouted 'land' that afternoon. It proved to be the Three Kings Islands we were heading for, and that night Cape Reinga lighthouse winked reassuringly through the gloom. Next afternoon, in continuing gales, we rounded North Cape and laid course for the Bay of Islands.

Not everyone was so lucky. That same day, we learned later, a large multihull en route for Australia broke up in the storm and sank. It must have been very near us, as the crew were taken up by a freighter bound for Newcastle — the reciprocal course to ours.

But we ourselves had seen the last of the bad weather. As we came under the shelter of land and turned south down the coast, Alby the Albatross circled the masthead one more time, then waggled his wings, something he had not done before.

'Goodbye Alby!' called Mary, as he flew away northwards. We never saw him again.

The next day, exactly two weeks after clearing Newcastle breakwater, and some 156 years after my great-grandfather James O'Neill, we ghosted into the bay on a perfect sunny morning.

The Customs at Opua were, as ever, courteous and kindly. That night we dined in style at the waterside restaurant. Then, after two days enjoying shore amenities, we zig-zagged among the islands and past wooded headlands to make fast alongside Curt's rakish schooner *Rat Bag* in Parekura Bay.

'Your boats are getting smaller as you grow older. Come to think of it, you are shrinking too,' Curt remarked with his usual delicacy.

'Why, what kind of boats does David like?' asked Jenny, camera in hand.

'Any kind. When he decides to do something, he uses whatever boat is at hand. "Suck it and see" is his motto. He fixes up some horrible little boat as best he can, and then goes on to do it. Just the opposite to those wealthy dills, the harbour Cape Horners!'

This was getting embarrassing. 'Will's double-ender is still here, I see. Whose is the big yacht?' I enquired.

'German George's. They will both be along to a party tonight, to celebrate your second trip back home in two years.'

After attempting a sustained discussion on such serious topics as the increasing inequality of contemporary New Zealand society, we went to the other extreme that evening: Jenny sang to

German George's guitar; Curt sank into a brandy haze; and all the while the red wine circulated. Suddenly, without a second's warning, George passed out. He had to return to his children on his own boat, so was revived with difficulty and helped down into his dinghy, where he promptly stepped onto the gunwale and flipped it. George and the soaked guitar were retrieved by Will Oldfield, the soberest of the party. He then dried off, changed and eventually rowed back to his boat, mourning his guitar.

A memorable party it had been, but it was a sorry crew nursing hangovers who set sail on the 140-mile leg to Auckland the next morning. We broke our journey for a night at anchor off Kawau Island, though by then normal health was pretty well restored.

The following day we traversed Rangitoto Channel to bring up at Hobson's Wharf, home of the hospitable National Maritime Museum, and in the evening celebrated our voyage at an expensive restaurant overlooking the harbour. We all felt a sense of achievement now that the stormy passage was over, but sadness too, for Mary had to return to her job in Sydney.

'I will be in Rarotonga next year,' I suggested, 'just as soon as the cyclone season is over — say in May. You could get time off to join the ship for a month, couldn't you?' Mary accepted eagerly.

'Who are all those identical young men, all in exactly the same blue suits?' Jenny wondered aloud.

'They are clones, in the uniform of the new business New Zealand,' I explained with distaste, ever nostalgic for our nation's less conformist and more individualistic past.

nine

Koro

Hearing aids! How I detest them! Background noises — traffic, restaurant clatter, wind, party hubbub — are so much clearer than words spoken. If you take them out sweet nothings whispered into your ear are inaudible, so that you answer with an unromantic 'Eh?'. Keep them in and they emit a piercing squeak when someone presses close. Either way, a no-win situation. Baldness! An open invitation to every mosquito to sting your vulnerable bare patch — an affront to your dignity. Yes, indeed, age does have its afflictions, despite brave words about challenges. And yes, I do have negative spells sometimes, losing zest and dwelling only on the downside. But such moods are temporary, the cause not infrequently turning out to be a virus rather than some incipient neurosis, and activity soon brings things back into proper proportion. And there was more than enough to do in Auckland that second half of 1995.

In the first place there were my university lectures at the departments of Maori Studies and Polynesian Studies at Auckland

University. These concerned navigation by natural means and the
unity of vegetable, animal and human systems. I found the lecture
format, where students scribbled conscientiously but asked no
questions, sadly lacking in feedback. Not so the Friday tutorials,
when we all gathered in the university *marae*, a magnificently carved
meeting house, in working groups, and I could really appreciate the
interplay of keen young minds. I was generally accompanied by
Sally Andrew, a wide-ranging maritime journalist who regularly
cruises the Pacific with her partner, Foster Goodfellow.

Before the lecture series had ended Jenny was back, filming
assiduously. One venue was my school's Old Boys dinner, where
I had been dragooned into speaking, ironically, since to my mind
no pupil could have been less distinguished, my only claim to fame
having been the kayak trip home after I left. However, having a
personable young female documentary-maker following me around
certainly aroused a good deal of interest and envy, for Jenny was
bombarded with questions as to our relationship. Thus belatedly,
I made my mark in school after all.

Jenny and I, later joined by her partner, Graham Chase, visited
my 1981–82 Antarctic shipmates Harry and Karen Keys. Later, we
cruised to the Mercury Islands, Great Barrier Island and Mayor
Island in *Southern Seas II*, to film, but Jenny's and Graham's
continual seasickness spoiled the trip. I could not but admire their
dedication in continuing to film when feeling so awful, but it was
becoming clear that the original storyline of a young woman's
introduction to the ocean by an old sea salt was not going well at all.
Despite Jenny's determination and courage, the sea was not really
her place.

I found the time to do some medical locums, both in Auckland
and up-country. The one I enjoyed most was at Waipu in Northland.
Here the nurses were all farmers' wives who hurried off home to do
the milking the moment the surgery closed. I particularly remember
one patient, a massively built farmer, who had sprained his right
shoulder.

'How did you do it?' I asked.

'I was picking up a cow by the tail,' explained the giant.

'Shouldn't you have used *both* hands?'

Then came October 1995 and a very special adventure. *Tohunga tarai waka* (canoe captain) Hekenukumai 'Hec' Busby invited me to join the crew of the *waka hourua* (double-hulled canoe) *Te Aurere* on a star-navigated voyage from Rarotonga to New Zealand, a virtual repeat of my passage in *Rehu Moana* thirty years earlier, but with one important difference: the navigator this time, Jacko Thatcher, had been trained by Hawaiian Nainoa Thompson and by Mau Piailug's son, so was heir to a very ancient tradition indeed, whereas back in 1965 my techniques had been entirely book-learned. Since that time canoe-voyaging had become the fulcrum of a great revival of Polynesian culture: the rituals and taboos associated with canoe-building and voyaging have come to provide a spiritual bridge between modern-day people and the traditions of their forefathers.

Inspired by Mau Piailug and *Hokule'a*, Hec had built *Te Aurere* in his backyard at Doubtless Bay in 1991. With traditional invocations, the permission of Tane, the god of the forest, was sought to cut the two twenty-metre kauri logs for the hulls. Hec explained: 'The logs had to be picked from the western side of a ridge, where the prevailing winter winds gave them a hammering. The side of the tree that faces the south-west winds is heavier, so you use this heavy part for the bottom. I'm a bridge builder by trade and did most of the cutting myself. It doesn't take long with a "Japanese adze" [chainsaw].'

Back in 1992 *Te Aurere* had been scheduled to sail to Rarotonga for the Festival of Pacific Arts, the event that Hurricane Iniki had so brutally prevented us from attending. Mau Piailug was navigator, Hec skipper, and a chase boat was in attendance. The star navigation was spot-on; Rarotonga is a tiny landfall after 1800 miles, and is complicated by having to steer east at least 1000 miles before turning north across the tradewinds. But the *waka hourua* faced a problem unknown in the days of old: a time deadline for the festival. Storms drove *Te Aurere* back so, in a last minute attempt to meet the schedule, it was towed south back into the westerlies by the chase boat. Films of this event were widely misinterpreted. Yachtsmen, who should know better, still refer to it as 'the canoe that was towed to Rarotonga', an undeserved slur on Mau Piailug's brilliant navigation.

We spread our two crab-claw sails outside Rarotonga's Avana reef pass in pouring rain on 9 November 1995, to follow Kupe in sailing 'a little left of the setting sun in early November', just as I had done before. An accompanying New Zealand yacht caught up with us the next day. Some rival canoe skippers (all these far-voyaging *waka* skippers are opinionated individualists, not excepting my friend Hec) have made a red herring out of chase boats, as if to suggest that their presence or absence has anything at all to do with star navigation as such. Their deployment has been mandatory on American-insured vessels ever since *Hokule'a*, sailing unaccompanied, was capsized and a crewman was lost. There is no such insurance requirement elsewhere. *Te Aurere* is rated Category 1 under the strict New Zealand Yachting Federation's offshore rules, and is at least as seaworthy as any other multihull — a good deal more so than most. The 'Japanese Paddler' (outboard), GPS, radio, EPIRB locator beacon and liferafts carried aboard are requirements under this category.

Our ship's company numbered twelve, including Jenny with her camera. There was Hec's niece (or 'daughter' in Maori culture) Theresa, who was one of the most skilled and active of the crew. Jacko was the sole navigator, with me 'theoretically' assisting him, though he was so competent and conscientious that I am afraid I did very little to help. For the whole three weeks that the voyage lasted, Jacko never once went below, simply catnapping on top of the lean-to fabric shelter over the port hull. Since its first voyage to Rarotonga, *Te Aurere* had been to Raiatea, the Marquesas and Hawaii, the last long leg back to Rarotonga having been navigated by Thatcher. Raiatea was once named Havaiki, and it is as 'Hawaiki' that it is recalled as the traditional homeland by the New Zealand Maori. Appropriately enough, it was on the high altar of Taputapuatea on Raiatea that Hec conducted a ceremony to lift the curse that tradition held had been placed on that temple by a Maori *tohunga* (shaman-like priest) 600 years earlier, when two Maori priests had been murdered. He concluded by placing a stone from Aotearoa (New Zealand) on the *marae* as a symbol of peace between the islands.

The crew was a cross-section of Maoridom — builder, farmer, computer programmer, meatworks employee, academic, entrepreneur — while the youngest and one of the most active was a youth of seventeen, who had once been a potential delinquent. Brailing up the crab-claw sails was strenuous work, as was steering. The heavy paddle blade was pushed down deeper to turn the vessel downwind, and the handle depressed and the blade lifted to steer upwind — an ancient steering system common to the great Tahitian and Fijian voyaging canoes and the sailing rafts of Vietnam, China and Peru. I, myself, found the kick of the great paddle nearly lifted me off my feet and soon abandoned my turn to my well-muscled young companions.

Everyone took turns at cooking, though the brunt fell on Theresa. There was a portable gas stove and, apart from bananas (while they lasted) and the fish we caught, the food was much the same as on any yacht voyage. However, the rules of *tapu* and *noa* were strictly enforced. There was a separate bucket for washing ourselves (in seawater) and our clothing, for the body and all that pertains to it is *tapu* or sacred, and one for food preparation and washing up, which are *noa* or secular/profane. A short prayer preceded all meals, after which Hec was brought his portion, then I was brought mine as *koro* or elder, after which the rest of the crew helped themselves. Regular four-hour watches were kept, and the alert company reacted like lightning to their ship's demands. They might not have known many nautical terms, calling dead eyes 'donuts', for instance, but they were about the most competent and willing crew I have ever sailed with.

We drove on under mostly cloudy skies. Hec and the navigator had marked out in segments the rails around the canoe, the more readily to estimate forced deviations from the course line. The time it took to pass foam patches was carefully noted, for this indicated our speed, which varied greatly, depending on the strength of the wind. In the rare intervals when much of the night sky was clear, the height above the horizon of star pairs like the Pointers to the Southern Cross was estimated by eye to gauge our latitude. Only at the very end of the voyage, beyond North Cape, would the whole Southern Cross constellation always remain above the horizon. Two fronts bringing wind changes under overcast skies did nothing to help Jacko's calculations, but he remained supremely confident.

A factor that could have complicated things was Hec's broadcasts to Maori schools, which required that our true positions from Hec's GPS be given to Kerikeri Radio. Thus Hec and Hotu Kerr, the radio operator, knew our actual positions, and no one else. I asked Jacko after the voyage if he had ever accidentally overheard these reports. 'Twice I did, but it only confirmed where I knew we were anyway,' he said. 'Of course, I couldn't help being heartened by the confirmation, but it did not affect my navigation in any way.'

As the voyage progressed it grew steadily colder and the fish became more plentiful. By the beginning of the third week our daily saltwater baths were becoming rather an ordeal. On the plus side for me, in a repeat of the *Rehu Moana* experience, the strenuous contortions needed to get in and out of my sleeping stretcher effectively 'oiled my hinges' and quite banished the aches and pains with which my ageing joints were beginning to be afflicted. By this time the crew were busy practicing a spirited *haka*, for people would soon be gathering at Doubtless Bay to greet our arrival. Only Theresa worried me a little. Her initial seasickness seemed to be recurring in the calmest weather. It is no tribute to my medical acumen that I never even thought of the obvious — that she was pregnant!

Nineteen days out from Rarotonga, a tense Jacko watched the sun setting in the south-west. We all joined him. Would the sun descend onto an unbroken sea horizon, or what? As it transpired, for the first time in weeks the horizon was not unbroken and the setting sun silhouetted the distant hump of North Cape.

Two days later, shortly after dawn on 30 November and twenty-one days from the Avana reef pass, we anchored just outside the break of the surf at Doubtless Bay. Ferried ashore, we stood ankle-deep in the surf waiting for the elders to assemble ashore. We waved to our friends, but could not yet join them, for we were still 'sea people' and strangers to the land. My friend Fran Gosnell was there, along with Graham Chase, and Sally Andrew and Foster Goodfellow in their yacht *Fellowship*. Then Hec stepped forward and laid down his *taiaha* (traditional weapon) on the sand. A chieftainess chanted the challenge. Our crew roared out and stamped the *haka*, foam splashing around our feet. We were home.

Only Maori radio reported *Te Aurere*'s arrival after 8000 miles of Pacific voyaging without instruments. The general public of New Zealand remain ignorant of her feat, and indeed, of the extraordinary renaissance of traditional voyaging that is so swelling the hearts of Maoris and Islanders alike. *Te Aurere* in the common view remains 'the canoe that was towed'.

After my return in the *waka* from Rarotonga and more filming with Jenny, *Southern Seas II* was 'put to bed' for several months while I looked after an Auckland medical practice. It was at Fran's brother's birthday party that I encountered Robyn Stewart. I was immediately drawn to her — looks, personality, style, everything! Of course, I invited her to go sailing (a kind of maritime 'come look at my etchings').

Robyn was then living at Waiwera by a picturesque estuary, which unfortunately dries out. However, within walking distance is another estuary, the Puhoi. It too is very shallow, though deep enough for *Southern Seas II* at high tide, but whether we could remain afloat at low water was another matter entirely.

Reconnaissance showed that there was one mooring marginally deep enough, provided our anchors and warps could hold us in position against racing tides and unpredictable crosswinds. We tried, and the result was a shambles.

At first we thought we had brought it off. As Robyn's little red MGB turned the corner we breathed a sigh of relief to see the mast still standing upright. A moment later, as we watched, it slowly leaned over and kept going right to a 65-degree angle. We could not help laughing, despite the hours of bailing out muddy water that we knew would necessarily follow. Altered mooring arrangements should have done the trick, but didn't. Once the tide even swept us helplessly into a macracarpa tree, entangling the mast and rigging, from which we had to be ignominiously rescued by the park keeper on his outboard. This was the last straw. We turned tail, abandoned Puhoi, and returned to Auckland and the National Maritime Museum.

Goodness knows why Robyn agreed to sail with me after that, but the gallant lady agreed to a plan to leave New Zealand in April after the cyclone season, and visit the Cooks, French Polynesia, Samoa and Tonga, returning to New Zealand in November, just one year after *Te Aurere*. Mary would fly over from Sydney and spend a month on the ship in Cook Islands waters — all the holiday time her job would allow. One object of the trip would be to spend September at the Festival of Pacific Arts in Samoa, where artist Robyn could not but be inspired.

Robyn is a potter; 'artist in clay' is perhaps a better term, for she handcrafts her shapes without benefit of wheel and often fires in the ancient way with cow dung. Her profession has seen her work with potters in Lombok, India and Zimbabwe. She had been ecstatic when I met her because one of her bowls had just been presented by the New Zealand Governor-General, Dame Catherine Tizard, as a gift from the nation to the visiting Nelson Mandela. I was gradually to realise that her art made manifest some essence of the ancient star-paths that I had long approached from an altogether different, more pedestrian angle. I had in a sense for a long time been 'living the raw material' of the age-old arts that her genius transmuted into powerful symbolism. We were complementary in a very deep sense, for her standing stones, anchor stones and 'shapes on the wind' evoked the epic past of the Polynesian far-voyagers with far more emotional impact than had all my own researches.

Singularly unpleasant weather accompanied our departure from Auckland on 18 April 1996; an easterly headwind, that failed to abate as forecast, and unheard-of fog in the Colville Channel, upon which all the world's freighters seemed to be converging. Westerlies followed soon enough, but were uncomfortably strong. It was the shock of the sea crashing against the hull that catapulted Robyn across the cabin, to crash headfirst into the bulkhead.

'Have you broken the GPS?' I called anxiously — me, all heart!

'You are NOT,' she began with enormous restraint, 'a Sweetie-Pie Captain ANY MORE! No, I didn't break it, only my head!'

I was horrified to see that she had sustained a whopping great bruise and a black eye, which had still not faded when we reached Rarotonga three weeks later.

I did not expect to be forgiven, but fortunately Robyn herself blotted her copybook shortly thereafter, so my offence could more easily be lived down. 'Lipstick in the loo' we called the incident — Robyn's lipstick had dropped into the toilet bowl, where it effectively blocked the outlet pipe and defied all attempts to remove it. Not many women would have cheerfully put up with a bucket or the rail. But Robyn did, for the next three months, until we got to a plumber in Samoa (more urgent problems in Rarotonga put it out of mind, and Tahiti was impossibly expensive).

Despite the 'Sweetie Pie Captain' contretemps, the voyage was going well with 100-plus-mile daily runs until into the third week, when there was less than 150 miles to go. Then, in place of the trades, strong headwinds from the north stopped us in our tracks. We tacked back and forth, the log recording such depressing daily runs as 'ten miles made good on course' or 'lost fifteen miles', so that three days later we still had 150 miles to cover. I was frustrated, fretful and impatient. Robyn, far more sensibly, was simply enjoying the ocean: the first *tevake* flapped by, trailing its long red tailfeather; there were bluebottles, flying fish, spectacular sunsets.

We were twenty-four days out from Auckland when at last we motored with the dawn into Avatiu Harbour, Rarotonga, and the debacle that followed quite eclipsed anything that had gone before. I was dead tired after a night hove-to awaiting daylight and the light was still poor. But nothing could excuse my abrogation of elementary seamanship. We had been allotted, via VHF radio, a berth against the sea wall, cramped it is true, but adequate. I still cannot understand my coming in much too fast, so that the loose gear linkage that failed to engage reverse was only the last straw. The yacht brought up violently against a piling and the bobstay fitting was torn off the bowsprit and part of the gunwale was ripped away.

Here was a welding job at least. In true South Sea Islands fashion, everyone was helpful; no one rubbed salt into the wound by commenting on my idiocy. It was only weeks later, after the damage had at last been repaired, that my friend Bobby Moeka'a told me how the whole community had been laughing at the 'great navigator who had tried to move the island with his bowsprit'.

With the help of old island hand Peter Nelson, repairs were effected within a week. I had already planned to leave the exposed commercial harbour of Avatiu for the shallow Avana anchorage in picturesque Ngatangiia Lagoon, the traditional owner having given his permission. This lagoon was the legendary staging post of the migration canoes from 'Hawaiki' (probably Raiatea) to New Zealand.

Then, on the eve of our move, a rare north-west gale swept the exposed commercial harbour, pounding us against the sea wall, breaking the bobstay fitting again and tearing away strips of gunwale. The next morning we belatedly motored round into the lagoon to look for a deepwater niche, much as we had done at Puhoi, and to dismantle everything for time-consuming welding ashore — a long-term project. This was particularly unfortunate because Robyn was off back to New Zealand to complete the sale of her house and Mary was due in Rarotonga for a month's cruising which, in the event, was spent making repairs in Avana anchorage. Mary accepted the necessity with good grace, and a land-based island holiday took the place of the promised cruise.

Not that there wasn't any excitement before *Southern Seas II* was securely moored. A fresh gale, an easterly one this time, sent seas bursting over the fringing reef and pouring out of Avana reef pass, close inside of which we were anchored, like a wild river. It was first light when our two anchors suddenly let go and we began bumping the shingle, miraculously missing the moored fishing boats. While I held us off with the motor, Mary struggled with a cat's cradle of intertwined anchors, a task that should have been far beyond her strength, but that with sheer guts she managed. We re-anchored securely, but it was some days before we could escape the torrent and come alongside in Avana Creek, where we could begin repairs.

The lagoon was familiar to me as our point of departure in *Te Aurere* the previous spring. The two Cook Islands voyaging canoes moored there now are of contrasting types. *Takitumu* is a *kalia*, a type introduced into Tonga and Samoa from Fiji at about the time of Captain Cook, which changes ends instead of tacking, thus gaining manoeuvrability and windward performance at the expense of carrying capacity. *Te Au O Tonga* (Mist from the South) is a Tahitian-type *tipairua* or travelling canoe, a double-hulled claw-sailed tacking vessel like *Te Aurere*. It was very possibly this type that colonised New Zealand.

Mary and I did all the tourist things in the intervals of repair work, and were family guests at the ceremony in which my cousin George Cowan was awarded an MBE. I gave a slide presentation at the crowded library museum, and then Mary's holiday was over and Robyn was back.

Robyn and I hoisted sail for Tahiti on 5 July, and the 14th found us nosing at dusk into Papeete Lagoon. We let go our bow anchor, then rowed a stern warp ashore in *Peanut*, our tiny red inflatable. I was eager to renew old friendships. After the *Hokule'a* voyage, I had stayed with Denise Valantin-Russell and her partner, before

National Geographic lured me unwillingly back
Denise is so well known that you only hav
'Chez Denise' to be dropped at her door. And
gave us! Denise is a singer and painter, and above a
unique style, even more flamboyant in her sixties than
twenty years earlier. Her personality quite overshadowed the ot
guest, the quiet and unassuming Princess Narcisse Pomare, heir to
the Tahitian throne. Tahitian lunches tend to be all-day affairs, and
this happy reunion was no exception.

Opunohu Bay, Moorea, is often claimed to be the most beautiful
spot on earth. Here we anchored in idyllic surroundings for ten days,
spending time with another old friend, Jean Shelsher, an artist who
lives at the head of the valley. Then came a long-awaited meeting
with Francis Cowan. He had once accompanied Eric de Bisschop on
the bamboo raft *Tahiti Nui* in his attempt to prove the opposite to
Kon-Tiki, and had almost made it from Tahiti to South America
before foundering. Since then he had constructed several deep-sea
canoe replicas with scrupulous attention to historical accuracy,
notably the *Hawaiki Nui* voyage from Tahiti to New Zealand.

'Yes, David, we are cousins, since we are both descended from
that Mary O'Neill from Mauke in the Cooks, who married a Cowan.
George, in Rarotonga, is too, of course,' he said. Francis has not
been well of late, but is still planning canoe voyages. When we dined
with him and his French wife Chantelle, I was interested to see that
they followed Tahitian custom in only eating *after* their guests —
a custom that Curt Ashford had long ago adopted. One new
acquaintance, Hinano, *'une chose de Gauguin'* in Denise's words, had
been picked out by her grandfather for her sensitivity to the spirits
of the *marae*, where he taught her ancient spiritual lore.

Raiatea, the legendary 'Hawaiki', was the next stop and our last
in French Polynesia. We delighted in the sleepy little capital town
of Uturoa. There is something very happy about the amalgam of
French and Polynesian culture, we thought, even if the same cannot
be said about France's heavy-handed colonial rule. We were awed by
the great Polynesian religious centre of Taputapuatea, where Hec

by had removed the ancient curse, though less impressed by the
ery deep water at the nearby anchorage. It was off Taputapuatea
with all our chain out that the windlass handle snapped. Robyn,
who had strained her back hauling up anchors, had by then firmly
laid down the law and meant it when she said, 'No more anchors
for me — NEVER!' Some husky Italians manning a charter boat
saved the day and hauled up the heavy chain and anchor for us.
The following day in Uturoa, our respective US$1000 bonds were
refunded and we said goodbye to those beautiful islands and laid
course for uninhabited Suwarrow in the northern Cooks.

The 750-mile passage to Suwarrow was a slow one in light airs,
so that it was ten days before we rounded the point of the 300-
metre-long main island in a rain squall to find no fewer than eight
yachts at anchor. On my previous visit in *Gryphon* there had been
only one.

Back in 1942 a hurricane had devastated Suwarrow, washing
away a large section of land from the islands fringing the nineteen-
kilometre-wide lagoon. From that time the atoll was for some
years the abode of the late hermit Tom Neale and, more recently,
numbers of caretaker families sent by the Cook Islands government.

The caretaker family encountered this time was different from
that in residence on our previous visit in *Gryphon*, but equally
hospitable and friendly. They took us in their outboard to Turtle
Island for coconut crabs and shared with us their fish and roast
frigate birds. A fellow yachtsman rewired our solar panel, thus
solving a longstanding battery problem. We swam, albeit cautiously,
in view of the local population of reef sharks, which were reputedly
harmless, and the occasional tiger shark, which was not.

A tiger shark had been responsible for the withdrawal of the last
caretaker. No one but a Polynesian would dare argue with a tiger
shark over the ownership of a fish impaled on his spear, but the old
Cook Islander had not only announced firmly, 'It is *my* fish,' but had
gone on to punch the tiger shark on the nose, whereupon it bit him
on the leg and he was evacuated to a hospital in Rarotonga, where
he eventually recovered.

All too soon we dragged ourselves away from this idyllic spot (bar the sharks) to attend the Festival of Pacific Arts at Apia in Samoa. Two hundred dancers, singers, musicians and artisans from twenty-one Pacific territories were taking part. I had thought I knew the South Seas backwards, but I now realised I had barely scratched the surface of its rich and varied cultures. I was amazed at the variety and vitality of the arts displayed. At the Aotearoa *marae* Robyn encountered no fewer than three Maori potters she had trained, while I was happy to meet again with the heavily tattooed Te Atu Rangi from *Te Aurere*, and to observe with amusement how he proudly showed off his magnificently decorated body to entranced teenagers. The financially strapped Cooks were unable to send their justly famous dancers, but the great *tipairua*, *Te Au O Tonga*, under joint command of my friend Piau and Sir Tom (Papa Tom) Davis, came in after a fast five-day sail from Aitutaki. The newly launched *alia* (Samoan double canoe), *Folauga O Samoa* (Navigations of Samoa) from American Samoa, came in soon afterwards on her maiden voyage. Before long, spacious Apia Harbour was host to seventy-five visiting yachts, that all had to be periodically repositioned to make room for paddling and rowing races.

There was so much happening that one could not see it all. I am left with an overwhelming impression of colour and dynamic spectacle. Surprisingly, not everyone was so impressed. The Papua New Guinea and Solomon Islands dancers had the distinction of arousing the ire of some fundamentalist Samoan Christians, who took violent objection to such 'pagan abominations' as penis gourds and topless women. But the narrow-minded minority failed to mar the overwhelming success of the great festival.

In a welcome break from the hurly burly at Apia, our friends Samoan artist Fatu Feu'u and his actress wife Bridget, with their two hyper-bright little boys, invited us to stay in the *fales* (traditional Samoan house) of a Samoan artist community on the windward coast of Upolu. Refreshed by this breathing space, we returned to Apia, Robyn to revel in the rich variety of the events, while I was co-opted by Hekenukumai Busby and Papa Tom Davis

into the Aotearoa and Cook Islands delegations for a poorly
organised navigational symposium. It would have been a total
mess, I wrote to my yachting journalist friend Sally Andrew, since
it mostly consisted of films of *Hokule'a*, that were of general
interest but irrelevant to star navigation, were it not for the last-
minute discovery of a Polowat delegation that included the
distinguished navigator-chief Manipy and his navigator 'son'
Sosthenes Emwalu. It was a delight to encounter the old pirate
again, who seemed unchanged, and as much in command of the
situation as ever. The last I heard he was back at sea again.

'How is Barry?' he enquired through the English-speaking
Sosthenes, and recalled the young man's turtle-catching expedition
in *Isbjorn*.

'Would you contribute to the symposium?' I asked eagerly
through Sosthenes.

Manipy thought for a while, then: 'We are old friends, so tell me,
if I send my son to explain about "ceremonial navigation", are these
people worthy of learning our secrets?'

'Yes, there are navigators from Aotearoa, Rarotonga, Tahiti Nui
and Hawaii, and they are fully worthy of your trust and deserve to
learn.'

'Very well then.'

Sosthenes's presentation, I felt, made the whole symposium
worthwhile.

'Because we don't have schools for apprentices, you live with your
father to acquire those skills. These take years of apprenticeship.
When my brother went to school in Hawaii I decided to stay on
Polowat and learn the traditional way. What I learnt from my father,
I taught my brother, and what he learned from outside, he taught
me,' he told the audience.

The old ways had been nearly lost to a whole generation, he
explained, when dangerous motor boats largely replaced canoes
and the churches forbade the teaching of 'ceremonial navigation'.
Now it was all coming back again. The Catholics, though not the
Protestants, had relented; two big voyaging canoes were under

construction; and traditional initiation ceremonies, banned by the churches for forty years, were currently being conducted on at least three islands. Sosthenes outlined some of the many-sided skills a trained navigator must master.

'We know the best weather before the overseas forecast. We know how to build canoes and how to fix them when they capsize. Other people just call "Mayday!" We learn housebuilding, because many of the islands we travel to are uninhabited. We know martial arts [*pwang*]; we know medicine to help us at sea. Fourteen different stars are used for each month, and waves and wind are used to indicate the direction where land lies. We know every island in our training. We look at the islands known in relation to other islands.'

So much I already knew, indeed, had written about exhaustively. But then Sosthenes went on to speak of spiritual aids to the seafarer. That these should be spoken of publicly, seemed to me to reveal a self-confidence which was quite new.

'The conch shell can call the Spirit of Navigation to put the canoe back in the right direction. In bad weather some navigators can call upon the thunder to break up the clouds. I know the chants but I am afraid to call the thunder down. Chants are also used for ensuring a safe journey; chants for leaving an island when the crew has done "something terrible"; chants for going in the right direction. All the crew wear magic pendants.'

When the festival was over and Robyn and I put to sea again, we had been so long at anchor that we seemed to have forgotten what sailing was like. But our next passage was a short one of a week's duration to the northern Tongan island of Vava'u. Short as it was, the trip gave scope for the sheet winches to 'freeze up' and for dirty diesel fuel to lead to an ignominious tow to a mooring off the town of Neiafu.

Vava'u is a yachtsman's paradise — lovely secluded anchorages everywhere. Helpful people who I had met at various times and places (the world of cruising yachting is a small one) repaired our winches and overhauled the motor without charge. For a sailing holiday Vava'u ranks with the Virgin Islands and Fiji's Yasawas, but is equally dislocated from place and people. Tonga here is, to some extent, a picturesque backdrop.

On the other hand, Nukualofa, the Tongan capital on Tongatapu, which we reached after an overnight passage and a weary night hove-to waiting for daylight, is a vital centre, if physically less attractive. The fact that it rained and stormed incessantly throughout our stay might help account for a rather jaundiced view, in spite of our visit being enriched by the hospitality of an old friend from my Canberra days, Noble Ulu Fusitu‘a, then Speaker of Parliament. Together we recalled the sunny hours that Barry and I had spent here so long ago. It was hard to credit that these rainswept streets were on the same island.

I will gloss over our return to New Zealand, to the Bay of Islands again, for the reader will by now be sick of voyages. Suffice it to say that we had reached that fateful distance of 150 miles to go in very good time, when strong southerlies stopped us, just as the northerlies had before Rarotonga, so that the passage of little more than 1000 miles took all of seventeen days.

My irritation at the frustratingly slow trip was eased by time spent with our Bay of Islands friends, before the last 140-mile leg to Auckland. We moored up at the National Maritime Museum on 13 November 1996. Soon afterwards I installed *Southern Seas II* in a mud berth behind a friend's house at Herald Island, where I began writing this book. The little ship had acquitted herself wonderfully well. Since leaving Australia two years before, she had weathered many gales and covered no less than 5500 miles of open ocean.

This latest Pacific Islands circuit with all its misadventures and fun had been completed by the end of 1996. 16 September 1997 was my eightieth birthday, which friends insisted on 'commiserating' with a barbecue. A good deal has happened since, not bold projects but, in the personal world of family and friends, deeply rewarding nonetheless.

Hearing that my daughter Susie, now living in the Spanish Balearic island of Ibiza, had given birth to a son, I flew to Spain in early 1997 to make the acquaintance of my new grandson, Dylan David, a snub-nosed little creature of great charm.

Equally significant for such a far-flung family as mine was the news that my eldest daughter Anna, a decade widowed and newly appointed to the European Commission, was entitled to a free trip to visit her nearest relative — me. Of course, her employers never imagined her next of kin to be so far away, but to their credit they honoured their commitment. So Anna came to New Zealand in December 1997, after which we both spent Christmas with Barry's family in Australia.

January 1998 found me unexpectedly in Antarctica as a guest lecturer aboard a Russian icebreaker. What a contrast to earlier trips! Aurora Travel, Everest climber Greg Mortimer's company, had chartered the 13 000-ton *Kapitan Khlebnikov* for a voyage to the Australian Antarctic sector. Familiar territory this from the Winterover Expedition — Larsemann Hills (now with Chinese, Australian and mothballed Russian bases), and the Mawson and Davis bases. As our helicopter descended into Winterover Bay memories came flooding back. Every rock and gully recalled its own story of *Explorer* and her crew, all silent now except for ghosts. After our return *Australian Geographic* magazine named me their 1998 'Adventurer of the Year'.

In the course of my visit to Susie and Dylan in Ibiza a crazy idea had begun to surface, so impractical as immediately to be suppressed. To sail to Spain in *Southern Seas II* would take ages; she was so small and slow, and besides I was beginning to need more comfort. There was no way I could afford to buy a larger yacht and I was much too old and not skilful enough to build one. Was there perhaps another way it could be done?

Only after living several months on Herald Island did I appreciate its real quality. It was a place, I found, where old sailors and shipwrights of every description had washed up among the mangroves and taken root. Suddenly my fanciful idea began to take shape.

If a partly completed ferro-cement hull became available, perhaps I could employ retired experts to help me finish it?

That, as it turned out, is exactly what happened. *Taniwha*, named after the mythical Maori water monster, is a monster indeed, forty-three-feet-long and weighing twenty tons. Trucking her up from Taranaki was itself a saga. She was propped up in a steel cradle in a field near Herald Island. Knowledgeable people joined the 'construction team' — Ken Moss, Mike Thomas, Alan Stevenson, Frank Brough, Richard Davis, the late Brian Barrett; a near endless list, some ludicrously underpaid, others volunteers. I was ensconced, meanwhile, in hospitable Ros Demas's garage, which I shared with her Mini. ('Something nasty in the woodshed,' said Ros.) Tim Brokenshire, my rock-climbing friend from Sydney, bought *Southern Seas II* and sailed her back to Australia. The little ship took with her some part of Mary, Jenny, Robyn and me.

The construction of *Taniwha* became something of a community project around Herald Island, where seafaring people, too numerous to mention individually, contributed labour and materials to her completion far beyond any market criteria.

The 60 h.p. Ford diesel engine predated *Taniwha* herself, having been marinised from some long-forgotten farm tractor and subsequently, in 1971, salvaged from a wrecked yacht and reconditioned. It ran perfectly. The steering assembly, too, was a survivor, having floated away from Frank Brough's son Wayne's catamaran when it was lost on Rakino. The compass had a particularly honourable pedigree. A gift from Sir Peter Blake, it had served Team New Zealand at the 1995 America's Cup in San Diego.

A controversial feature of *Taniwha* was her Chinese junk rig. Despite multiple disasters I am more than ever 'sold on' this venerable system, with its instant 'Venetian blind' reefing, easy tacking and fair performance even to windward. The downside is that it depends on the correct functioning of innumerable lines. The main and foresail sheets alone each measured sixty-five metres, and a plethora of lazy jacks, yard hauls and parrel lines each had its essential role. Break or misplace even one of them and utter chaos ensues. Equally vital were the full length battens. Ours were five-centimetre-diameter bamboo, which served well for a similar sail on Keith Levy's *Shoestring*, but proved hopelessly inadequate for our vastly heavier twenty-ton craft with its enormous momentum-induced stresses. The steel bracing beneath the deck that supported our unstayed masts was an unqualified success and had nothing to do with the subsequent failure of the black poplar foremast — light and flexible but, we were to find, about as strong as cardboard.

On 19 February 1999 a *karakia* was chanted and Robyn broke the traditional bottle of champagne over the bow as the travel lift lowered *Taniwha* into the water at Westpark Marina. With Gary Russell, we motored to Robert Purchas's wharf on Herald Island, and after an expensive gearbox debacle, began setting up the rig. John Channings had sailed his junk-rigged 26-footer *Liu Shueng* to Alaska and back, but his friend John Thomson now owned her and sailed with commercial fisherman Wally Langdon. The first two put the complex rig together expertly, and sailing trials in Hauraki Gulf went well. I was impatient to be gone (my failing, as we have seen), so we could have done with more trials when we cleared Customs and put to sea from the National Maritime Museum on 9 May. The crew comprised Wally Langdon, John Thomson and myself.

High hopes and light hearts set the tone as we raced along under full sail. All this ended abruptly at 1900 hours off Bream Tail, when a north-west squall snapped the foremast clean off one metre above the deck. What a wonderful crew! The wreckage was retrieved and both agreed that the word 'dismasting' was taboo. We had only experienced 'a little bit of mast trouble'. So we motor-sailed to Opua in the Bay of Islands, where we tied up at the Customs wharf twenty-four hours after leaving Auckland.

The mast stump was extracted and a very much shortened foremast stepped from square-rigger R. Tucker Thompson's main yard. John Channings helped us rig a lighter and smaller foresail, which was to last out the trip well enough but was too small to be of much use. On 13 May we sailed again. By now the weather had broken, so that I was bounced out of my bunk, grazing my forehead and breaking my glasses. By morning we were off North Cape wrestling with an annoying chain reaction of leaking stern gland and blocked bilge pump, when it was dwarfed by a far more serious crisis. The fifty-two-year-old John suffered a coronary heart attack. The agonising pain, clammy pallor and thready pulse were unmistakable. Northland Radio responded magnificently to our call on VHF radio. A sports-fishing boat came out for John, the nearest harbour being barred to our near seven-foot draft. He was rushed to hospital in Kaitaia and subsequently flown to Green Lane, Auckland. Here angioplasty (dilating the coronary arteries) was successfully performed. Meanwhile, *Taniwha* wallowed back to Opua again, her depleted crew considerably shaken by their experience.

It was now 15 May. Friends from Auckland and Ken McAlpine from the yacht *Myschief* rallied round, but it was not until 3 June — full winter — that we were able to set out again. The staunch Wally, this time accompanied by his wife Kay, and myself made up the crew. North-west headwinds now became our portion. It was very rough and soon the bamboo battens began breaking quicker than we could replace them. Neither would the windvane self-steering work properly with the tiny foresail, and weary hours at the exposed steering position exhausted us all.

My eighty-one-year-old eyesight seemed to be deteriorating alarmingly, so much so that I could barely make out the Southern Cross itself one night. 'The stars are going out one by one,' I thought gloomily, feeling very sorry for myself. However, the next night the haze I hadn't noticed had cleared away and the stars were back as bright as ever. I still had a little time to go after all!

Eleven days out on 14 June and still no more than 500 miles from Opua, and 700 from Australia, we hove-to under three mainsail panels before a savage 50-plus-knot gale. The seas, while not enormous, were steep and breaking heavily. The next day we gloomily surveyed the damage. Every single batten had broken or gone overboard; topping lifts and yard hauls were hopelessly snarled; the stern rail with its sheet attachments had been bodily wrenched away; the self-steering paddle had gone; a wave had stove-in the dinghy; the VHF radio was dead. Two days of risky and vertiginous attempts to fix the rig finally convinced even the tireless Wally that it was irreparable at sea.

Strong north-west winds continued blasting into our teeth, as indeed we should have expected, this being the prevailing midwinter direction. There was no way we could patch up the rig well enough to make headway against such winds, but we could run before them. There was no need for discussion. Back to New Zealand it would have to be. On 17 June, after two weeks at sea, we headed back home. The 21st found us coasting in the shadows of Cape Reinga and North Cape.

Fuel was now very short, but if the north-west wind held there would be no difficulty in reaching Mangonui or even Opua. However, the wind did not hold. Instead, an unseasonable south-east gale stopped us dead in our tracks and drove us relentlessly back out to sea until we were 130 miles north-west of New Zealand. How we once would have welcomed this fair wind to Australia! But what to do now? Every day we were being driven fifteen to twenty miles further offshore. Our damaged sails could not serve us and our fuel was almost gone. The VHF radio was out of action.

Our solution on 25 June was to activate the EPIRB emergency beacon. Kay and Wally prepared a notice while we waited. It read:

TANIWHA NZ 502
NEED FUEL
RADIO U.S.
JURY RIG

At noon we heard the beat of a helicopter's rotors. It circled while the pilot read our notice, then he spoke into his radio. After some minutes he gave us a thumbs-up sign and departed. It was 1700 hours when the massive tanker *British Strength* hove over the horizon, while the French yacht *Savanah* stood by in case of need.

I steered *Taniwha* under the tanker's stern, rigid with tension, as the seas crashed over the huge square rudder that was so close ahead. My only control over our speed was to shout down to Kay at the noisy engine, because the Morse cables from gearbox and throttle had come adrift. Everything depended on the tanker. Nor did she fail us. With superb seamanship the chief engineer (a massive Scotsman) and the helmsman held the giant ship steady, matching her speed to ours.

Wally, who had a stiff knee, slithered to and fro along the reeling foredeck, retrieving and making fast the messenger line, then hauling aboard and securing five 20-litre plastic cans of diesel. It was dark when we were done and the tanker drew cautiously away, leaving us to fill our fuel tank and reflect with gratitude and not a little humility on our debt to the satellite EPIRB system, the rescue helicopter and the crew of *British Strength*.

We finally reached Mangonui without incident on 28 June, nineteen days after leaving Opua. Our arrival at the wharf was somewhat complicated by the absence of gear and throttle controls, but was accomplished safely with the aid of some sturdy fishermen.

Kay and Wally were overdue back at work and had to hurry south, surprisingly assuring me of their eagerness to join me again. A 'delegation' from Herald Island headed by Ros Demas brought welcome support. Then, after essential repairs by helpful Mangonui seamen, I headed back to Auckland with Paul LeNoel, an old shipmate from *Te Aurere*. A happy addition to the party on the very last leg from Gulf Harbour was a revitalised John Thomson. On 14 July we moored at Herald Island after the not-uneventful two-month shakedown cruise.

Now *Taniwha* is no more. No more afloat, that is, for she lies broken in ten fathoms off Tryphena Bay, Great Barrier Island, some fifty nautical miles to seaward of Auckland. What happened? This is the story.

Way back around 1976 I found myself in the Caroline Islands of Micronesia, home to my clan brother Hipour of Polowat, Mau Piailug of Satawal, and of another great Satawal star-path navigator, Repunglap. I wrote about this occasion in *The Voyaging Stars*:

At Pigailoe the next day we dropped anchor half a mile out in the placid lagoon and swam ashore to be entertained by Repunglap and his crew to a feast of turtle, breadfruit and coconuts. It was at this meeting that the celebrated navigator gave his rokeyok *into my keeping. This was the little stone or shell container of special red clay from Yap used in the navigators' initiation ceremony and also used at sea, with the appropriate charm, to ward off impending bad weather. I had in fact seen one so used not long before, when sailing with Hipour. A tropical rainstorm had swept down towards the canoe, and a crewman had smeared red streaks of clay down his cheeks, while chanting and motioning to the rain squall to divide and pass on each side of us. It must have been apparent from my expression that I had little faith in the efficacy of this procedure because, after the black drenching clouds had duly split asunder and swept harmlessly by on either side, he favoured me with a triumphant look, which said as clearly as any words, 'You see!'*

Repunglap's reason for pressing this very special object upon me became clear when he said it might get broken, clearly implying that such a pagan object was no longer safe on the island. Also, I think he doubted its continuing effectiveness, for he explained: 'Formerly I could not go to sea without it and it worked very well. Now I have become a Christian and it won't work anymore.'

When this had been said I agreed to hold the sacred vessel in trust. The time will hopefully come when such a precious cultural object will be preserved in its proper home and I can return it to Satawal.*

**The Voyaging Stars: Secrets of the Pacific Island Navigators*, Collins, Sydney, 1978, pp. 158–59.

I duly took custody of the *rokeyok*, later putting it in the more secure care of Te Papa, the National Museum in Wellington. Over the ensuing years the religious climate in the now-independent Federated States of Micronesia changed. No longer did the church forbid such pagan rites as the initiation of navigators.

The American documentary producer Eric Metzgar now enters the picture. He had captured Caroline Islands initiation ceremonies in his video *Spirits of the Voyage*. One initiate was Repunglap's son (his father had died). It was clearly time for the *rokeyok* to come home. The whole of Satawal awaited it eagerly. Metzgar suggested that the *rokeyok*'s return be featured in his new documentary. Obviously it was the right project for *Taniwha*. I at once began to make ready for the voyage.

Before long, New Zealand film producer Paul Gorsuch had arranged an exchange of footage with Metzgar and got busy filming our preparations. Moreover, he drummed up amazing support from maritime firms, whose generosity was overwhelming.*

The *rokeyok*, soon christened 'The Magic Barnacle' by the media, aroused so much public interest that I cannot even begin to list all the generous people who helped me. All I can do is give one example: The Amazons. Charlotte, an American midwife, who had sailed on one of our sea trials, asked diffidently if I minded if she cleaned the yacht. 'Delighted,' I replied, guiltily aware that my bachelor boat-keeping left a good deal to be desired. Even so, I was not prepared for the assault when it came. *Taniwha* was hauled out, courtesy of Salthouse's Yard, when three personable and determined American women arrived, heavily laden with vacuum cleaners, brushes, mops, buckets and detergent. For two whole days they took over the vessel. The shipwrights were speechless. They had never seen anything like it. Nor had I. A new, spotless *Taniwha* was revealed.

While in the yard the first official inspection took place. It was meticulous. The ship was examined above and below and a formidable

---

*Sponsors included BP Oil, Pure Dew Water, Bowden Marine, Clarke Equipment, Logan Clothing, Manson Marine, Reid Technology, RFD Marine, Electronic Navigation Ltd, Southern Ocean Ropes, Hutch Wilco, Benjamin Moore, Salthouse Boatbuilders, Great Barrier Airlines, Fullers Ferries, Donnaghys Ropes and Epson New Zealand.

list of requirements was ticked off. The two inspectors were among the most experienced yachtsmen in New Zealand. How was it then that a structural weakness was missed? It was not their fault. The sole responsibility for what was an ultimately fatal mistake was mine. What I want to emphasise, however, is the futility of ticking off endless lists of bureaucratic requirements, a sure formula for missing the really important points in any but the most standard craft. And our Chinese junk rig was unusual.

To explain where I went wrong I have to be more detailed.

The too-fragile foremast that had broken the previous year had been as much responsible as John's heart attack for aborting the cruise. Determined that the new foremast should not break, I used steel pipe. Sir Peter Blake paid for it to the tune of NZ$1000. It was the inadequate way that I fastened down the heavy spar that was at fault. It passed through the strengthened deck two metres down to a steel shoe that was bedded in cement and bolted to the hull. The butt of the mast was in turn bolted to the shoe and the gaps packed with wooden wedges, cemented together with Sealastic compound. Sufficiently anchored, I thought. I was wrong.

Our crew comprised Wally and Kay Langdon, my loyal companions from the previous season's antics; Ros Demas, a replacement for Hotu Kerr, my shipmate from *Te Aurere* who at the last moment suffered a crippling knee accident; and Robyn, then spending two months as Artist-in-Residence at Christchurch University, who would join us in Micronesia together with Eric Metzgar.

On Sunday 8 April 2000 the Speaker of the House of Representatives, Jonathan Hunt, flew up from Wellington to farewell the 'barnacle' and the next morning we motor-sailed ten miles down the muddy upper harbour channel to clear Customs at Queen's Wharf, escorted all the way by an NZAF helicopter.

Then we were off! The rest is soon told. At 2 a.m. on 10 April we were some fifteen miles out to sea, clear of Great Barrier Island, running before a fresh south-wester through choppy seas, when Wally found that the foremast had sheered its wedges and was dangerously unsupported. He was unable to replace them in the sea that was running, so we lowered sail and turned back towards the nearest shelter, Tryphena Bay in Great Barrier Island, where we could make repairs in calm water and, if necessary, have welding done. The seas were steep and we motored slowly to avoid plunging, so that it was not until about 10 a.m. that we closed in on Tryphena. Safety was very near — ten minutes away, perhaps. Unfortunately, the wind-driven waves were funnelling into the bay, growing steeper as they felt the ground. With a crash a big one broke against the bow and we saw the foremast lean, first one way then the other. The remaining wedges were scattered and Wally reported there was a great rent torn in the hull.

I in turn went below and engaged the engine bilge pump, reaching down to the seacock through the floorboards already floating about my knees. A futile effort. The engine soon flooded and stopped. I grabbed the emergency EPIRB beacon and scrambled on deck, where lifejackets were being donned and Wally was making a distress call, while Kay had freed the liferaft's lashing with the attached knife dedicated to the purpose.

'Launch it now!' I said, and the inflating raft was drawn alongside. Kay misjudged her jump and went into the water. Ros, Wally and then I boarded the raft successfully. No sooner was Kay aboard the raft than it was time to push clear of *Taniwha*, as with two mighty explosions of air she slid out of sight and into the depths of Tryphena Bay.

A sports-fishing boat called *Bounty Hunter* took us ashore, damp, barefooted and bewildered, but overwhelmingly thankful at being alive. Possessions can be replaced, but people cannot be remade. Our fortunes had nowhere to go but up. My memory of the rest of that day is a little hazy — dry clothes from the island's emergency store; the startling coincidence that Wally and the island health officer Peter Sporle were old friends; our stumbling walk through the bush to the Sporles' home.

Salvage diving to the uninsured vessel began that very afternoon. The team comprised the harbourmaster Sam Opie, Peter Sporle and Kevin Reynolds. Much was recovered in the week we spent as guests of Peter and Wendy Sporle: all the diesel, propane gas and oil; Wally and Kay's US banknotes in a plastic bag; and Mayor of Waitakere Bob Harvey's case of wine, an occasion tempered somewhat by the discovery that the water pressure at twenty metres had bypassed the intact corks to effectively salinate the vintage. My clothes and shoes were also brought up, but sadly no passports, credit cards or address books, as well as most of my personal possessions, for *Taniwha* was my floating home. The media came to life again when 'The Magic Barnacle' was recovered, for it was far more newsworthy than our own predicament. Later, I donated *Taniwha*'s shattered hull to Great Barrier Island as a scuba diving site. Then, on 19 May, the *rokeyok* and I set off by air for Micronesia with Robyn to meet with Eric and the navigators.

Finally, on 9 June 2000, I handed the *rokeyok* back to the senior navigator of Satawal, the late Repunglap's elder brother, *ppalu* (initiated navigator) Urupiy and his own son Ali, himself an initiated navigator, as participant and interpreter.

The very private little ceremony was held on Yap, where Urupiy was receiving medical treatment. Touching each of us in turn with a coconut leaf tied in a sacred knot, he chanted an invocation to the spirits to protect us all, for forces of great power and portent were involved here. Then, taking the *rokeyok* in hands that trembled, he examined it long and thoroughly. At last he spoke: 'Yes, this is the one.'

It had been passed down from his great-grandfather, through his grandfather, to him. He clasped my hand, beaming with joy. Ali translated: 'It is as if part of one's body had been cut away and has now been restored. We are whole again.'

It is time to wrap up this book, and it seems only appropriate to end with more general thoughts on the challenge of ageing, a subject, it seems to me, of vital interest to society as a whole. Now that life expectancy in Australia and New Zealand is approaching eighty, we can anticipate *half* our lives to extend beyond forty after our children have mostly become independent, with but little physical or mental deterioration in prospect, provided we use our faculties fully and draw on the wisdom of experience. It seems to me that we are only beginning to tap this almost bottomless resource in ways that are a challenge to social thinkers and to every one of us.

So, what have I, myself, learned through this varied life? A very hard question, indeed, for I continue to make the same mistakes, equally in seamanship and in human relations. 'Mad' Don Logan once asked me, 'When will you ever grow up?' This, too, is as far from being answered as it ever was. 'Never,' I suppose, is the succinct reply. At least, I remind myself as I look back, my errors have generally been not of passivity, but of *commission*, of *doing*, of *daring* to undertake fresh ventures and not holding back for fear they collapse round my ears; and of daring to love and to not be afraid of commitment or heartache. So I hope to remain as actively engaged in this life, fully, and as long as possible, right to the very end.

P.S. Am looking for a sound little cruising yacht, *very cheap*. Any offers?

t e n

Apocalypse
Tin Can Bay

> *Do not go gentle into that good night*
> *Old age should burn and rave at close of day;*
> *Rage, rage against the dying of the light.*
> — Dylan Thomas,
> 'Do Not Go Gentle Into That Good Night'

Some time after restoring the *rokeyok* to Urupiy, I was putting the finishing touches to *Shapes on the Wind* when I had a rebellious afterthought — what if there was life after *Taniwha* after all? So I ended the book with the note:

> *P.S. Am looking for a sound little cruising yacht,* very cheap.
> *Any offers?*

Thereupon began what I called 'The Senile Sailor's Refloating Project', to which Dick Smith and *Australian Geographic* responded nobly to the tune of $3000 and $2000 respectively, and old and new friends rallied around to refit for me a sadly decrepit 47-year-old wooden Herreshoff H28 (actually a 29-foot version the designer designated a 'Solitaire') called *Leander*.

I bought *Leander* on 9 October 2000, just after *Shapes on the Wind* was published, well knowing she had been allowed to seriously deteriorate.

'By the way, I couldn't turn over the motor this morning,' remarked the vendor. Not surprising since the stern must have been half-flooded for months, leaving the gearbox locked solid with corroded aluminium.

First stop was Fenwick's Marina, Brooklyn, where Gordon Lewins and Steve Ramsey set to reaming out seams until the hull was flooded with sunlight, cutting out patches of worm and later recaulking with oakum and cotton. The 15 h.p. two-cylinder Yanmar engine was carted off to Newcastle for rebuilding. An army of friends was enlisted for scraping and painting, including dancer Penny Prior from Hollywood via Hawaii, who was still jetlagged when presented with scraper and paintbrush, Sue Olsen, whom I had met on the *Kapitan Khlebnikov*, and Tim Brokenshire, my rock-climbing friend who had purchased *Southern Seas II*.

A month later a sound *Leander*, no longer leaking, was afloat once more, bound for Spencer on the Hawkesbury River for David Thurston to rebuild the rotten cabin top. The circuitous road to Spencer leads through Central Mangrove, Mangrove Mountain and Lower Mangrove. By water it is twenty kilometres. Colin Putt's 9 h.p. tinny towed alongside, with us almost rubbing our noses on the markers to make out their colours, since neither of us was blessed with acute eyesight. We were thankful when Spencer's Pub — a tree with benches beneath — came into view and we could drop anchor.

Four weeks later, with a new cabin top installed, Colin again came to the rescue, to tow the yacht across Broken Bay and up to

Brisbane Water to my son Barry's home at Empire Bay. At a tender age my daughter Susie was wont to count 'one, two, three, another more!' Our running aground en route came under the category 'more' — five, to be exact.

Much interior carpentry followed. The metho (alcohol) stove went much better once a mud wasps' nest had been removed from a burner. The reconditioned engine was reinstalled and by April *Leander* was pronounced fit to proceed to Lake Macquarie near Newcastle for further work.

Robyn Stewart had now joined us from New Zealand, so I proudly demonstrated the yacht's paces in nearby Brisbane Water, blotting my copybook when I confused the marks in gathering darkness and ran aground. It was 2 a.m. before we floated off. The debacle was forgotten when, two days later, we stormed across Broken Bay before a south-easter, to moor up in beautiful Refuge Bay. We swam in the still-warm autumn water and showered under a waterfall. Two self-possessed kookaburras shared our supper in the cockpit.

A feature of the H28's design is sharply cut away sections which make it extremely difficult to clamber on board from the water. We decided to try out a rope ladder. Prudently, Robyn would stand by in the dinghy in case I needed rescuing. Imagine my surprise when, having dived overboard, I saw that Robyn was swimming too and the dinghy was floating upside down. This was no reflection on her boatmanship; the borrowed dinghy had caught its rail under the yacht's overhang. Laughing we scrambled up the ladder, which worked.

The yacht's bottom now being fouled, we sailed to Dangar Island, where, under Colin's direction, we ran onto a rock shelf at high tide and dried out — supported by a network of ropes, wires and a pair of stout wooden legs — to scrape antifoul.

'We need a strong young man to sail with us nowadays,' said Robyn, looking at me disparagingly. My counter-suggestion of a strong young woman was treated with the contempt it deserved.

Tim was the strong young man. He came aboard at Brooklyn one morning and we set sail for Lake Macquarie, running fast before a steady, strengthening southerly which soon put paid to the oldest jib that had come with the boat. I was confident of finding shelter before the weather deteriorated further. I was wrong. Evening found the bar breaking off the entrance to Lake Macquarie. We turned offshore and hove-to under staysail, as I used to do in *Southern Seas II*. A mistake, for *Leander* only heaves-to under close-reefed main and she forereached so fast that we were past Newcastle by dawn. 'Gusts of 60 knots plus, with cross seas from a cyclone moving down the Tasman,' the coastguard told us. They were not exaggerating. 'Make for Port Stephens,' they advised. *Leander* was proving a magnificent sea boat and it was not her fault that approaching unfamiliar Port Stephens in the dusk, we ran right through a formidable bombora where towering walls of water came crashing aboard. We were grateful when we encountered a coastguard vessel, which escorted us to the wharf at Nelson Bay. 'A motel!' said Robyn firmly to a waiting taxi driver and a bedraggled ship's company piled gratefully into the cab.

After Robyn had returned to New Zealand and Tim to Sydney, a Port Stephens yachtie, Mike Hughes, piloted me to Lemon Tree Passage, where a veritable nest of retired Kiwis took me to their hearts, refusing to let me pay for my marina berth and showering me with gifts of gear.

Then on Anzac Day, 2001, with James Couston and Gary Henschel, we set off for Lake Macquarie. The trip was uneventful except for the disintegration of the second oldest jib (the staysail had not survived the trip to Port Stephens).

Dora Creek became my home until July. Thanks to neighbours who were as kindly as those at Lemon Tree Passage, I was able to use electricity and lie alongside free of charge, thus materially lowering the drain on my pension and book advance. Pelicans, ibis, egrets and herons lined the wooded parkland fringing Dora Creek as I walked to the village each morning to work out at the local gym. James, under Gordon's supervision, took on the major jobs, assisted by Gary. James was nominally being paid (and inadequately at that), but even then he kept cheating himself. Bruce Morley of the beautiful Vertue-class cutter *Tui of Opua* presented me with a heavy anchor as well as the metal framework for a roller jib. This last was beyond price and enabled me to commission the jib from a sailmaker who also made me a staysail and a pram hood to shelter the companionway.

A major project was the construction of stout floors and frames in way of the mast and the after end of the cabin. To install them we would have to be lifted out of the water at Marmong Cove Marina before setting off up to Queensland.

There was an unexpected time constraint now, because I learned I had been awarded a New Zealand honour and would have to fly out of Brisbane to attend the investiture. My air ticket was booked for 10 August. Coastal passages are largely dependent on wind and weather and if not a total masochist one must make best use of them.

So no sooner was the hull stiffening installed at Marmong and fresh antifouling applied, than we tied up at a disused jetty outside James's house, stocked up with provisions and water, and promptly put to sea.

There were four of us, rather a crush — James, Gary, myself, and an ABC-TV filmmaker, Scott Bevan. He had been lent a highly sophisticated video camera to shoot open sea film footage for an episode of *Australian Story*. At 9 a.m. on 2 August, we left Lake Macquarie, passing under the lifting road bridge at Swansea with a fair wind. By nightfall we were off Port Stephens. Soon after, a predicted southerly change caught up with us, with quite unpredicted ferocity — 60 knots-plus again. Stripped of all canvas, *Leander* surfed at hull speed. As she became more difficult to control we trailed two car-tyre fenders astern to make her more manageable. This ordeal so soon after setting out intimidated us, so that we were far too slow making sail again after the southerly buster had moderated.

A calm succeeded the storm, then relentless headwinds, both of which were heavy on diesel, so it was 8 August before we pulled into Tweed Heads to refuel and land Gary and Scott, whose onshore commitments were well overdue. A delightful day's sail with a long-awaited fair wind, during which James fitted Barry's autopilot and the solar panel I had purchased just before sailing, took us to Southport Yacht Club Marina. Here David Edmondson and Ian MacKenzie took us under their wings.

It was a happy coincidence that my friend Donna Goodwin (now a PhD student), with whom I had shared the uncanny incident of mask and snorkel in Kauai, was attending a conference in Brisbane. She drove me to the airport and then flew out to New Zealand herself the next day, where we met briefly. Barry joined me in New Zealand, flying over from Sydney, and we were both met by the long-suffering Ros Demas of Herald Island, whereupon I found myself back in her garage where I had lived so long building the ill-fated *Taniwha*. Sadly, Ros's father Bill Owen had died aged 103. On meeting Donna when she arrived at Herald Island independently, Ros declared, 'She's gorgeous!' Indeed, now that Donna had embarked on a career she was far more attractive than the rather rootless young woman of eight years earlier.

The honour which brought me to New Zealand was the Distinguished Companion of the New Zealand Order of Merit (DCNZM). The ceremony was to be held in Wellington and I was allowed to invite several guests. Unfortunately, the Maori navigators Hec Busby and Hotu Kerr were either involved in Treaty of Waitangi business or out of the country. However there was Barry, of course, Ros and her daughter Rachel, and my cousin Rhonda Bosworth. It was fortunate that no one was going by car to Wellington because heavy snowfalls blocked all roads and delayed our train, though it gave Barry and I some unusual views of snow-covered farmlands. I should add here that on our return the snowy Mount Ruapehu stood out brilliantly against a blue sky. Paretetaitonga (Bird of the Southern Sea), the highest peak of Ruapehu, had been my first mountain as a schoolboy climber and I was grateful for this glimpse back into my boyhood, a sight that I am not likely to see again.

The ceremony at Government House was moving. There were just four of us receiving the DCNZM, which had been a knighthood until the previous year. I was only acquainted with one of my fellow recipients, Professor Ranginui Walker. Some years before, he had refused a knighthood, saying these honours were granted to people who made a lot of money and donated it to charities approved by the ruling political party. I was glad that he thought things had changed and the new honour was now respectable. Amusingly, I had letters from a number of National Party MPs reminding me that I would now have been a 'Sir' if they had not been voted out of office.

After the ceremony I was whisked away to be interviewed for Paul Holmes's TV show, *Holmes*, on a freezing deck in the harbour. I thawed out in Speaker of the House of Representatives Jonathan Hunt's flat in Parliament House where he threw a party for us, and the excited Rhonda pretty well danced him off his feet. My main memory is of extreme discomfort as my underpants (a pair of old Bill's taken by mistake) kept slipping down, hobbling me. After removing them in the lavatory at The Backbencher Pub and Cafe, a consensus of our table decided to stuff them under the table and leave the staff to speculate as to what their MP customers had been up to.

Back in Auckland, the highlight for me was a party jointly hosted by HarperCollins and the Auckland Observatory, the wine being donated by my cousin David Hopkins from his Herons Flight vineyard. The rest of our stay was spent driving around Northland. Barry was a different person in New Zealand and seemed in a way come to life more. It was his first visit to the homeland of so many of his ancestors. Barry and I flew back to Australia after a memorable fortnight's stay.

On returning to Australia and being reunited with *Leander* in Southport, I was able to do a little local cruising with various new friends as well as doing more filming for *Australian Story*.

Accompanied by James Couston, who had driven from Lake Macquarie, we sailed up the Broadwater toward Brisbane. Now this is a 50-mile passage all on inland waters, broad at the beginning, later tortuous and with a narrower channel in which you have to be careful; we did actually run aground once, which is not bad for the record. We spent the night at Manly Harbour in Moreton Bay, near Brisbane.

Moreton Bay is a deceptive place because it looks like a great expanse of open water but in fact it's a maze of sandbanks and channels, for which you have to watch the markers meticulously or you are in trouble. From Moreton Bay itself we motored up the Brisbane River; no problems there, everything was very well marked and buoyed. We tied up opposite the Botanic Gardens, where you moor bow and stern on piles. It's difficult to land because your dinghy gets jostled for position on a ferry landing and the tide races very quickly. This was a bit hair-raising at times. The other disadvantage was the fast ferries called CityCats, whose design supposedly cuts down the surface wash they make but actually produces an enormous underwater surge that crashes against your boat, making it very uncomfortable.

Be that as it may, I enjoyed being in Brisbane and the company of other yachties who were tied up there. My eyesight was worrying me so I did get around to going to get new glasses, to be tested and so on. It's better not to dwell too much on this because of course I was doing exactly the wrong thing. I should have realised just how serious this deterioration was and gone straight away for eye specialist assessment and treatment.

But it was most definitely a question of denial, of denying how bad things were getting. Some days I could see better and some days I couldn't, and this led to a fair bit of blindness in the mental sense. No matter if you are doctor and should know better, you still make these same very human mistakes.

When I sailed back to Southport with Sue Olsen I realised with a shock how sharply my vision had deteriorated. I found I was unable to read the echo sounder, an essential instrument in these confined waters and the pilotage was left almost entirely to Sue. It is a tribute to her that we only grounded once. In Southport we anchored in a cove popularly known as Bums Bay after seagoing bums like myself who make good use of the free anchorage. Ros Demas came to join me and it was shortly after her arrival that it was brought home dramatically just how bad things were. My right eye lost central vision ages ago, leaving only peripheral vision, but it was clear that my left one, damaged in the past through a detached retina, was failing too. Both eyes had glaucoma and artificial lenses, but these were not issues.

I was following another boat into a new anchorage, but because my alternator belt was slipping I couldn't keep up with it and it became just a blur ahead. I mistook another great white blur, which seemed to be dropping back towards us, for our guide boat. It was in fact a huge motorboat coming directly towards me. I recognised the situation at the last moment and swerved across the channel. The man on the powerboat didn't slow down or anything and had no reason to. I was doing something abnormal to get out of his way. I was very lucky to escape unhurt. It had been a dangerous situation.

Shortly thereafter Ros and I were ready to head offshore towards Tin Can Bay. Our objective was to go cruising in the Great Sandy Strait inside Fraser Island, about which I'd heard a great deal. There was a fellow yachtsman called Fin the Fin — I can't remember his surname — who volunteered to come with Ros and me on this trip. We left rather hurriedly because of a favourable weather forecast that gave us a window to get into Great Sandy Strait through Wide Bay Bar. The bar is best negotiated by GPS as only someone with super vision can see the tiny beacons even in the best light conditions. So you don't want to tackle the bar in bad weather, as there's nowhere to hang back in any safety whatsoever before you arrive there.

Our strategy was to get on our way as soon as possible, so we left with a southerly change anticipated. We still had a northerly headwind so we tucked out to sea in the evening and got bashed around a little. The change arrived with moderate intensity and we ran away up the coast past Point Lookout and from there direct to the coordinates outside Wide Bay Bar in a gradually dying wind. The yacht ran beautifully, self-steering with a rather elaborate arrangement of sheets to the tiller and came through Wide Bay Bar mid morning. We anchored at Tin Can Bay, where Ros and I didn't know a soul. It had become obvious that I urgently needed to see an eye specialist, so soon after we anchored I saw a local doctor and thereafter started a progression of examinations, first in Maroochydore, later in Brisbane, and then the treatment.

What turned out to be wrong was macular degeneration, a condition which occurs where the nerves and blood vessels connect the retina to the brain. There was an overgrowth of small blood vessels that bleed and obscure the only part of the eye that gives acute vision. The treatment recommended was visudyne therapy, and expensive treatment involving injection of a light-sensitive substance. Then after the offending little artery has been identified it is zapped with laser. This has to be repeated every three months for some time and it doesn't necessarily give you any improvement but it does stop things getting worse.

So for poor Ros the whole of her couple of months' holiday in Australia, apart from that one voyage, was involved in carting me back and forth by bus to Maroochydore, Brisbane, and other places for treatment. This was unfair to her because the only other time she had sailed offshore with me was on the *Taniwha*, on the fatal voyage — fatal as far as the boat was concerned. After it had sunk Ros had come ashore in the life raft. I had promised her that this time it would be a nice peaceful safe holiday, but I wasn't quite right.

Journeys on the bus were so frequent that on one trip to Brisbane the bus driver said, 'You know the road better than me, would you like to drive?' I replied breezily, 'Sure, there are plenty of blind drivers nowadays.'

One thing that was unexpected was the tremendous warmth and support I received for being blind. It's rather different when you're deaf. When you're deaf people tend to shout and say, 'Stupid old bugger, he's such a nuisance', whereas blindness, happily for me at least, seems to elicit protective instincts in others. For instance, the official in charge of regulating moorings found out a little later that I was using one to which I was not strictly entitled. He asked the owner Mike Davidson if the offending yacht belonged to the old blind bugger. When Mike assured him it did, he replied, 'Well, let him have it.'

The support I have received in Tin Can Bay has been beyond all measure and the kindness from so many people impels me to make a big point that for anyone who is going blind the best thing they can do is sail their boat to Tin Can Bay.

The whole impact of what has happened is enormous. I can't disguise that, nor would I want to. The state of my sight now is that I am legally blind and carry a white stick, but I can distinguish shapes, walk about and so on, short of reading. I am unable to read and that means I can't use a telephone without help, or decipher most nautical instruments, but for general things I don't manage too badly. I have certain problems, like I can't clearly see butter as I spread it on a piece of bread and as a result the cabin floorboards of *Leander* are rather like a skating rink of spilt butter. One time I tried to shave with a toothbrush. Another time, while lathering up in preparation for a shave, I unwittingly covered my face with toothpaste. This lighter side of things has been quite unexpected. I may not see the funny side at the time, but appreciate it later. Going out to the boat at moorings I am quite doubtful about finding my way, especially at night. I find it easier to row than use the small outboard, so I can creep along gradually and if necessary feel the way along the boats, until I bump into my own.

When lying at mooring surrounded by the misty shapes of the land and other vessels, I get the illusion that other people cannot see me, so I tend to pee over the side and perform my ablutions without any modesty whatsoever. Friends have pointed out my error.

Ros and I were later made honorary members of Tin Can Bay Yacht Club, and among new friends who came sailing with me was Commodore Mike Harrison, who, when my daughter Anna came out from Europe to visit, piloted us to Fraser Island. Anna and I were able to sail a long way up the Great Sandy Strait in quite rough conditions. All this was a wonderful break from being anchored and static, while helplessly watching the other boats going past.

After Ros left, Mike and his wife Denise took me to their home at Tin Can Bay for Christmas Day. Larry Bardsley put *Leander* on his slip for nothing and he and his wife Heidi helped me materially in telephoning.

I was walking along the footpath one day when a car pulled up alongside me and the driver said, 'Last time we met we were skiing down a road in Alaska.' It was Bill Blake, whose wife Jill had lent me her MGB car in which Don Logan and I had driven to Mount Rainier and I had discovered the gaff cutter *Gryphon*. After Ros's return to New Zealand it was Jill Blake, and later her daughter Janet, who looked after me on the treatment trips to Brisbane.

A major problem I think is how to live in a situation where you are dependent on other people and for someone who has always been very independent, it's not exactly easy having to get someone to metaphorically wipe your bottom for you — or damn near.

It is no less an impossible burden on anyone unfortunate enough to have to do the wiping. 'Fussy old man,' they say, irritated by your constant demands. For in a situation where you cannot make notes, a list of trivial daily necessities must constantly be borne in mind.

The question of whether impairment of vision enhances the other senses comes very much to the fore. The sense of touch in my fingertips has been blunted ever since my hands were frostbitten aboard *Ice Bird* but nevertheless, together with the sense of pressure, remains very important. Smells have always been significant for me. Smells of the earth and the sea and the fragrance of women loom no less large in my life, perhaps larger than they did before.

In April 2002 I sailed north out of Great Sandy Strait with Jo Solomon and Brian Sweeney. After the usual mishaps we stopped off

at the Burnett River that flows out from Bundaberg and from there we made the 60-mile passage to Lady Musgrave Reef. Though I can barely read a compass I can use the angles of the wind and waves to steer by. The sun is obvious, as well as the major stars. Constellations, however, have lost their outlines because the many small stars that compose the patterns have disappeared. However, once I have learned to identify the remaining big stars, steering with their aid is easy. Happily ships' lights are visible at a considerable distance. Being out in the open sea is less complicated and easier than skirting the land. The 60-mile open sea passage to Lady Musgrave Reef was a joy. At the reef itself it was wonderful snorkelling in the lagoon, where I did, with some difficulty, actually see a small turtle under the water. Mostly I could see the shapes of the coral and the flashing of the electric blue fish, which brought back so vividly the many atolls where I have dived and sailed throughout the Pacific. We left Lady Musgrave Reef hurriedly because of a bad weather forecast that predicted accurately that stormwaves would soon be sweeping right across the shallow reef lagoon. A night's sailing before a fair wind took us to Gladstone. From here Brian had to return to Tin Can Bay while Jo and I continued to Rockhampton, where we moored.

The passage between Curtis Island and the mainland is called The Narrows. Tides and the ship's draft have to be calculated very carefully indeed because the central portion dries out. This is a cattle crossing. 'Who has right of way at the crossing?' I asked Jo. 'Nobody silly,' she answered. 'The cattle cross at low tide and we at high tide.' The passage was completed successfully and we anchored in Pacific Creek on the northern aspect of Curtis Island. The lighthouse here is notable in being of the classic shape but being constructed completely of corrugated iron.

Rockhampton lies thirty miles inland up the Fitzroy River, distinguished by its shallow patches and somnolent crocodiles sunning themselves on the banks at low tide. We grounded only twice, being ignominiously towed back into deep water by a passing motorboat on both occasions, and moored at the hospitable Fitzroy Motor Boat Club, where, as of June 2002, I am now based.

In the chapter that finished the original edition of this book I predicted correctly that life would continue to offer challenges, but was unaware of how big they were going to be. Being able to live as I am doing, to be able to do it at sea or at anchor, doing the things I love, not restricted to living in a home or some very protected environment, this is the challenge I face now and I find it not depressing but stimulating and exciting. People keep asking me what is my next adventure. Everything is an adventure now.

Editor's Note

David Lewis died on 22 October 2002 in Gympie Hospital. He had suffered a stroke while on board *Leander* at anchor in Tin Can Bay and lapsed into a coma from which he did not regain consciousness.

David had been very excited about the impending publication of the updated edition of his autobiography, and despite his almost total blindness had just learned to communicate by email, albeit with the help of his friend, Anne Cross.

In his last email to me, sent during a sailing trip in the Keppel Islands, he responded to a question regarding the state of his eyesight in his inimitable fashion:

Eyesight no worse, needs more rum. Ciao, David.

Right until the end, he lived his life to the fullest. Cheers, Dr Lewis.

Jesse Fink
October 2002

Index